LONDON: A LITERARY COMPANION

Other books by the author

LONDON
A Literary Companion

Peter Vansittart

JOHN MURRAY

Dedicated, with much love, to Yolanta and Derwent May

First published in 1992
by John Murray (Publishers) Ltd.,
50 Albemarle Street, London W1X 4BD

A catalogue record for this book is available from the British Library

ISBN 0-7195-5014 9

Typeset in 12½/12½ pt Bembo by Colset Pte Ltd, Singapore
Printed and bound in Great Britain by
Biddles Limited, Guildford and King's Lynn

CONTENTS

ILLUSTRATIONS

(between pages 152 and 153)

PREFACE

With so vast a subject I have not attempted to be comprehensive, and have small interest in cataloguing famous names in verbal blue plaques. This is a personal London derived from my favourite writers and prejudices, geared to my own limitations and, very largely, to my own library. It cannot be comprehensive. My chief desire is not to preach or assert, but to entertain and, at times, move. Some may carp at inattention paid to Fielding, to Conrad . . . the list could fill the page, but pages are limited. I hope sufficient remains. My problem has been to prevent Boswell, Johnson, Dickens, Henry James, Virginia Woolf and V. S. Pritchett from hogging the limelight.

I am grateful to friends for help, loans and suggestions, notably Justine Brener, Jane Bush, Thomas Hinde, Kirsty McCleod, Allan Massie, Roger Lubbock, Jeremy Lewis, James and Jean MacGibbon, Frederick Grubb, John Ashe, Peter Johnson, Margot Strickland, Anthea Zeman, Ruth Montague, Hubert Picarda, Nicholas Shakespeare, Elizabeth Jenkins, Mary Fyvel, my step-daughter Mary Stephens, and the staff and library at Mount Pleasant, and above all my editors, first Ariane Goodman, then Gail Pirkis, unfailingly patient, stern but practical. My dependence on Terry Jordan's typing is absolute. My friend Margot Walmsley has been invaluable in very kindly consenting to read the proofs, one of many acts of generosity. Douglas Matthews, yet again, needs special thanks for the Index. I hope that my chapter arrangements, simple enough, will not leave the reader growling for a map. I like to think that a few readers may be stimulated to map out the routes for themselves and relish the discoveries that begin by getting lost. There are certain authors, Diana Witherby and Dunstan Thompson among them, whom I have quoted without permission, their original publishers having vanished. I can only beg their forbearance.

INTRODUCTION

> A mighty mass of brick, and smoke, and shipping,
>   Dirty and dusty, but as wide as eye
> Could reach, and here and there a sail just skipping
>   In sight, then lost amid the forestry
> Of masts, wilderness of steeples peeping
>   On tiptoe through their sea-coal canopy;
> A huge, dun Cupola, like a foolscap crown
>   On a fool's head – and there is London Town!
>   Lord Byron, *Don Juan*

PANORAMIC LONDON

Many Londons exist: mythical, historical, literary, topographical, at times so personal as to become mystical. Until Tudor times, what most Londoners knew of their city's past derived more from the tall stories of such chroniclers as Geoffrey of Monmouth than from fact. His London was founded by Brutus, a Trojan prince, and fortified by King Lud, who echoes Lugus, the Celtic Apollo. The sixteenth-century Scottish poet, William Dunbar, could still refer to London as 'New Troy', and his audience might remember the capital of an imaginary Britain once terrified by 'a travelling shriek'.

Unlike Venice or Florence or Bath, London has no single dominating personality. The atmosphere, the texture, tone and voice, continually alter, along the lines of ancient villages. 'London is a muddle,' E.M. Forster wrote, adding, 'The city has piled itself up, like a geological series, and perhaps the process will continue until a skin of unsmashable glass is stretched over her, as in H.G. Wells' dream.'

H.V. Morton remarked:

Of course, no living man has seen London. London has ceased to be visible since Stuart days. It was then possible for the last time in history to stand among the water meadows at Westminster and to see London riding on Ludgate Hill escorted by her church towers and spires. Plantagenet London must have been the best of all the Londons for the purposes of a farewell speech: a city behind its wall, something definite to see and address. To-day, even if you climb to the dome of St Paul's you see, not London the City of State but London the labyrinth. The nearest approach to a real view of London is that from the tower of Southwark Cathedral, or better still, from a boat on the Thames at night when darkness lends an ancient enchantment to the roof lines.

In crisis, plague, fire, bombing or riot, a further London transcends the literal and everyday, not always comforting, as in Blake's 'Prophetic Books'.

Jerusalem came down in a dire rain over all the Earth,
She felt cold from Lambeth's Vale in groans and dewy
    death –
The dew of anxious souls, the death sweat of the dying –
In every pillar'd hall and arched roof of Albion's skies.

A modern writer, Andrew Sinclair, in his novel *King Ludd* fuses past and present, myth and politics, the visionary and the quotidien, and sweeps King Arthur into the Wapping newspaper strike.

Arthur is in the front line of the comrades with the black knights on their police horses facing them. It is the final battle and Sir Mordred and the minions of Sir Magog and Lord Mowler confront the king of the Round Table and his flying pickets. And as the grim delivery lorries roll out with their armoured windscreens, the stones and the shouts fly, and as the black buses roll in bearing the strikebreakers, the rivets and bolts and the curses are hurled at the barred windows.

Legendary London throve on illiteracy, vigorous hearsay and popular song. Iago's song in *Othello* did not appeal to historical truth: 'King Stephen was a worthy peer, His breeches cost him but a crown . . .'

Today, poets, novelists and dramatists have created another London, and the simplicity of the twelfth-century monk, William FitzStephen, is hard to recapture: 'The most noble City of London . . . where the mild sky doth soften the hearts of men'. Chelsea and Southwark, Limehouse and Newgate, Baker Street, Bloomsbury and the Bayswater Road are so stamped with the inventions of writers that, for many, it is difficult to see them unadorned with stories and images.

Though sordid and vile, displaying the sores of poverty and the reek of injustice, London was possessed of a lyrical grace and gaiety, as Virginia Woolf described in this memory of London in 1880, in her novel *The Years*:

It was an uncertain spring. The weather, perpetually changing, sent clouds of blue and purple flying over the land. In the country farmers, looking at the fields, were apprehensive; in London, umbrellas were opened and then shut by people looking up at the sky. But in April such weather was to be expected. Thousands of shop assistants made that remark, as they handed neat parcels to ladies in flounced dresses standing on the other side of the counter at Whiteley's and the Army and Navy Stores. Interminable processions of shoppers in the West End, of business men in the East, paraded the pavements, like caravans perpetually marching, – so it seemed to those who had any reason to pause, say, to post a letter, or at a club window in Piccadilly. The stream of landaus, Victorias and hansom cabs was incessant; for the season was beginning. In the quieter streets musicians doled out their frail and for the most part melancholy pipe of sound, which was echoed, or parodied, here in the trees of Hyde Park, here in St James's, by the twitter of sparrows and the sudden outbursts of the amorous but intermittent thrush. The pigeons in the squares shuffled in the tree tops, letting fall a twig or two, and crooned over and over again the lullaby that was always interrupted. The gates at the

Marble Arch and Apsley House were blocked in the afternoon by ladies in many-coloured dresses wearing bustles, and by gentlemen in frock coats carrying canes, wearing carnations. Here came the Princess, and as she passed hats were lifted. In the basements of the long avenues of the residential quarters servant girls in cap and apron prepared tea. Deviously ascending from the basement the silver teapot was placed on the table, and virgins and spinsters with hands that had staunched the sores of Bermondsey and Hoxton carefully measured out one, two, three, four spoonfuls of tea. When the sun went down a million little gaslights, shaped like the eyes in peacocks' feathers, opened in their glass cages, but nevertheless broad stretches of darkness were left on the pavement. The mixed light of the lamps and the setting sun were reflected equally in the placid waters of the Round Pond and the Serpentine.

'London' includes Royal London, Imperial London, Commercial London, Clubland, patrician Belgravia, seething Whitechapel, criminal London. Much of its past is that of rookery and sponging-house, bagnio and workhouse, gaunt hospital, opulent church and mournful chapel; the canal, the wasteland, the railway. De Quincey lamented 'the stony-hearted city'. Different societies existed within a few steps of each other. Jewelled high heels tripped daintily, avoiding the naked feet of those slumped in shadows; frontiers on no map but solid as the Traitors' Gate. Dostoevsky summed up London in 1862 after his sojourn there:

The vast town, always in movement night and day, wide as an ocean, with the grind and howl of machinery, railways shooting above houses and soon to go beneath them, commercial adventure, disorder superficially unrestrained though in reality controlled by the strictest bourgeois discipline, the Thames befouled, the atmosphere packed with coal dust; the superb squares and parks, metropolitan spaces that freeze the blood – Whitechapel with a populace half-naked, brutal and famished, the City with its vast moneybags, the Crystal Palace.

Virginia Woolf's Elizabeth Barrett dwelt in sedate Wimpole Street but, 'You might see sights and hear language and smell smells not a stone's throw from Wimpole Street that threw doubt upon the solidity of Wimpole Street itself.' And in the same novel, *Flush*, she continued: 'Splendid buildings raised themselves in Westminster, yet just behind them were ruined sheds in which human beings lived herded together above herds of cows.'

Dostoevsky also noticed drastic contrasts:

> The poor are not even allowed inside a church, being unable to afford a pew. Usually, working-class couples live in illicit union as marriages are expensive. Many husbands, by the way, beat their women very brutally, disfiguring them almost to the point of death – usually with a poker, which they apparently see as tools made for this purpose. Certainly, newspaper accounts of domestic rows, invariably refer to pokers. Pauper children still very young, often leave for the streets, join the passing crowd and never return.

If London could be callous to its own impoverished citizens, it was often hostile to foreigners, as many can still testify. Long before Dostoevsky, an anonymous Venetian diplomat, in a letter from London written in 1500, had commented:

> The English are great lovers of themselves and of everything belonging to them; they think that there are no other men than themselves, and no other world but England; and whenever they see a handsome foreigner they say that 'He looks like an Englishman . . .' They have an antipathy to foreigners, and imagine that they never come into their island, but to make themselves masters of it.

Boswell, attending Bickerstaffe's *Love in a Village* at Covent Garden in 1762, mentioned in his Journal: 'Just before the overture began to be played, two Highland officers came in. The mob in the upper gallery roared out: "No Scots! No Scots! Out with them!" – Hissed and pelted them with apples.'

Earlier, in 1726, Voltaire had been in London as an exile. He
possessed a genius, John Masefield considered, not for giving
light but for shattering darkness, and he fell foul of Londoners.

London swarmed at this time with Huguenot refugees
who made Frenchmen excessively unpopular with the
masses by their readiness to work at less than the prevail-
ing rates of wages. Some workers, detecting Voltaire's
nationality as he walked the streets, began throwing mud
at him. He made them a flattering and amusing speech.
'Is it not misfortune enough for me,' he began, 'that I was
not born among you?' And went on until they chaired
him and carried him in triumph to his lodging. Even in
the England he had so lavishly praised, life had dark risks
and incongruities. On another day a Thames waterman
insulted him, bawling that all Frenchmen were slaves.
Next day, he saw the fellow in the grip of the press-gang.
(H.N. Brailsford)

Dostoevsky's great compatriot, Leo Tolstoy, was in London
in 1861. His French biographer, Henri Troyat, tells how

he went out to mix with the people in order to learn and
criticize. The foggy, smoky town, with yellow gas lamps
glowing here and there, impressed him by its orderliness,
discipline and tedium. Not one curious glance in the
street, and not one over-hasty movement, not a cry, not
a smile. Nothing but measured, sober citizens hiding their
souls and going about their business with no concern for
that of others. Although London instilled in him 'a
loathing for modern civilization', he was fascinated by the
cockfights and boxing matches, by a sitting in the House
of Commons during which Lord Palmerston spoke for
three solid hours, and by a lecture on education given by
Dickens.

Dickens himself provided, in *Our Mutual Friend*, a classic
confrontation of Londoners with a foreigner, classic in that it
has scarcely dated:

The majority of the guests were like the plate and
included several heavy articles weighing ever so much.
But there was a foreign gentleman among them: whom

Mr Podsnap had invited after much debate with himself –
believing the whole European continent to be in mortal
alliance against the young person [his daughter] – and
there was a droll disposition, not only in the part of
Mr Podsnap, but of everybody else, to treat him as if he
were a child who was hard of hearing.

As a delicate concession to this unfortunately-born
foreigner, Mr Podsnap, in receiving him, had presented
his wife as 'Madame Podsnap', with some inclination
to add, 'Ma fille', in which bold venture, however, he
checked himself. The Veneerings being at that time the
only other arrivals, he had added (in a condescendingly
explanatory manner), 'Monsieur Vey-nair-reeng', and had
then subsided into English.

'How do you like London?' Mr Podsnap now inquired
from his station as host, as if he were administering
something in the nature of a powder or potion to the deaf
child; 'London, Londres, London?'

The foreign gentleman admired it.

'You Find it Very Large?' said Mr Podsnap, spaciously.

The foreign gentleman found it very large.

'And Very Rich?'

The foreign gentleman found it, without doubt,
enormément riche.

'Enormously Rich, we say,' returned Mr Podsnap, in
a condescending manner. 'Our English adverbs do Not
terminate in Mong and We Pronounce the "ch" as if there
were a "t" before it. We Say Ritch.'

'Reetch,' remarked the foreign gentleman.

'And Do You Find, Sir,' pursued Mr Podsnap, with
dignity, 'Many Evidences that Strike You, of our British
Constitution in the Streets of the World's Metropolis,
London, Londres, London?'

The foreign gentleman begged to be pardoned, but did
not altogether understand.

'The Constitution Britannique,' Mr Podsnap explained, as if he were teaching in an infants' school. 'We
say British, But You Say Britannique, You Know,'
(forgivingly as if that were not his fault). 'The Constitution, Sir.'

The foreign gentleman said, 'Mais, yees; I know eem.'

A youngish sallowish gentleman in spectacles, with a lumpy forehead, seated in a supplementary chair at a corner of the table, here caused a profound sensation by saying, in a raised voice, 'ESKER', and then stopping dead.

'Mais oui,' said the foreign gentleman turning towards him. 'Est-ce-que? Quoi donc?'

But the gentleman with the lumpy forehead having for the time delivered himself of all that he found behind his lumps, spoke for the time no more.

Mr Podsnap considered foreigners 'a Mistake'. Throughout London's history they were useful scapegoats for price rises, black markets, the Great Fire, the spread of disease and general immorality.

More reassuringly, the biographer Leon Edel imagines another foreigner, Henry James, as a small boy lying on his stomach, evoking a London which he would one day enter, to be honoured and humiliated, praised and mocked, and about which he elaborated lasting descriptions and reflections. Edel writes:

And here he read *Punch*. All England seemed to unfold from its pages, but mainly London – the names of the London streets and theatres, Kensington Gardens and Drury Lane, the sounds of Piccadilly seemed to be there, people riding in the Row, cabmen and costermongers, little pages in buttons, small boys in tall hats and Eton jackets, pretty girls in striped petticoats with their hair dressed in the shape of mushrooms.

At that early age, James may not have imagined London under threat: from violence and social angers, from pollution of environment and spirit. But long before George Orwell's dismal vision of 1984, Richard Jefferies, in his novel, *After London* of 1885, envisaged the capital collapsed, through corrupt materialism, moral blindness and disregard of nature:

These skeletons were the miserable relics of men who had ventured, in search of ancient treasure, into the deadly marches over the site of the mightiest city of former days. The deserted and mostly extinct city of London was under his feet.

He had penetrated into the midst of that dreadful place, of which he had heard many a tradition: how the earth was poison, the water poison, the air poison, the very light of heaven, falling through such an atmosphere, poison. There were said to be places where the earth was on fire and belched forth sulphurous fumes, supposed to be from the combustion of the enormous stores of strange and unknown chemicals collected by the wonderful people of those times. Upon the surface of the water there was a greenish-yellow oil, to touch which was death to any creature; it was the very essence of corruption – sometimes it floated before the wind, and fragments became attached to reeds or flags far from the place itself. If a moorhen or duck chanced to rub the reed, and but one drop stuck to its feathers, it forthwith died. Of the red water he had not heard, nor of the black, into which he had unwittingly sailed.

Ghastly beings haunted the site of so many crimes, shapeless monsters, hovering by night, and weaving a fearful dance. Frequently they caught fire, as it seemed, and burned as they flew and floated in the air.

Sixty years later, however, in a London befouled, bombed and impoverished by war, Cyril Connolly, in *The Unquiet Grave*, could yet rejoice: 'Sunshine streams into the room, the dove grinds her love-song on the roof, in the square the grass turns green, the earth has been cleared round the daffodils as a stage is cleared for the dancers, and under a clean blue sky the streets remember Canaletto; London spring is on its way.'

London is strewn with details, often insignificant yet memorable, occasionally brilliant. The dates of the following miscellanea are jumbled, for chronology can mislead. Macaulay declared that late-seventeenth-century foreign princes were carried to see Bloomsbury Square as one of the wonders of England. At a charity breakfast in Fulham, for public wash-houses, Louis Napoleon first met a fellow author, Queen Victoria. In Ranelagh Gardens, Tobias Smollett's *Humphry*

Clinker saw the castrato, Tenducci: 'A thing from Italy. It looks for all the world like a man, though they say it is not. The voice, to be sure, is neither man's nor woman's; but it is more melodious than either; and it warbled so divinely that, while I listened, I really thought myself in Paradise.' W.J. Loftie once looked up at the balcony of No. 1, Grosvenor Gate, and saw Disraeli unexpectedly emerge 'in a gorgeous long dressing-gown and a velvet cap with a golden tassel'. Baroness Orczy, in the Temple underground station, suddenly 'saw' Sir Percy Blakeney and was soon at work on *The Scarlet Pimpernel*. 'A momentary vision I had of a room high above the leaping lights of Piccadilly' spontaneously gave Hugh Walpole his melodrama *Above the Dark Circus*. In Soho Square a policeman rebuked T.E. Hulme for urinating publicly, but apologized when the philosopher retorted: 'Do you realise you're address-ing a member of the Middle Class?' In the year of Victoria's Diamond Jubilee, John Masefield saw a leper selling hot pig's trotters outside Charing Cross Station. Also in Charing Cross, during the seventeenth century, had been exhibited the Dutch Boy. Thomas Burke, in *The Streets of London*, explains:

> He had on the iris of one eye the words, in small letters, 'Deus Meus'; and on the iris of the other, in Hebrew letters, 'Elohim'. Physicians and philosophers examined the boy and, as usual, disagreed; some saying it was natural, others that it had been done since birth, though, since the boy's sight was unimpaired, they could not imagine how.

An art critic, Mr Thomas Griffith Wainwright, murdered his uncle, mother-in-law and, having insured her life for £18,000, his sister-in-law. 'Yes,' he agreed, before execution, 'it was a dreadful thing to do. But she had very thick ankles.' His case fascinated Oscar Wilde. Gervase Markham wrote so many identical books that publishers forced him to sign a docu-ment that is probably unique: 'Memorandum that I Gervase Markham of London gent Do promise hereafter never to write any more book or bookes to be printed, of the Deseases or cures of any cattle, as Horse, Oxe, Cows, Sheepe, Swine and Goates etc.'

Human oddity persisted, against odds barely possible. Beautifully crafted handwriting issued from half-starved clerks going blind by candlelight. From the condemned cell in Holloway, Edith Thompson wrote moving, troubled letters; and the Elizabethan dissident, Chidiock Tichborne, lamented in a poem written the night before his execution:

> My tale was heard and yet it was not told,
>   My fruit is fallen and yet my leaves are green,
> My youth is spent and yet I am not old,
>   I saw the world and yet I was not seen;
>   My thread is cut and yet it is not spun,
>   And now I live, and now my life is done.

At the pre-1914 Tour Eiffel restaurant in Percy Street, decorated by Wyndham Lewis, Ronald Firbank could be seen dining alone on champagne and musing aloud about art. Here, the management placed a screen round one table to shelter other diners from Ezra Pound declaiming his 'Sestina: Altaforte':

> Damn it all! All this our South stinks peace.
> You whoreson dog, Papiole, come! Let's to music!
> I have no life save where the swords clash.
> But ah! When I see the standards gold, vair, purple,
>   appearing
> And the broad fields beneath them turn crimson,
> Then howls my heart nigh mad with rejoicing.

LONDON AS THEATRE

With its moods and unpredictabilities, its polyglot traditions of independence, its leisured clubs and rowdy dram-shops, its elegant creatures upright in carriages and its slumping bodies (Henry James rated London poverty 'the hard prose of misery'), London is a depthless quarry for writers. There is always the

London just beyond reach, a London of dreams containing a substantial and fateful truth. It is liable to appear at any instant, only to flicker, dissolve, often remain unrecorded, though in *Delight* J.B. Priestley did capture this illusionistic or phantom city:

> There is to me a curious pleasure, sometimes leaping to a delight, in coming upon a real street scene that looks like a good stage set. The older parts of London are rich in these illusions, especially on a clear early evening. You turn a corner, and there happens to be nobody about and the noise of traffic is falling in a theatrical fashion, and for a moment, you seem to be in a theatre, waiting for the opening scene of a masterpiece. There is a bit of St. James's that I must have caught a score of times at these moments, all deserted, and exquisitely lit, and I have loitered there, half-expecting some Fainall or Whitwould to make a sauntering entrance in full Restoration costume.

London indeed has always been a theatre, an exhibition. On streets, in parks and taverns, and chocolate-houses, Londoners sought love and mirth, sex and companionship. Mayhew in 1862 estimated that there were 80,000 London street-walkers. The streets were a living frieze of whores, beggars, talented animals, spangled acrobats, touts, jokers, muggers, ballad-singers, pickpockets, flower-girls – 'Here's your fine rosemary, sage and thyme. Come, buy my ground-ivy.' – visionaries, sausage-vendors, piemen, midgets, contortionists. In *The London Encyclopaedia*, Weinreb and Hibbert mention 'The human lavatory . . . who offered for a small fee the use of a pail and his voluminous cape as a screen for passers-by.'
Gibbon, in his *Memoirs*, reflected:

> The metropolis affords many amusements which are open to all: it is itself an astonishing and perpetual spectacle to the curious eye; and each taste, each sense may be gratified by the variety of objects that will occur in the long circuit of a morning walk.

He added:

> The pleasures of a town life, the daily round from tavern
> to the play, from the play to the coffee-house, from the
> coffee-house to the bagnio are within the reach of every
> man who is regardless of his health, his money and his
> company.

Commemorated in Bleeding Heart Lane, Hatton Garden,
Lady Hatton was feared as a witch and had her heart ripped out
in the street, supposedly by the Devil. Londoners could observe
Lord Macaulay walking from Piccadilly to Clapham reading
Sophocles. Continuous were hectic interruptions from fire,
hue and cry, brawls, funeral processions and bizarre appari-
tions. In St Botolph's, Cripplegate, 'Arise' Evans announced
that he was Jesus. The highway man James Dalton, of lower
station, rode to Tyburn holding his five-year-old son for the
boy to see his execution. Another felon, Roger Johnson, was
brought from Newcastle to Newgate strapped to a horse's
belly.

None knew London better than Defoe, butcher's son,
perhaps a Monmouth rebel, journalist, pamphleteer, government agent, hosier, brickmaker, itinerant salesman, accountant
and novelist. *Hymn to the Pillory* exploited personal experience.
His *Moll Flanders* shows the tough struggle for existence in old
London. She had one chancy encounter,

> with a young fellow woman and a fellow that went for
> her husband, though, as it appeared afterwards, she was
> not his wife, but they were partners, it seems, in the trade
> they carried on, and partners in something else too. In
> short, they robbed together, lay together, were taken
> together, and at last were hanged together.

Spectators of this could also have seen the Restoration Lord
Buckhurst who celebrated his killing a tanner in a street brawl
with a banquet at Oxford Kate's Cock and Pie Tavern, Bond
Street, afterwards from a high window preaching to the crowd
before urinating on it. Pepys records a day commonplace
enough:

To the Comptroller's, and with him by coach to White Hall; in our way meeting Venner and Pritchard upon a sledge, who with two more Fifth Monarchy men were hanged to-day, and the first two drawn and quartered. Went to the Theatre, where I saw *The Lost Lady* which do not please me much. Here I was troubled to be seen by four of our office clerks, which sat in the half-crown box, and I in the 1 and 6. From hence by link and bought two mousetraps of Thomas Pepys the turner.

His friend John Evelyn had seen an accused man pressed to death for refusing to plead. More happily, John McManners records: 'The widow who died in 1781, leaving a small legacy to each of the clerks at her obsequies on condition that they did not laugh, ensured for herself the most hilarious funeral of the century.'

Swift, in *Description of the Morning*, 1709, wrote about a London morning:

> Now hardly here and there a hackney coach
> Appearing, show'd the ruddy morn's approach,
> Now Betty from her Master's bed had flown,
> And softly crept to discompose her own.

ending:

> The watchful bailiffs take their silent stands,
> And schoolboys lag with satchells in their hands.

All London knew the story of the grandee, usually though not invariably applied to Wellington, when George IV was divorcing his wife for unseemly behaviour. A pro-Caroline crowd confronted the Duke as he was riding down Piccadilly to his home, 'No. 1, London', at Hyde Park Corner.

'Your Grace, if you don't shout with us "God save the Queen", we'll . . . pull you off your horse!'

The conqueror of Napoleon touched his hat. 'Gentleman, I see how the matter stands. Very well, then. "God save the Queen . . . and may all your wives be like her!"'

Popular speech had exuberance. In Dekker's *The Shoemaker's*

Holiday of 1609 Eyre grumbles in a manner appreciated by all classes from every London region:

> Where be these boys, these girls, these scoundrels? They wallow in the flat brewis of my bounty, and lick up the crumbs of my table, yet will not rise to see my walks cleansed. Come out, you powder-beef queans! What, Nan! What, Madge Mumblecrust! Come out, you fat midriff-swag-belly-whore, and sweep me these kennels that the noisome stench offend not the noses of my neighbours. What, Firk, I say; What Hodge! Open my shop-windows!

Ned Ward, in *The London Spy*, shows the quotidien drama of Fleet Bridge, where '*Nuts, Gingerbread, Oranges* and *Oysters*, lay Pil'd up in moveable shops that run upon wheeles, attended by ill-looking Fellows, some with but one Eye, and others without Noses. Over against there stood a parcel of *Trug-moldies, Straw Hats* and *Flat-Caps*, selling *Socks* and *Furmity, Night-Caps* and *Plumb-Pudding*.'

For a populace still at best semi-literate, puppetries on streets, under bridges, in parks or on commons sustained old tales. Jonson and Fielding wrote for them; Dr Johnson, like Goethe, admired them. *Macbeth* was in Rowe's repertory until about 1800. Perhaps the most skilful was Powell's Puppet Show, in the Little Piazza, Covent Garden, watched by Swift in 1710. Marlowe and Webster were performed by puppets. All ages swarmed for the antics of Paul Pry, St George, the Witch of Endor, the King of Spain, Dick Whittington, Solomon and Balkis, Fair Rosamund, Jane Shore. George Speaight mentions a London puppet-drama of 1660 which presented an aerial view of Norwich, songs, accidents and a fight between Tamerlaine the Great and the Catholic Duc de Guise, instigator of the St Batholomew Massacre. The puppets' quasi-magical skills and startling and licentious humour broke taboos, ventilated resentments, squared the circle of existence, so patently unjust, ludicrous, lustful, tormenting and joyous.

Falstaff of the streets was Mr Punch, anti-hero, thumbing his nose at the Chesterfields and Brummells and, in a more recent text, Winston Churchill, mocking honour, nobility, authority, convention and marriage. Libidinous, murderous, vindictive, cowardly, braggardly, not eloquent but loquacious, free of prudery and guilt, Punch, though of French and Italian ancestry, was very much a Londoner, well appreciated by Pepys.

Free entertainment was everywhere. At Will's Coffee Rooms, Bow Street, 'those who frequented the place had been astonished, day after day, by the entry of a clergyman, unknown to any there, who laid his hat on the table and strode up and down the room with a rapid step, heeding no one and absorbed in his own thoughts. His strange manner earned him, unknown as he was, the name of "the mad parson".' This was the still unknown Jonathan Swift, as recorded by a biographer, Henry Craik.

Voltaire, in London, encountered more than chauvinist rudeness. As a writer he abhorred 'details', calling them the vermin that destroy important literary work. As a visitor, however, he enjoyed plenty of details of the theatre of London streets. In E.M. Forster's words, he was moved 'to respect and admiration by inoculation, a woman who bore rabbits, and an Irishman who saw worms through a microscope in mutton broth'. The gifted woman was Mary Tofts, pictured in her performance in 1727, in a famous Hogarthian print.

Dr Johnson rated Voltaire, like Rousseau, 'an arrant rogue'. Henry Mayhew went further, ranging all authors with 'desiccation, anti-dry rot Preservers, Scourers, Calenderers and French Polishers'. He discovered that writers who sold best on London street-stalls were Shakespeare, Pope, Thomson, Goldsmith, Byron, Scott and Burns. Less popular were Milton, Dryden, Wordsworth and Shelley.

Two centuries after Voltaire, Dorothy Burnham, in her autobiography, recalled 'details' common to all quarters of early twentieth-century London. Muffin-men then walked with their trays of muffins balanced on their heads:

We children would follow the muffin-man hopefully waiting for the tray to fall off its precarious perch, but it never did. He was completely in control, a dedicated circus performer, every movement an astonishing feat of suspension. From time to time he steadied the tray with his left hand as, with his right, he swung a small handbell. . . .

After tea, Sunday evening and church bells again. This was the only sound that drifted through the half-dark as the lamplighter came along with his ten-foot taper. We watched fascinated as, holding his wand poised over the darkened glass, he made the gas mantle shiver and hiss before glowing into soft golden light. I was a little afraid of the lamplighter for, like the Roman god Janus, he had two faces. At dusk, a Promethean bringer of flame, but on winter mornings he came out of the frosty grey Unknown to put out the lamps; a Plutonian bringer of darkness then with a long, black-handled snuffer. This was a pole with a neat cone on the end which fitted over the top of the street lamp and hovered gracefully above the flame until it flickered and dimmed and finally went out.

Periodically, the capital erupted into wild rejoicings – Mafeking Night, or the cessation of the Great War, when the American playwright Robert Sherwood wrote to his mother: 'The well-known British phlegm went west. There was a wild conglomeration of Tommies, Jocks, Australians, Yanks, sailors, wounded men, Italians, Belgians, Indians, French, Portuguese, land-girls, "Waacs", "Wrens", munition girls, and everyone else in uniform parading and howling and hooting and dancing through the streets and breaking things and hurting each other.'

Stanley Weintraub, in his account of the last day of the Great War, describes an all-night party at the Adelphi, to which Osbert Sitwell brought his guests, after talk of Nijinsky and Bolshevism. There they greeted Lytton Strachey

who was as if 'pleasantly awakening from a trance, jigging about with an amiable debility' – also Augustus John, cheered for his officer's uniform, an unlikely apparel, David Garnett, Duncan Grant, Carrington, D.H. Lawrence in a dark mood. 'It makes me sick to see you rejoicing like a butterfly in the last rays of the sun before the winter. The crowd outside thinks that

Germany is crushed forever. But the Germans will soon rise again. Europe is done for; England most of all.'

Elsewhere in the bacchantic streets, Weintraub observes,

> caught up in the enthusiasm was an American citizen, Ezra Pound. A Londoner since 1907, and increasingly cranky because of real and imagined literary affronts and frustrations, he surprised himself. Roused at his Kensington flat by Stella Bowen, Ford Madox Ford's current mistress, he had hopped onto an open-topped bus to central London with her. 'Ezra with his hair on end, smacking the bus-front with his stick and shouting to the other people packed on the tops of other buses jammed alongside ours.' Pound would remain out in the rain so long that he acquired a cold; but he found himself once within a few feet of the King's carriage, which was without escort except for a few policemen. To his friend John Quin in New York, he wrote, attempting to appear more cynical than he had felt at the moment, 'Poor devil was looking happy, I should think for the first time in his life.' Forty years later he recalled the experience in a *Canto*:

> > George the Fifth under the drizzle,
> > As in one November
> > A man who had willed no wrong.

Royal occasions, like executions, evoked savagery, ribaldry or dutiful respect. Also speculation and rumour; the last so important that Shakespeare gave it a speaking part in *Henry IV*. A newspaper report on the attendance of the King of Romania at the state funeral of George V in 1936 provoked speculation to a fantastical degree; in Robert Graves and Alan Hodges' *The Long Weekend*:

> It appears that King Carol, who does not often get among the lights of London, woke up on the funeral morning feeling not too well. Resourceful attachés succeeded in securing the services of an able and energetic masseur of Romanian origin, who worked hard on the King. Thinking that a last-minute work-over might do good,

the masseur accompanied the King in his car – the late-
ness of Carol had caused considerable confusion round
Westminster Hall. The masseur, bewildered by the
marching troops, lost his head and, thinking escape
impossible, lined up with lesser diplomats, generals, and
foreign attachés, and marched a considerable distance . . .
and was described vaguely in the newspaper as 'a representative of Transylvania'.

Politics were always an opportunity for inventive display.
Jean and James MacGibbon took part in a May Day march from
Hammersmith to Hyde Park in 1938. Jean MacGibbon writes:

The surrealists and the A.I.A. [Artists International
Association] had put on a spectacular display: gigantic
figures of Hitler, Mussolini and Franco weaved among
the trade union banners and scarlet flags. There were
tableaux mounted on vans; on one was a cage in which
hung a skeleton and a loudspeaker that played Spanish
Republican records. A quartet of lifesize Chamberlains,
Julian Trevelyan among them, wearing masks designed
by F.E. MacWilliam the sculptor, waved their rolled
umbrellas, shouting 'Chamberlain must go!' and danced
a minuet together when the procession halted.

The Clean Air Act has removed another theatrical feature
of London. The 'pea-souper' fog has vanished. Dickens used
it in *Bleak House* as a symbol of the cruel obfuscations of legal
and public life. Sherlock Holmes distrusted it, in 'The Bruce
Partington Plans':

Look out of this window, Watson. See how the figures
loom up, are dimly seen, and then blend once more into
the cloud-bank. The thief or the murderer could roam
London on such a day as the tiger does the jungle, unseen
until he pounces, and then evident only to his victim.

Monet, in the 1890s, was painting Charing Cross and the
London bridges, the Houses of Parliament and the Thames. To
René Gimpel he wrote: 'What I like most of all in London is

the fog. Without the fog, London would not be a beautiful city. It is the fog that gives it its magnificent breadth.'

That was the late Victorian city of fog, flaring gas-lamps and carriage lamps. An American journalist, Bayard Taylor, compared London to the gloom of Hades, wrapped in a dense mist of dirty yellow, the air as if suddenly thick and mouldy, gas-lamps in shops white and ghastly: 'As I stood in the centre of Trafalgar Square, with every object invisible around me, it reminded me of Satan resting in the middle of Chaos.' Yet in his Journal in 1888, Henry James enthused: 'The atmosphere, with its magnificent mystifications, which flatters and super-fuses, makes everything brown, rich, vague, magnifies distances and minimises details.'

Perhaps this fog's last appearance was in 1952, when it abruptly descended on a brilliant summer morning: silent, ominous, eerie. People were lost a few yards from home. From darkness at noon sounded moans, whimpers, cries for help. Dim forms were visible, kneeling and praying.

Of fog's converse, resplendent London skies, Oscar Wilde, in 'The Decay of Lying', had his own perception:

Yesterday evening Mrs Arundel insisted on my going to the window and looking at the glorious sky, as she called it. Of course I had to look at it. She is one of those absurdly pretty Philistines to whom one can deny nothing. And what was it? It was simply a very second-rate Turner, a Turner of a bad period, with all the painter's worst faults exaggerated and over-emphasised.

Wilde and Mrs Arundel could have also watched a scene, at pre-Victorian Greenwich, but older than Thebes and Rome, as contemporary as tomorrow's Oxford Street, described by 'Boz':

Pedestrians linger in groups at the roadside, unable to resist the allurements of the stout proprietress of the 'jack-in-the-box, three shies a penny,' or the more splendid offers of the man with three thimbles and a pea on a little round board, who astonishes the bewildered crowd with some such address as, 'Here's the sort o' game to

make you laugh seven years arter you're dead, and turn
ev'ry air on your 'ed grey with delight! Three thimbles
and vun little pea – with a vun, two, three, and a two,
three, vun: catch him who can, look on, keep your eyes
open, and niver say die! Niver mind the change, and the
expense: all fair and above board: them as don't play can't
vin, and luck attend the ryal sportsman! Bet any gen'lm'n
any sum of money, from half-a-crown up to a suverin, as
he doesn't name the thimble as kivers the pea.' Here some
greenhorn whispers to his friend that he distinctly saw the
pea roll under the middle thimble – an impression which
is immediately confirmed by a gentleman in the top-
boots, who is standing by, and who, in a low tone,
regrets his own ability to bet, in consequence of having
unfortunately left his purse at home, but strongly urges
the stranger not to neglect such a golden opportunity.
The 'plant' is successful, the bet is made, the stranger
of course loses: and the gentleman with the thimbles
consoles him, as he pockets the money, with an assurance
that it's 'all the fortin of war! This time I vin, next time
you vin; niver mind the loss of two bob and a bender!
Do it up in a small parcel, and break out in a fresh
place.'

In parks, public gardens and fairgrounds, Londoners heard
plenty of music, 'Promenade Concerts'. From the Restoration
onwards, programmes included Handel, J.C. Bach, Purcell,
Boyce, Arne, Locke, Alvison and Clarke. None of this would
have gratified Dr Johnson. 'Music excites in my mind no ideas,
and hinders me from contemplating my own.' He demanded
of the great musicologist, Dr Burney, father of the novelist
Fanny, herself praised by Johnson, 'And pray, sir, who is Bach?
Is he a piper?'
     Together with the music was dancing, a favourite London
occupation, one function of which, in the late sixteenth century, apparently was to discover whether one's partner smelt
like bad meat. Eighteenth-century music was condemned by
a Mr Peter Bedford for exciting female sensitivity and the
tête-à-tête.
     A unique mingling of fair, carnival and pleasure-ground was

imagined by Virginia Woolf, in *Orlando*, which loses little by
not being literally true:

> Near London Bridge, where the river had frozen to a
> depth of some twenty fathoms, a wrecked wherry boat
> was plainly visible, lying on the bed of the river where
> it had sunk last autumn, overlaid with apples. The old
> bumboat woman, who was carrying her fruit to market
> on the Surrey side, sat there in her plaids and farthingales
> with her lap full of apples, for all the world as if she were
> about to serve a customer, though a certain blueness about
> the lips hinted the truth. 'Twas a sight King James
> especially liked to look upon, and he would bring a troupe
> of courtiers to gaze with him. In short, nothing could
> exceed the brilliancy and gaiety of the scene by day. But
> it was at night that the carnival was at its merriest. For
> the frost continued unbroken; the nights were of perfect
> stillness; the moon and stars blazed with the hard fixity
> of diamonds, and to the fine music of flute and trumpet
> the courtiers danced.

Smollett, in *Humphry Clinker*, praised Ranelagh Gardens,
Chelsea:

> Ranelagh looks like the enchanted palace of a genie,
> adorned with the most exquisite performance of painting,
> carving, and gilding, enlightened with a thousand golden
> lamps, that emulate the noon-day sun; crowded with the
> great, the rich, the gay, the happy, and the fair; glittering
> with cloth of gold and silver, lace, embroidery, and
> precious stones. While these exciting sons and daughters
> of felicity tread this round of pleasure, or regale in dif-
> ferent parties, and separate lodges, with fine imperial tea
> and other delicious refreshments, their ears are entertained
> with the most ravishing delights of musick, both instru-
> mental and vocal.

Such places offered unexpectedly varied entertainment,
including a hare that played a tabor. Rivalling Ranelagh was
Vauxhall Gardens, Lambeth, which a character in Fanny

Burney's *Evelina* called the first pleasure in life. The place was originally named Spring Gardens. In 1662 Pepys,

> With my wife and the two maids and the boy took boat to Vauxhall, where I had not been a great while. To the old Spring Garden, and there walked long, and the wenches gathered pinks. Here we stayed, and seeing that we could not have anything to eat but very dear and with long stay, we went forth again without any notice taken of us, and so we might have done if we had had anything. Thence to the new one, where I never was before, which much exceeds the other; and here we also walked, and the boy crept through the hedge and gathered abundance of roses, and after a long walk passed out of doors as we did in the other place, and so to another house that was an ordinary house, and there we had cakes and powdered beef, and so home again by water, with much pleasure.

Here too was brilliance for eye and ear: fireworks, masked balls, acrobatics, the attentions of press-gang and pimp; imitation pagodas, Greek temples, Chinese pavilions. 'Boz' saw Vauxhall Gardens in 1837:

> A small party of dismal men in cocked hats were 'executing' the overture to 'Tancredi', and a numerous assemblance of ladies and gentlemen, and their families, had rushed from their half-emptied stout mugs in the supper boxes, and crowded to the spot. Intense was the low murmur of appreciation when a particularly small gentleman in a dress coat led on a particularly tall lady in a blue sarcanet pelisse and bonnet of the same ornamented with large white feathers, and forthwith commenced a plaintive duet.

Thackeray's Becky Sharp and her friends wandered through the Gardens and saw:

> The three hundred thousand extra lamps, which were always lighted; the fiddlers in cocked hats, who played ravishing melodies under the gilded cockle-shell in the

midst of the Gardens; the singers, both of comic and
sentimental ballads, who charmed the ears there; the
country dances, formed by bounding cockneys and cock-
neyesses, and executed amidst jumping, thumping, and
laughter; the signal that announced that Madame Saqui
was about to mount skyward on a slack-rope ascending
to the stars; the hermit that always sat in the illuminated
hermitage; the dark walks so favourable to the attentions
of young lovers; the pots of stout handed about by the
people in the shabby old liveries; and the twinkling boxes,
in which the happy feasters make-believe to eat slices of
almost invisible ham.

The decline of the gardens and huge fairs assisted the rise of
the music-halls, from Battersea to Edgeware Road, Hoxton to
Camden Town, Shoreditch to Leicester Square, developing
from eighteenth-century tavern back rooms and supper rooms,
drink always encouraging an atmosphere of belligerent patriotism, sentimentality, guile, insolence and humour; taking the
strain in the fight for survival, making tolerable the intolerable,
transforming the vicious to mirth.

> It's the same the whole world over,
>   It's the poor that gets the blame,
> It's the rich that gets the pleasure,
>   Ain't it all a bloomin' shame.

Of the rich, Will Fyffe would demand: 'What do they *do*? I'll
tell you what they do! They do *us*!'
  Popular humour, based on shrewd observation and disrespect
for pedigree and unearned honours, reaches back to Chaucer.
Music-hall jokes were aged, with themes even older. Broadcasting in 1942, a dark time of the war, Sir Max Beerbohm
reminisced:

Mr Harry Freeman, dear man, sounded no depths, and
scaled no heights, and indeed had no pretentions of any
kind except a thorough knowledge of his business, which
was the singing of songs about Beer, about the Lodger,
about being had up before the Beak, about the Missus,

about the sea-side and all the other safest and surest themes.

Outsize wives and timid or erring husbands, the rent-collector, mothers-in-law, in a smoky, boozy haze, with rumbustious double-entendres, sly winks, robust sexuality, gallows humour, with the incongruous and absurd demolishing the stuffy and rigid – all this was the stuff of the music-hall.

Beerbohm lastingly remembered the glum Gus Elen, with his song 'Well, It's a Grite Big Shame' and his reflection 'Wot's the good of ennyfink? Why, nuffink.'

Bedecked with bars and promenades, opulent mirrors and dashing sales-girls, the music-halls also, however, sheltered prostitution. Here in Arnold Bennett's *The Pretty Lady* in wartime London is the Empire, Leicester Square:

> She surveyed the Promenade with a professional eye. It instantly shocked her, not as it might have shocked one ignorant of human nature and history, but by reason of its frigidity, its constraint, its solemnity, its pretence. In one glance she embraced all the figures, moving or stationary, against the hedge of shoulders in front and against the mirrors behind – all of them: the programme girls, the cigarette girls, the chocolate girls, the cloak-room girls, the waiters, the overseers, as well as the vivid courtesans and their clientele in black, tweed, or khaki. With scarcely an exception they all had the same strange look, the same absence of gesture. They were northern, blond, self-contained, terribly impassive. Christine impulsively exclaimed – and the faint cry was dragged out of her, out of the bottom of her heart, by what she saw.
>
> 'My God! How mournful it is!'

Nevertheless, music-hall songs, some still sung, sublimated poverty, injustice, violence and old age. 'I'm one o' the Ruins that Cromwell knocked abaht a bit.' They were unbreakable foils to the hoity-toity and la-di-da. They influenced Dickens and Kipling. T.S. Eliot thought that through comedians the poor found the expression and dignity of their own lives.

George Orwell believed that the song 'Two Lovely Black Eyes' would outlast Virginia Woolf:

> Two Lovely Black Eyes,
>   Oh, what a surprise!
> Simply for telling a man he was wrong –
>   Two Lovely Black Eyes.

Almost everywhere, London was lightened at intervals not only by entertainment marts but also by private gardens, some large, many tiny, all colourful. Stefan Zweig, in London in 1906, considered that the English, with their gardens, art collections, schools – he might have added sports – were nearer the ancient Greeks than any other contemporary people. The squares and public parks also provided room to breathe and to dawdle, and evidence for Hannah More's strictures: 'The substitution of the word "Gallantry" for that crime which stabs domestic happiness and conjugal virtue, is one of the most dangerous of all the modern abuses of the language.'

London has long rejoiced in its parks, each one with its particular flavour, particular colour; each with a slightly different note. Of St James's Park, Henry James wrote, in *English Hours*:

> Much of its character comes from the nearness to the Westminster slums. It is a park of intimacy, and perhaps the most democratic corner of London, in spite of its being in the royal and military quarter and close to all kinds of stateliness. There are few hours of the day when a thousand smutty children are not sprawling over it, and the unemployed lie thick on the grass and cover the benches with a brotherhood of greasy corduroys. In the London parks are the drawing-rooms and clubs of the poor . . . these particular grass-plots and alleys may be said to constitute the very *salon* of the slums.

In Virginia Woolf's *The Years* characters revive lost times and many-faced Time as they reflect on their pasts in Regent's Park. In *Mrs Dalloway*, a man sees more than grass and water, children and birds:

He had only to open his eyes; but a weight was on them;
a fear. He strained; he pushed; he looked; he saw Regent's
Park before him. Long streamers of sunlight fawned at his
feet. The trees waved, brandished. We welcome, the
world seemed to say; we accept; we create. Beauty, the
world seemed to say. And as if to prove it (scientifically)
wherever he looked, at the houses, at the railings, at
the antelopes stretching over the palings, beauty sprang
instantly. To watch a leaf quivering in the rush of air was
an exquisite joy. Up in the sky swallows swooping,
swerving, flinging themselves in and out, round and
round, yet always with perfect control as if elastics held
them; and the flies rising and falling; and the sun spotting
now this leaf, now that, in mockery, dazzling it with soft
gold in pure good temper; and now and again some chime
(it might be a motor-horn) tinkling divinely on the grass
stalks – all this, calm and reasonable as it was, made out
of ordinary things as it was, was the truth now; beauty,
that was the truth now. Beauty was everywhere.

London parks, with their grass, trees, water, show the most
obvious beauties. Everyone has a favourite. George Bernard
Shaw, who always had an eye cocked for commonplace drama
and zest for life, in old age told Stephen Winsten:

A man of fashion only knew Hyde Park. The Regent's
Park held the Zoo, and the other places the riff-raff in my
days. You did not walk in Hyde Park when the season
was over; if you did, you were regarded as a man lost to
society and that was all that mattered. I was to be found
every season of the year in Hyde Park because that was
where I learnt my English. As a foreigner, I enjoyed ideas
and every idea was thrashed out in the Park. You could
learn more by mixing with the riff-raff at Marble Arch
in one hour than by a thousand walks from Hyde Park
Corner to Albert Gate in the season. Besides you could
take your lectures lying down at Marble Arch. The
greensward is the natural couch of man and the people for
whose sake you had to avoid everything that was natural
were not to be seen.

The parks supply lecturers, grumblers, extortionists, seducers, lovers, ribald children – all have something to declare. William Sansom had a flair for London speech:

> Parks! Don't give me none of them things thanks! Parks I've had, and thank you very much. There's things go on in parks I wouldn't know, I know there is, and I wasn't Keeper thirty year, and not know more I don't want none of them, you keep 'em, keep your parks. . . .
>   Parks isn't only fairies taking ladies' pewdle-dogs to air, parks is no dear old lady in a chair. Sweet lavender no! Nor is it banstands on a sunny day nor reds and whites at football play, nor forty winks in a threepenny deck, nor snowdrops ring-a-ding in spring, no nor the white Tomtiddler's day folks thinks parks is . . . parks is a pest, parks has a shady side nor do I mean the shade beneath a leafy tree, there's a darker shade than that in parks.

Henry James, intimate with patrician London, had also known Second Empire Paris and the passions seething beneath surfaces outwardly controlled. He too realized something of London's darker shade, the melodrama threatening to invade the mannered comedy and reasonable debate. Hyacinth, in *The Princess Casamassima*, is a young Frenchman embroiled in London anarchism, conspiracy and bombs: the sub-world of political cells, cheap cafés and dingy pubs. Here the theatre of popular life lacked a comedian.

> The season was terribly hard; and as in that lower world one walked with one's ear nearer the ground the deep perpetual groan of London misery seemed to swell and swell and form the whole undertone to life. The filthy air reached the place in the damp coats of silent men and hung there till it was brewed to a nauseous warmth and ugly serious faces squared themselves through it, and strong-smelling pipes contributed their element in a fierce dogged manner which appeared to say that it now had to stand for everything – for bread and meat and beer, for shoes and blankets and the poor things at the pawn-broker's and the smokeless chimney at home.

Nevertheless, as so often in an old and vast city, perhaps in the next street would be living a fellow quite different, seen by Ford Madox Ford:

> Late in the (Sunday) afternoon he would get up, dress himself carefully in his best; wrap his chaffinch cages in old handkerchiefs, and, carrying them, saunter along Petticoat Lane, look restfully at the cages of birds exposed for sale, meditating a purchase for next year, passing the time of day with a Jew or two, and losing himself, stolid, quiet, and observant, in the thick crowd. He would come to a greengrocer's shop, the door open, the interior a black and odorous darkness, where you trod upon cabbage leaves and orange paper. Behind this was another dark room, in the centre of which a ladder stood up, going into an upper loft through a trap-door. This loft was the 'Cave of Harmony' where, in the light of brilliant gas jets were held the contests of the piping chaffinches. There, taking the gas jets for a fiercer sun, the little birds sang shrilly and furiously one against another, the attentive crowd of faces around them, thrown into deep shadows and strong lights, hard featured and intense, with every eye fixed upon the small and straining singer, fingersticking offturns in the song and a silence broken by no shuffling of feet and no clearing of throats.

There was another obsession, far from politics, in what Henry James called 'the roaring vortex of London'. Louis Blanc, French politician and journalist, wrote of the London he saw in the 1860s, that there existed

> a number of unsavoury dens where old women as ugly, decrepit, dirty and dubious as business permits, all told Milady the exact moment when she would see her husband again, or Miss So-and-So that she could dry her eyes as she was still loved and that the quarrel would not last. Would you believe that in London exists a number of dark dens, all of them situated in lonely parts of the city, to which duchesses, countesses, society ladies and others stealthily crept to have their fortunes told by these witches in rags?

Throughout, London was in constant change. The motor-car displaced the hansom, the railway the coach. For the novelist Compton Mackenzie, the London Tube opened a new angle of perception, revealing:

> The Cyclopean eye of the advancing train, the adventure of boarding, the fastidiousness in the choice of a neighbour, the sense of equality, the mysterious and flattering reflection of oneself in the opposite windows, even of the colours of the various stations – from the orange and lemon of Covent Garden to the bistre melancholy of Caledonian Road or Camden Town, faint cerulean like an autumnal sky.

Material changes have never overcome London's appetite for drama: in the planned and vicious, the random and improvised, the grotesque. William Sansom's London, heightened to a fusion of fantasy and detailed realism, is a city of unpredict-abilities, in which the familiar is abruptly wrenched askew. A gasometer is minutely observed – by a man climbing it. Murderous hatred flashes amongst the mirrors and scissors in a barber's. A lion rears up amid trim Maida Vale daisies. His is a metropolis of decayed hotels where forbidden meals are cooked between sheets on electric blankets; of faded Edwardian conservatories, edgy office parties, a razor-gang's pad. A vision of wonder, of small clues, enlarges into the bizarre and mysteri-ous; unforeseen cravings and chance recognitions are told in language precise as an engineer's yet excited as a child venturing amongst extraordinary secrets. In his collection of short stories, *South*, one reads:

> Once a snake escaped from an animal warehouse in London. It made its way at speed down the length of Tottenham Court Road, proceeded over into Charing Cross Road, and thence in the same straight determined line to Trafalgar Square and the Nelson monument, about whose plinth it was captured. Then there was the thief, who chose, among all the pockets of the crowd, that of a zoological student; he drew forth a thin, green grass-snake.

THE WAR AND AFTER

The Second World War could create that further, visionary
London, briefly held, tragedy and horror suspended for an
instant, amongst blazing streets, toppling buildings, vistas
almost supernatural gliding between wreckage, or, in some
tense, prolonged interval, spreading over the capital an
atmosphere both shared and momentous, and very personal.
Elizabeth Bowen's short story, 'Mysterious Kor', captures it:

> Full moonlight drenched the city and searched it; there
> was not a niche left to stand in. The effect was remorse-
> less: London looked like the moon's capital – shallow,
> cratered, extinct. It was late, but not yet midnight; now
> the buses had stopped, the polished roads and streets in
> this region sent for minutes together a ghostly unbroken
> reflection up. The soaring new flats and the crouching old
> shops and houses looked equally brittle under the moon,
> which blazed in windows that looked its way. The
> futility of the black-out became laughable: from the sky,
> presumably, you could see every slate on the roofs, every
> whited kerb, every contour of the naked winter flower-
> beds in the park; and the lake, with its shining twists and
> tree-darkened islands would be a landmark for miles, yes,
> miles, overhead.
>   However, the sky, in whose glassiness floated no clouds
> but only opaque balloons, remained glassy-silent. The
> Germans no longer came by the full moon. Something
> more immaterial seemed to threaten, and to be keeping
> people at home. This day between days, this extra tax,
> was perhaps more than senses and nerves could bear. Peo-
> ple stayed indoors with a fervour that could be felt: the
> buildings strained with battened-down human life, but
> not a beam, not a voice, not a note from a radio escaped.
> Now and then under streets and buildings the earth
> rumbled: the Underground sounded loudest at this time.

Rose Macaulay describes the bombed City, the ruins
relapsing into a haunt for wild nature, wild animals, wild
children:

The maze of little streets threading through the wilderness, the broken walls, the great pits with their dense forests of bracken and bramble, golden ragwort and coltsfoot, fennel and foxglove and vetch, all the wild rambling shrubs that spring from ruin, the vaults and cellars and deep caves, the wrecked guild halls that had belonged to saddlers, merchant tailors, haberdashers, waxhandlers, barbers, brewers, coopers and coachmakers, all the ancient City fraternities, the broken office stairways that spiralled steeply past empty doorways and rubbled closets into the sky, empty shells of churches with their towers still strangely spiring above the wilderness, their empty window arches where green boughs pushed in, their broken pavement floors – St Vedast's, St Alban's, St Anne's and St Agnes's, St Giles Cripplegate, its tower high above the rest, the ghosts of churches burnt in an earlier fire, St Olave's and St John Zachary's, haunting the green-flowered churchyards that bore their names, the ghosts of taverns where merchants and clerks had drunk, of restaurants where they had eaten – all this scarred and haunted green and stone and brambled wilderness lying under the August sun, a-hum with insects and astir with secret, darting, burrowing life, received the returned traveller into its dwellings with a wrecked, indifferent calm. Here, its cliffs and chasms and caves seemed to say, is your home; here you belong; you cannot get away, you do not wish to get away.

William Sansom, a fireman during the London Blitz, saw strange agonies, related in his short story 'Building Alive':

The bomb fell.
  Swiftly the life of the house blossomed. The trickling from the pipes gushed free, cascading noisily into the courtyard. Tiles, plaster, gutter fragments and more glass lurched off the roof. A new growth was sprouting everywhere, sprouting like the naked plumbing, as if these leaden entrails were the worm at the core of a birth, struggling to emerge, thrusting everything else aside. But

the house held. It must have blossomed, opened, subsided upon itself.

In his Blitz poem, 'The Streets of Laredo', another survivor, Louis MacNeice, was sardonically apocalyptic:

Then twangling their Bibles with wrath in their nostrils
From Bunhill Fields came Bunyan and Blake.
'Laredo the golden is fallen, is fallen;
   Your flame will not quench and your thirst will not
                                                    slake.

A sometimes feline witness to post-war London was Sir Angus Wilson. His south-west or north-west Londoners grapple with socialist austerity, grumble at shortages, complain of social upstarts, rate Churchill's friends 'common'. In stories and novels he misses few affectations of the 'new poor' and of leftish intellectuals, academic snobs, chilly do-gooders. His story 'The Wrong Set' has period exactitude:

After closing time she had a drink with Terry and Mrs Lippiatt. Mrs Lippiatt said what was the good of having money, there was nothing to spend it on. Vi thought to herself what she would like was to have some money to spend, but aloud she said in her smart voice 'Yes, isn't it awful? With this government you have to be grateful for the air you breathe. Look at the things we can't have – food, clothes, foreign travel.' 'Ah, yes, foreign travel,' said Mrs Lippiatt, though she knew damned well Vi had never been abroad. 'It's bad enough for you and me, Mrs Cawston, but think of this poor boy' and she put her fat, beringed hand on Terry's knee 'he's never been out of England. Never mind, darling, you shall have your trip to Nice the day we get a proper government back.' Mr Pontresoli and Trevor joined them. Trevor was the real public schoolboy with his monocle and calling Mrs Lippiatt 'my dear lady', Vi could see that Terry was worried – he was frightened that Trevor was muscling in; but that was just Trevor's natural way with women – he had perfect manners. Later in the evening he asked Vi who the hell the old trout was.

'The Major's got a good one about Attlee,' said Mr Pontresoli, in his thick, adenoidal Italian cockney, his series of blue stubbed chins wobbling as he spoke.

'It's impossible to be as funny about this government as they are themselves,' said Trevor. He had *such* a quiet sense of humour. 'They're a regular Fred Karno show.' But they all begged to hear the story, so he gave it to them. 'An empty taxi drove up to No. 10,' he said 'and Mr Attlee got out.' Beautifully told it was, with his monocle taken out of his eye and polished just at the right moment.

Older Londoners will recognize a particular tone in Sir Angus' short story, 'Mother's Sense of Fun': 'Nonsense, Cook, you know very well you like standing in those queues, you take to them like a duck to water, they're just up your street.'

Some of the battered, perilous London reappears in Muriel Spark's novel, *The Girls of Slender Means*:

Long ago in 1945 all the nice people in England were poor, allowing for exceptions. The streets of the cities were lined with buildings in bad repair or in no repair at all, bomb-sites piled with stony rubble, houses like giant teeth in which decay had been drilled like the ruins of ancient castles until, at a closer view, the wallpapers of various quite normal rooms would be visible, room above room, exposed, as on a stage, with one wall missing; sometimes a lavatory chain would dangle over nothing from a fourth – or fifth – floor ceiling; most of all the staircases survived like a new art-form, leading up and up to an unspecified destination that made unusual demands on the mind's eye. All the nice people were poor; at least, that was a general axiom, the best of the rich being poor in spirit.

There was absolutely no point in feeling depressed about the scene, it would have been like feeling depressed about the Grand Canyon or some event of the earth outside everybody's scope. People continued to exchange assurances of depressed feelings about the weather or the news, or the Albert Memorial which had not been hit, not even shaken, by any bomb from first to last.

London, after Blitz and shortages, suffered severe changes, in architecture, racial distribution, political debate, readjustment of class values. Yet historical change, if often severe, is seldom sensational and never absolute. To this day, sections of London remain virtually unchanged. Even Irish bombs have not dislocated the scene in London parks. A pale mosque with a golden dome has risen alongside Regent's Park, but still the military bands play to audiences slanted dreamily in deckchairs, inhaling sounds largely familiar to their grandparents – Sullivan, Lehar, Offenbach, Lionel Monkton, Rossini, Sousa, Suppé, Strauss: a scene, amongst trees and water and roses, which would have been instantly recognized by Shaw and Pinero, Wells and Compton Mackenzie, tunes poignant as a girl's scent reaching you only after she has passed. On shop windows in Holloway Road, Camden Road, Hammersmith and Hackney, advertisements remain unchanged: masseurs and models, clairvoyants, faith-healers and animal-fanciers. A North London statue of Gandhi is added to that of John Wesley. Receptions continue at the Palace, not always to the comfort of literary London. Elizabeth Longford, in her autobiography *The Pebbled Shore*, described one, in the Sixties:

My worst experience of the doghouse at a Buckingham Palace garden party was when I was officially presenting Valerie Eliot, recently married to the poet, T.S. Eliot. We were bitterly disappointed to find that 'presentation' carried no guarantee of meeting the Queen, Prince Philip or any other member of the Royal Family. In vain Frank waylaid every official he knew. 'This is our greatest living poet. Please present him and Mrs Eliot to someone royal . . .' The official did not actually reply, 'Never heard of him,' but that was the unspoken message.

Cecil Beaton knew royal London, though also its artistic and Bohemian circles, the clubs and restaurants. An entry in his 1955 diary tells:

A neighbour told me of an argument that Augustus John had with Philip Dunn, a very rich and brilliant money-maker, with whom he was dining at the Eiffel Tower in London. This was the expensive restaurant presided over by the great character, Stulik, where Augustus when in London was most likely to be seen. Philip suddenly said: 'I'll bet you whatever money we have in our pockets that you are wrong.' Philip found that he had about twenty pounds in his own pocket. To his astonishment, Augustus laid down eleven hundred pounds in crisp, white, high-denomination notes. Stulik, the Hungarian promoter of the Club-Restaurant, who had doubtless run a 'tick' with Augustus that had mounted with the years, had eyes like a rocket. In a flash the vast Stulik was hovering over the pile of money. Philip, when he had recovered from his surprise, said: 'You'd better let me have that money to invest for you.' But neither Philip nor Stulik got their hands on any of it. Augustus summed up: 'I like carrying a bit of pin money on me.'

Recovering from the Blitz, London at night showed some unchanged externals, particularly the London verging on heightened, even visionary perception. A girl in Nina Bawden's novel, *Familiar Passions*, observed from her Islington flat:

> From the window at night, the view was beautiful: the mysterious, dark canal below and, in the distance, tower blocks lit like fairy castles dwarfing the spires of city churches and the squat dome of St Paul's.

To this day, undeterred by the bombs of wartime and indeed peacetime, official London, the London of Whitehall, Westminster, the Abbey, has set a measured pace. This is instantly recognizable in the start of C.P. Snow's novel, *The Corridors of Power*:

> I stopped the taxi at the corner of Lord North Street. My wife and I had the habit of being obsessively punctual, and

that night we had, as usual, overdone it. There was a quarter of an hour to kill, so we dawdled down to the river. It was a pleasant evening, I said, conciliating the moment. The air was warm against the cheek, the trees on the Embankment garden stood bulky, leaves filling out although it was only March, against the incandescent skyline. The light above Big Ben shone beneath the cloud-cap; the House was sitting.

We walked a few yards further, in the direction of Whitehall. Across Parliament Square, in the Treasury building, another light was shining. A room lit up on the third storey, someone working late.

There was nothing special about the evening, either for my wife or me. We had dined with the Quaifes several times before. Roger Quaife was a youngish Conservative member who was beginning to be talked about. I had met him through one of my official jobs, and thought him an interesting man. It was the kind of friendly acquaintanceship, no more than that, which we all picked up, officials, politicians of both parties: not meeting often, but enough to make us feel at home in what they sometimes called 'this part of London.'

Prompt to the last stroke of eight, we were back in Lord North Street. A maid took us upstairs to the drawing-room, bright with chandeliers, drink-trays, the dinner-shirts of the two men already standing there, the necklace of Caro Quaife glittering as she took our hands.

'I expect you know everyone, don't you?' she said. 'Of course you do!'

For many other Londoners, perhaps most, there was no such *of course*. Frances, one of Anita Brookner's lonely, perceptive women, dreads 'all those terrible public holidays – Christmas, Easter – when I could never, ever, ever, find an adequate means of using up all the available time.' In *Look at Me* (1983) Frances, on one of her many solitary, brooding walks, goes, not to a lively dinner-party, but merely to remain deep within herself, hoping that exhaustion will induce a sound sleep at the end. She traverses the underground tunnel at Marble Arch, with its

Iranian slogans and vomiting drunk, looks up Oxford Street,
'like a dull chasm, with ghostly Christmas trees in shop
windows illuminated only by those terrible overhead lights'.
Midnight has gone. She passes the sex shop and ethnic hair-
dresser in Edgware Road. Finally, with frightened steps, she
reaches an underpass:

> I was shaking so much that I had to cling to the railing,
> feeling for every step with my foot, and then, when I had
> reached the tunnel, keeping close to the wall, the dirty
> tiles, ready at the slightest sound to retreat, or, when I
> had passed the halfway mark, to fling myself forward. It
> took a long time, that I know; I also know that when I
> reached the steps at the other end I could hardly lift my
> feet to climb them. At one point I was overcome with a
> sort of vertigo and had to stand still until I found the will
> to go on. I emerged upwards into the blackest night I had
> ever seen.
> This must be the most terrible hour, the hour when
> people die in hospitals. No sound. No light, the vital
> forces ebbing away, even the memory indistinct.

Martin Amis contributes to the medley of London voices in
his novel, *Money*:

> And now I am one of the unemployed. What do we do
> all day? We sit on stoops and pause in loose knots on the
> stained pavements. The pavements are like threadless
> carpets after some atrocious rout of flesh-frazzled food
> and emetic drink: last night the weather gods all drowned
> their sorrows, and then threw up from thirty thousand
> feet. We sit flummoxed in the parks, among low-caste
> flowers. Whew (we think), this life is slow. I came of age
> in the Sixties, when there were chances, when it was all
> there waiting. Now they seep out of school – to what?
> To nothing, to fuck-all. The young (you can see it in their
> faces), the stegosaurus-rugged no-hopers, the parrot-
> crested blankies – they've come up with an appropriate
> response to this, which is nothing. Which is nothing,
> which is fuck-all. The dole-queue starts at the exit to

the playground. Riots are their rumpus-room, sombre London their jungle-gym. Life is hoarded elsewhere by others – you can only press your face against the glass. In my day, if you wanted, you could just drop out. You can't drop out any more. Money has seen to that. There's nowhere to go. You cannot hide from money. You just cannot hide out from money any more. And so sometimes, when the nights are hot, they smash and grab.

To end this section on such a note would mislead. Post-war London has had many literary chroniclers, exploring its varied social layers, its juxtapositions and changes, its adventurers, victims, rivals, cynics, buffoons and comedians. Readers may recall Anthony Powell's elaborate social comedies, Doris Lessing's serious young people striving to find themselves, detect political and moral certainties, adjust to a London of bomb-sites, grim housing, violence, long debates in an era of immigrants, go-getters, prophets, squatters, rebels, proselytizers, the puzzled. London flashes and subsides, emits mirth and pathos, complex dilemmas and unexpected solutions, in the work of Muriel Spark, Gillian Tindall, Margaret Drabble, a list too lengthy to continue. A.S. Byatt's novel, *Still Life*, is more exuberant than Martin Amis:

London excited Frederica. She knew little of it, and could not connect the parts she knew into a coherent map in her head. What she liked, being young and strong and curious and greedy, was the anonymity and variety of her possible journeys from territory to territory. She liked hurling in bright boxes amongst endlessly various strangers from Camden Town to Oxford Circus, from Liverpool Street to Leicester Square or, after the *Vogue* luncheon, from Hyde Park to St Paul's to see Nigel Reiver in the City. Differences delighted her.

1

LONDON RIVER

This is a broad slippery fellow; rest he affects not,
for he is always in motion: he seems something like
a carrier, for he is still either going or coming, and
once in six or eight hours salutes the sea his mother,
and then brings tidings from her . . .

Merchandise he likes and loves; and therefore
sends forth ships and traffic to most parts of the
earth; his subjects and inhabitants live by oppres-
sion like hard landlords at land, the greater rule,
and many times devour the less; the city is won-
drously beholden to it, for she is furnished with
almost all necessaries by it.

Donald Lupton, *London and the Country
Carbonadoed*, 1632

HAMPTON COURT, TWICKENHAM AND HAMMERSMITH

No longer London's commercial spine, the Thames has lost
vitality. The tourist steamer and water-bus have deposed the
East Indiaman, the clipper and the powerful steamships. The
nineteen important quays that Boswell could have seen are
submerging beneath towering slabs of glass and steel. Yet,
freed from much of its old business, the river may yet, as
William Morris and H.G. Wells hoped, regain its sparkle and
purity once praised by Dunbar and Spencer and still visible
between Oxford and Richmond, and, increasingly, beyond.

At Hampton Court, with its tall red chimneys, square
battlements and forty-four acres of garden, Jerome K. Jerome
in *Three Men in a Boat* discerned the 'mellow, bright, sweet old
wall' alongside the river, 'with fifty shades and tints and hues

in every ten yards', shared indeed by the water. Here, in
Virginia Woolf's *The Waves*, ageing friends reassemble, each
with a private vision:

> 'The gold has faded between the trees', said Rhoda,
> 'and a slice of green lies between them, elongated like the
> blade of a knife seen in dreams, or some tapering island
> on which nobody sets foot. Now the cars begin to wink
> and flicker, coming down the avenue; the boles of the
> trees are swollen, are obscene with lovers.'

From riverside Twickenham, Pope had, in 'Ombre at
Hampton Court', celebrated the Palace in his unmistakable
way, beginning:

> Close by those meads, for ever crown'd with flow'rs,
> Where THAMES with pride surveys his rising tow'rs,
> There stands a structure of majestic frame,
> Which from the neighb'ring HAMPTON takes its name.
> Here BRITAIN'S statesmen oft' the fall foredoom
> Of foreign tyrants, and of nymphs at home;
> Here thou great ANNA! Whom three realms obey,
> Dost sometimes counsel take – and sometimes tea.

Pope's house at Twickenham – where Gay is buried – has
vanished. Not so Strawberry Hill, Horace Walpole's villa,
which he bought from Mrs Chevenix, a provider of toys, and
an authority on them. Writing to H.S. Conway in 1747, he
praised it as

> a little plaything-house that I got out of Mrs Chevenix's
> shop, and is the prettiest bauble you ever saw. It is set in
> enamelled meadows with filigree hedges:
> > 'A small Euphrates through the piece is rolled,
> > And little finches wave their wings in gold.'
> Two delightful roads, that you would call dusty, supply
> me continually with coaches and chaises: barges as solemn
> as Barons of the Exchequer move under my windows;
> Richmond Hill and Ham Walk bound my prospect; but,
> thank God! the Thames is between me and the Duchess

of Queensberry. Dowagers as plenty as flounders inhabit
all around, and Pope's ghost is just now skimming under
my window by a most poetical moonlight. I have about
land enough to keep such a farm as Noah's, when he set
up in the ark with a pair of each kind; but my cottage is
rather cleaner than I believe his was after they had been
cooped up together forty days. The Chevenixes had
tricked it out for themselves: up two pairs of stairs is what
they call Mr Chevenix's library, furnished with three
maps, one shelf, a bust of Sir Isaac Newton and a lame
telescope without any glasses.

Naomi Mitchison, future novelist, lived nearer London by
the river at Hammersmith, between the wars (she remembered
a homosexual friend being given a Guardsman for his birth-
day). Her autobiography, *You May Well Ask*, begins in
childhood:

Hammersmith was presumably thought in other circles to
be very avant-garde and we had a good share of love and
hate affairs, rushing in and out of one another's lives,
having parties and from time to time swimming in the
Thames which was surely much dirtier then than now.
But it was fun to be swept up with the slightly buoyant
tide past Chiswick Eyot. Muddy to land on, across to the
towpath and then the run downstream to a good starting
point for getting back. It was thick brown water, stick-
and bubble-streaked, but if we kept our mouths shut, not
swallowing so much as a cigarette package or an old
French letter, nothing went wrong.
    There was also the Doves and a pub in Black Lion Lane
where people played bowls. And there was an amiable
confectioner and newspaper shop along at the end of
Hammersmith Terrace where Lois and the Kennington
boy attempted to disguise pennies as half-crowns with
silver paper. The parents were discreetly told! All the
people along the river had Boat Race parties and there was
a cake shop that made us decorated Boat Race cakes. They
also made a wedding cake for my cousin Charlotte when
she married Michael Hope. My mother disapproved

because he was 'in trade' – Hope's Windows! But I
approved strongly and the cake had pink windows
opening on a foam of perilous seas in tossing white icing,
and on the bottom layer the sweet Thames flowing
sweetly . . .

[In later years] There was always argument, admiration, dressing up and parties. Those at St Peter's Square
were like to-day's: beer and bangers rather than claret cup
and sandwiches as they would have been at more ordinary
houses. Here were the poets and painters; here was
Robert Graves, who might be delightful or might bite,
according doubtless to his current relationship with the
White Goddess. Here was Dylan Thomas holding forth,
never sober. Here sometimes was Augustus John, who
once suggested that as I had so many children I might
have one by him. I felt this was an interesting party
approach, but he had a glass of beer in each hand which
inhibited the next step.

BRIDGES

Thenceforward succeed London's bridges: Kew, Battersea,
Albert, Chelsea, Vauxhall, Lambeth, Westminster, Hunger-
ford, Waterloo, Blackfriars, Southwark, London, Tower . . .
of different dates and history, all with lingering associations.
Smollett knew London, Westminster and Blackfriars. In
Humphry Clinker he displays them:

You see three stupendous bridges, joining the opposite
banks of a broad, deep and rapid river; so vast, so stately,
that they seem to be the work of giants: betwixt them,
the whole surface of the Thames is covered with small
vessels, barges, boats, and wherries, passing to and fro;
and below the three bridges, such a prodigious forest of
masts, for miles together, that you would think all the
ships of the universe and grandeur, in the Arabian Nights'
Entertainment, and the Persian tales concerning Baghdad,
Diarbekir, Damascus, Ispahan and Samarkand, is here
realised.

The bridges yield vistas of continual, often dramatic movement. George Gissing's Gilbert Grail crossed Lambeth Bridge
in evening gloom in the 1880s:

> Unsightliest of all bridges crossing the Thames, the
> red hue of its iron superstructure, which in daylight
> only enhances the meanness of its appearance, at night
> invests it with a certain grim severity; the archway, with
> its bolted metal plates, its wire-woven cables, over-
> glimmered with the yellowness of the gas-lamps which
> it supports, might be the entrance to some fastness of
> ignoble misery. The road is narrow, and after nightfall has
> but little traffic.
>
> Gilbert walked as far as the middle of the bridge, there
> leaned upon the parapet and looked northwards. The tide
> was running out; it swept darkly onwards to the span of
> Westminster Bridge, whose crescent of lights it repeated
> in long unsteady rays. Along the base of the Houses of
> Parliament the few sparse lamps contrasted with the line
> of brightness on the Embankment opposite. The Houses
> themselves rose grandly in obscure magnitude; the clock-
> tower beaconed with two red circles against the black sky,
> the greater tower stood night-clad, and between them
> were the dim pinnacles, multiplied in shadowy grace.
> Farther away Gilbert could just discern a low, grey shape,
> that resting-place of poets and of kings which to look
> upon filled his heart with worship.
>
> In front of the Embankment, a few yards out into the
> stream, was moored a string of barges; between them and
> the shore the reflected lamp-light made one unbroken
> breadth of radiance, blackening the mid-current. From
> that the eye rose to St Thomas's Hospital, spreading block
> after block, the windows telling of the manifold woe
> within. Nearer was the Archbishop's Palace, dark, lifeless;
> the roofs were defined against a sky made lurid by
> the streets of Lambeth. On the pier below signalled two
> crimson lights.
>
> The church bells kept up their clangorous discord,
> softened at times by the wind. A steamboat came fretting
> up the stream; when it had passed under the bridge, its

spreading track caught the reflected gleams and flung them away to die on unsearchable depths. Then issued from beneath a barge with set sail, making way with wind and tide; in silence it moved onwards, its sail dark and ghastly, till the further bridge swallowed it.

To cross the Thames has for centuries been to realize the immense variety of the capital's lives and livelihoods, particularly in early morning and late afternoon. In her novel *Jacob's Room*, Virginia Woolf reflected on the purpose of London's bridges:

All the time the stream of people never ceases passing from the Surrey side to the Strand, from the Strand to the Surrey side. It seems as if the poor had gone raiding the town, and now traipsed back to their own quarters, like beetles scurrying to their holes, for that old woman fairly hobbles towards Waterloo, grasping a shiny bag, as if she had been out into the light and now made off with some scraped chicken bones to her hovel underground. On the other hand, though the wind is rough and blowing in their faces, those girls there, striding hand in hand, shouting out a song, seem to feel neither cold nor shame. They are hatless. They triumph.

The wind has blown up the waves. The river races beneath us, and the men standing on the barges have to lean all their weight on the tiller. A black tarpaulin is tied down over a swelling load of gold. Avalanches of coal glitter blackly. As usual, painters are slung on planks across the great riverside hotels, and the hotel windows have already points of light in them. On the other side the city is white as if with age: St Paul's swells white above the fretted, pointed or oblong buildings beside it. The cross alone shines rosy-gilt. But what century have we reached? Has this procession from the Surrey side to the Strand gone on for ever? That old man has been crossing the Bridge these six hundred years, with the rabble of little boys at his heels, for he is drunk, or blind with misery, and tied round with clouts of clothing such as pilgrims might have worn. He shuffles on. No one stands still. It seems as if we marched to the sound of music; perhaps the wind and the river; perhaps these same drums and trumpets – the ecstasy and hubbub of the soul.

In *The Waste Land*, T.S. Eliot envisaged a crowd of the dead flowing over London Bridge, in an

> Unreal city
> Under the brown fog of a winter dawn.

a luminous moment which, in his autobiography, Bertrand Russell traced to some remarks he had made to Eliot, after having watched wartime troop-trains leaving Waterloo:

> I used to have strange visions of London as a place of unreality. I used in imagination to see the bridges collapse and sink, and the whole great city vanish in morning mist, and where the Londoners began to resemble hallucinations.

THE LOST RIVER

To visit the Thames today is to find glittering offices, apartment blocks and housing projects where trees and flowers grew in the gardens of nobles and bishops. Palaces have gone, as have many warehouses and markets and small-scale houses. 'Manor' now has a changed significance.

The gardens of Tudor grandees and institutions once decorated the Strand bank, from Chelsea to the Temple, the bank of monumental London, of authority and wealth, facing the south bank, more irresponsible and libertarian. The dramatist John Heywood compared the shrubs and orchards of Thomas More's 34-acre estate, at Beaufort House, Chelsea, to a tapestry woven by Nature herself; Lady More described it as a 'right fair house, library, books, garden, orchard, and all other necessaries so handsome about you'. Of the rosemary, More himself wrote: 'I let it runne all over my garden walls, not onlie because my bees love it, but because it is the herb

sacred to remembrance and to friendship, whence a sprigg of
it hath a dumb language.'

More's son-in-law, William Roper, in his *Life*, records the
final departure of More to the Tower and death in 1534:

> Whereas he evermore used before at his departure from
> his wife and children, whom he tenderly loved, to have
> them bring him to his boat, and there to kiss them all, and
> bid them farewell, then would he suffer none of them
> forth from the gate to follow him, but he pulled the
> wicket after him, and shut them all from him, and with
> a heavy heart, as by his countenance it appeared, with me
> and our four servants there he took his boat towards
> Lambeth.

Over a century later, Evelyn mentions 'divers Gardens and
Orchards planted in the very heart of London', though the
river was to darken hideously with the upsurge of industrialism. Dickens's Rogue Riderhood and Gaffer Hexham, in *Our
Mutual Friend*, gained some of their squalid rewards by hoisting
corpses from the Thames:

> The squall had come up like a spiteful messenger before
> the morning; there followed in its wake a ragged tier of
> light which ripped the dark clouds until they showed a
> great grey hole of day.
>   They were all shivering, and everything about them
> seemed to be shivering; the river itself, craft, rigging,
> sails, such early smoke as there yet was on the shore. Black
> with wet, and altered to the eye by white patches of hail
> and sleet, the huddled buildings looked lower than usual
> as if they were cowering, and had shrunk with the cold.
> Very little life was to be seen on either bank, windows
> and doors were shut, and the staring black and white
> letters upon wharves and warehouses 'Looked,' said
> Eugene to Mortimer, 'like inscriptions over the graves of
> dead businesses.'
>   As they glided slowly on, keeping water shore, and
> sneaking in and out among the shipping, by back-alleys
> of water, in a pilfering way that seemed to be their

boatman's normal manner of progression, all the objects among which they crept were so huge in contrast with their wretched boat as to threaten to crush it. Not a ship's hull, with its rusty iron links of cable run out of hawse-holes, but seemed to be there with a fell intention. Not a figure-head but had the menacing look of bursting forward to run them down. Not a sluice-gate, or a painted scale upon a post or wall, showing the depth of water, but seemed to hint, like the dreadfully facetious Wolf in bed in Grandmamma's cottage. 'That's to drown you in, my dears!' Not a lumbering black barge, with its cracked and blistered side impending over them, but seemed to suck at the river with a thirst for sucking them under. And everything so vaunted the spoiling influence of water – discoloured copper, rotten wood, honey-combed stone, green dank deposit – that the after-consequences of being crushed, sucked under, and drawn down, looked as ugly to the imagination as the main event.

Spenser had written of the 'sweet Thames' but for Dickens, and for James Thomson, the river, with its suicides, filth and oily darkness, now symbolized a road to death, through a corrupted society which had largely lost contact with trees and hedges, pure water, even a clear view of the stars. In 1858, London suffered 'the Great Stench', the outcome of uncontrolled factory smoke, countless coal fires and the new railways. In Blake Ehrlich's *London on the Thames*, we read: 'The windows of the Houses of Parliament were hung with sheets soaked in chloride of lime, and near the sewer outlets 250 tons of lime were dumped daily. The stench was so overpowering that at times the House was forced to adjourn.'

Industrial London bred other unwholesome careers. Mayhew reported of the mudlarks in his Victorian survey of the London poor:

They generally consisted of boys and girls, varying in age from eight to fourteen or fifteen, with some persons of more advanced years. For the most part they are ragged, and in a very filthy state, and are a peculiar class,

confined to the river. The parents of many of them
are coalwhippers – Irish cockneys – employed getting
coals out of the ships, and their mothers frequently sell
fruit in the street. Their practice is to get between the
barges, and one of them lifting the other up will knock
lumps of coal into the mud, which they pick up afterwards; or if a barge is ladened with iron, one will get into
it and throw iron out to the other, and watch an opportunity to carry away the plunder in bags to the nearest
marine-storeshop. They sell the coals among the lowest
class of people for a few halfpence. The police make
numerous detections of these offences. Some of the mudlarks receive a short term of imprisonment, from three
weeks to a month, and others two months with years in
a reformatory. Some of them are old women of the lowest
grade, from fifty to sixty, who occasionally wade in the
mud up to the knees. One of them may be seen beside
the Thames Police-office, Wapping, picking up coals in
the bed of the river, who appears to be about sixty-five
years of age. She is a robust woman, dressed in an old cotton gown, with an old straw bonnet tied round with a
handkerchief, and wanders about without shoes and
stockings. This person has never been in custody. She may
often be seen walking through the streets of the
neighbourhood with a bag of coals on her head.

In the neighbourhood of Blackfriars Bridge clusters of
mudlarks of various ages may be seen from ten to fifty
years, young girls and old women, as well as boys. They
are mostly at work along the coal wharves where the
barges are lying aground, such as Shadwell and Wapping,
along Bankside, borough; above Waterloo Bridge and
from the Temple down to St Paul's wharf. Some of them
pay visits to the City Gasworks and steal coke and coal
from their barges.

Another long-vanished Thames institution was the hulk.
Hulks were superannuated vessels used as temporary stages for
convicts awaiting transportation. The *Bellerophon* and Captain
Cook's *Discovery* were thus degraded. An eighteenth-century
hulk was moored off Woolwich. Like Bedlam, they were

Dostoevskyan, a peepshow for the salacious and sadistic. Boys, old men, the crippled and diseased, were herded together, some naked, even in midwinter, as a result of gambling. In *Great Expectations* Pip sees a hulk, which Dickens removed from the Medway to the Thames:

> By the light of the torches, we saw the black hulk lying out a little way from the mud of the shore like a wicked Noah's ark. Cribbed and barred and moored by massive rusty chains, the prison-ship seemed in my young eyes to be ironed like the prisoners.

However, had the later river comprised only stench, corpses and mud, its literature would have been less lively. The Thames always excited writers, with its importance, its varied and expert activities, the shapes of vessels and the dark of flamboyant skies. Masts bobbing against the sky, sails unfurling, a bowsprit pointing east, riding lamps at night, a wheel, bollards on an empty wharf, warehouses hung with dim mustiness of cloves, cinnamon, tar, woodshavings and sawdust, a cat flitting along the shabby foreshore, stale slopping water adrift with straw, a plank, a coil of rope, a sodden cap – all these could stir memories of old yearnings, other lives. Hilaire Belloc, in *The River of London*, saw the larger implications, now outdated, after so long:

> To the sailor the river is but a continuation of, or an access to, his port, and the Lower Thames is thus universally known as London River. The term is an accidental one, but it contains the true history of the connection between the stream and the town. The Thames made London. London is a function of the Thames . . . [the] great crossing place of the Thames, the custodian and fruit of what early may have been the chief ferry, but has for nearly two thousand years been the chief bridge; London, the market of which the Thames is the approach and the port; London a habitation of which the great street is the Thames . . . London the civil and religious head of revenues which were drawn from the Thames Valley;

London the determinant, through its position upon the
Thames, of English military history.

Water, sky and human pursuits retained their allure. Any
moment can reveal a small drama, a flash of beauty, a muted
fear. Watching the 1876 Boat Race, Henry James saw 'great
white, water-swimming birds, with eight-feathered wings'.
The Thames also retained powers of hazard and adventure, as
in the chase of criminals down river at night by Holmes and
Watson in a police boat, through the Pool, past the West India
Docks, down Deptford Reach, round the Isle of Dogs:

At Greenwich we were about three hundred paces behind
them. At Blackwall we could not have been more than
two hundred and fifty. I have coursed many creatures in
many countries during my chequered career, but never did
sport give me such a wild thrill as this mad, flying man-
hunt down the Thames. Steadily we drew in upon them,
yard by yard. In the silence of the night we could hear the
panting and clanking of their machinery. The man in the
stern still crouched upon the deck, and his arms were
moving as though he were busy, while every now and
then he would look up and measure with a glance the
distance that still separated us. Nearer we came and
nearer. Jones yelled to them to stop. We were not more
than four boat's lengths behind them, both boats flying
at a tremendous pace. It was a clear reach of the river,
with Barking Level upon one side and the melancholy
Plumstead Marshes upon the other. At our hail the man
in the stern sprang up from the deck and shook his two
clenched fists at us, cursing the while in a high, cracked
voice. He was a good-sized powerful man, and as he stood
poising himself with legs astride, I could see that, from
the thigh downwards, there was but a wooden stump
upon the right side. At the sound of his strident, angry
cries, there was a movement in the huddled bundle upon
the deck. It straightened itself into a little black man – the
smallest I have ever seen – with a great, misshapen head
and a shock of tangled dishevelled hair. Holmes had
already drawn his revolver, and I whipped out mine at the

sight of this savage, distorted creature. He was wrapped
in some sort of dark ulster or blanket, which left only his
face exposed; but that face was enough to give a man a
sleepless night. Never have I seen features so deeply
marked with all bestiality and cruelty. His small eyes
glowed and burned with a sombre light, and his thick lips
were writhed back from his teeth, which grinned and
chattered at us with half-animal fury.

'Fire if he raises his hand,' said Holmes quietly.

THE TOWER

Dominating the river and old wooden London, the Tower
was uncompromising in massive stone: fortress, palace, chapel,
menagerie, prison. For some writers it was an image of
romance, preserved by distance and personal security. Harrison
Ainsworth's *The Tower of London*, published in 1840 and
centering round Jane Grey, affected several generations. Henry
James would recall his early enchantment, in the Luxembourg,
with Delaroche's *Les Enfants d'Edouard*, the Princes in the
Tower, 'the long-drawn odd face of the elder prince, sad and
sore and sick'.

The Tower was traditionally, though erroneously, held to
have been founded by Julius Caesar who, in doing so, dug up
the magic head of the Celtic hero Bran, upon the protection
of which London had depended. In 1757, Thomas Gray could
still write, in 'The Bard':

> Ye towers of Julius, London's lasting shame
> With many a foul and midnight murder fed.

These lines puncture the romantic.

From the Tower, Sir Thomas More, a prolific London
writer, hailed as the best story-teller between Chaucer and
Shakespeare, on his last night alive wrote to his favourite child,
Margaret Roper:

> I cumber you good Margaret much, but I would be sorry
> if it should be any longer than to-morrow. For it is

St Thomas's Eve and the Utas of St Peter, and therefore
to-morrow long I to go to God; it were a day very mete
and convenient to me. I never liked your manner towards
me better, than when you kissed me last. For I love when
daughterly love and dear charity, hath no leisure to look
to worldly courtesy. Farewell my dear child, and pray for
me, and I shall for you and all your friends, that we may
merrily meet in heaven.

A man, the ex-Chancellor had said, may lose his head yet
come to no harm. Human dignity in a nutshell. Awaiting the
axe, he pushed aside his beard, commenting that it should not
be injured, as it had committed no treason. Usually, the victim,
if executed in public, died well. Bishop Burnet described Lord
William Russell in the Tower before execution in 1683: 'He
drank a little tea and some sherry. He wound up his watch and
said, now he had done with time and was going to eternity.'
    Walter Ralegh had been unjustly imprisoned here for years,
bitter and angry, once attempting suicide, his body waning but
retaining a grip on life, indomitably undeterred by an unforgiv-
ing King and a wretched future, writing his *History of the
World*. From the Tower he wrote: 'Whosoever, in writing a
modern history, shall follow truth too near the heels, it may
haply strike out his teeth.'
    The romance of the Tower eludes a contemporary writer,
V.S. Pritchett, in *London Perceived*:

It is a citadel with a king's palace and court in flushed
brick in the centre – that winey brick, like the blood royal
itself, that looks so rich and post-prandial in England, as
if it had been copied from the cheeks of Henry VIII. Here
are the pleasant velvety lawns over which the great ravens
stalk and squawk like dilapidated Tudors. These deadly
birds parade like familiars around what, one feels, might
be a satisfaction to them: the executioner's block. Ring-
ing the centre is a maze of stone, a stone that is as grey
and cruel as frost in a wicked season. There is no grimmer
sight in England than this terrible building; the women's
prison at Holloway is child's play compared with this
horror. For centuries it was the national slaughter-house,

but more frightening to us, no doubt, than to the long
procession of men who went there to be imprisoned for
years, to be poisoned, strangled, drowned, tortured, and
decapitated, for they were used to Death walking beside
them in their short lives and their religion celebrated
suffering . . .

I find no glamour in the Tower. It appals . . . We are
now closer to the Middle Ages than the Victorians were.
These picturesque lumps bristle and wake up. In what
way does the medieval ethos now differ from that of
Europe or, indeed, the greater part of the world? The
Tower means murder *now*, torture *now*, stranglings,
treacheries, massacre, the solitary cell, the kick of the
policeman's boot. The scratchings on the walls of the
Tower are the scratchings of Auschwitz. We are
reminded of what the words 'struggle for power' mean in
our own age. It may have astonished Victorians that
Wren's uncle, a harmless, dull, and climbing bishop, was
shut up here for eighteen years; but that sort of thing does
not astonish us today. It is normal. I say nothing of the
Great. The Tower, grey and nasty, is awake again, and
the dirty water of the Thames lapping under Traitors'
Gate, where they rowed the fellows in, looks sly and has
the light of a conniving modern eye.

DOCKLANDS

The eighteenth-century Port of London is glimpsed in
Lawrence Norfolk's novel, *Lemprière's Dictionary*:

It was late afternoon. The light was beginning to fail. His
eyes travelled over the jostling ships crammed together in
the Upper Pool of the Thames. His spirits were strangely
sunk. The legal quays were full as ever. The suffrance
wharves on the southside likewise. Three-masters, little
brigs and sloops, a few colliers, they were all jammed,
prow to stern against one another. Only the steps separating the wharves offered a space. Barges nosed clumsily
about the larger ships moored in mid-stream like sightless

fish . . . Captain Guardian looked over the shambling
mess of wharves, piers, stairs and watergates, the greater
and lesser vessels with their masts and rigging, their
varying states of disrepair, and saw hierarchies, prece-
dences, pecking-orders: all the intricate sub-divisions and
degrees of standing which were the sea's secret language
made wood, canvas and rope, different responses to its
vagaries . . .

So many ships and boats. So many secrets.

The Captain warns a novice:

He thought how he might explain it, that he was not in
the Strand or the Adelphi, that he was here, in the docks,
at the river's edge where the laws and rules and codes of
the land grew ragged and frayed as the land itself when
it petered out into water, and became the mudbanks which
the tide said were both land and water. To the outsider,
a dubious area with its own rules, its own privacies and
penalties. They would throw him in the Pool, nail him
in a crate and throw him in. They would not think twice.

In *Tono-Bungay*, H.G. Wells saw the same Pool, but not the
same scene:

One goes down the widening reaches through a monstrous variety of shipping, great steamers, great sailing
ships, trailing the flags of all the world, a monstrous
confusion of lighters, witches' conferences of brown-
sailed barges, wallowing lugs, a tumultuous crowding
and jostling of cranes and spars, and wharves and stores,
and assertive inscriptions. Huge vistas of dock open right
and left of one, and here and there beyond and amidst it
all are church towers, little patches of indescribably old-
fashioned and worn-out houses, riverside pubs and the
like, vestiges of townships that were long since torn to
fragments and submerged in these new growths.

Today, all this has surrendered to newer growths, not
yet completed, as another London takes the succession. At

Wapping, London merchants stored wines and Jamaica rum, and many historical romances ended there with pirates, purple-faced and with jutting tongues, hanging from gibbets, washed by the high tide at Execution Dock. Also at the Red Cow, Wapping, a biter was bit. In 1688, a scared man, disguised as a collier, crouched to defend himself from a furious revolutionary crowd – George, Lord Jeffreys, Lord Chancellor of England. He died in the Tower, worn out, diseased, already a legend. As scarlet-robed judge in the Bloody Assizes, he remains the villain of popular fiction that fattens on ill-researched history. 'Speak up,' he ordered some wretch in the dock, adding inauspiciously, 'I love to know men's names.'

In his *The English at Home* (1861), the traveller Alphonse Esquires trudged through

> that poorest, most ill-famed, ugliest part of London. Here you see docks, suffrance wharfs, sail, anchor, and rope factories; sailors of every country and colour lodge in equivocal houses in narrow streets; a muddy pavement, crushed by the wheels, see every day the riches of a universe passing by on heavy carts. We went down Wapping Old Stairs, celebrated in sailors' songs; the moon shed a sickly light over the Thames, and except the voice of the river, all was silent. On the muddy, worn steps we witnessed a fight between two rats of a different colour.

John Masefield, briefly a sailor, though hating it, loved those sailors' songs:

> Don't put your feet in the port wine, Joe,
> There's plenty of stale old beer.

Brunel's tunnel beneath the river links Wapping with Rotherhithe, on the opposite bank, from where many seventeenth-century dissidents sailed to the New World. Here, rivermen jeered at the dropsical Henry Fielding. 'A lively picture,' he considered, 'of that cruelty and inhumanity in the Nature of Man which I have often contemplated with concern.' As a magistrate and as brother to the blind John, founder of

the Bow Street Runners, he must have contemplated it very
often.

Iain Sinclair's novel, *Downriver* (1991), exhibits a Stygian
riverside London where Canaletto and Turner have been pole-
axed by Gustave Doré and Albert Speer. Of Rotherhithe
Tunnel:

> If you want to sample the worst London can offer,
> follow me down that slow incline. The tunnel drips with
> warnings. DO NOT STOP. Seal your windows. Hold
> your breath. This is not reassuring to the pedestrian
> who wobbles along a thin strip of paving, fearing to
> let go of the tiled wall; working the grime into his
> hand. Your heart fills your mouth like a shelled and
> pulsing crab. Why are there no other walkers? Traffic
> scrapes so narrowly past. The drivers are mean-faced and
> locked into sadistic fantasies. White abattoir walls solicit
> vivid splashes of blood. You feel the brain-stem ineluc-
> tably dying, releasing, at its margins, dim and flaccid
> hallucinations.

Further on, past Poplar and Blackwall, from the horse-
bus toiling over the bridge which crosses Bow Creek, near
Limehouse, into Canning Town, H.M. Tomlinson saw,
beyond the mudflats, gasometers, barge-builders' yards and
ranges of marsh weed, a battleship ready for launching:

> Towering higher and mightier as we approached it, a
> little awe-inspiring in its magnitude, the chief work of the
> Thames. So massively was she elevated that you could
> have imagined she had drawn up the substance of the
> place, had diminished what was about her as her belly
> swelled. The greater she grew, then the meaner became
> the homes beneath her shadow. She had taken their vir-
> tue, as she had absorbed from their inhabitants their time,
> their skill, and their energy. The goodness of the parish
> might have been drawn up to put upon the sky the form
> of a brooding giant. She lorded it over us, haughty and
> terrible, and her gaily fluttering bunting was a sign of the
> buoyancy with which she possessed her threatening

strength. She was called forth by us, and she was there, ready to be furnished with her guns. The timbers in which we had caged her could no more hold her now than cobwebs. When I stood under her, amid the litter of industry, dust and rust and chips of wood and scraps of metal, and looked up past the projection of her smooth body, it was as though black calamity were impending and might fall upon us through the chance of an unlucky jolt. Yet that was only the doubt of a witness who stood nervously under a shape so dark and vast; his confidence that his fellows knew what they were doing faltered when threatened by so ominous a symbol of their faith. I took my eyes from the giddy height of her, and a group of workmen paused near me; and one, an evident leader, with a mallet in his fist, contemplated Leviathan for some moments, contemplated her calmly, and with fond approbation. One of the men spoke. 'Does she want another touch there, Mr Bolt?' The leader considered this. 'No. She'll do. She's all right.'

Docklands bred generations of stories: in taverns, grubby back kitchens, genteel, seldom-used parlours, in small shops and in ambiguous cellars, stories of female bruisers, reluctant bridegrooms, ribald insults and energetic repartee, dignified liars and outsize drinkers. W.W. Jacobs wrote from a world of now forgotten ships and lost patois, slow cynical ruminations, revenges skilfully, even delicately contrived, and of a humour grounded in the clear-sighted reality essential to watermen:

'Love?' said the nightwatchman, as he watched in an abstracted fashion the efforts of a skipper to reach a brother skipper on a passing barge with a boat hook. 'Don't talk to me about love, because I have suffered enough through it. There ought to be teetotalers for love the same as wot there is for drink and they ought to wear a piece of ribbon to show it, as teetotalers do.'

He adds that sailors are particularly prone to love, but: 'Wait until they become nightwatchmen.'

DEPTFORD AND GREENWICH

Deptford has sunk since the days when Peter the Great
destroyed John Evelyn's fine hedge at Sayes Court by continually charging through it with a wheelbarrow, and when
Pepys, as Master of Trinity House, attended the annual Trinity
Monday sermon and banquet of the Deptford Corporation,
partaking of duck pottage, salmon with fried fish and roast
turkey, Lombard Pie, lobsters, prawns, Westphalian ham,
creams and syllabubs, reinforced with claret, champagne,
rhenish and canary. Here, in 1593, Christopher Marlowe was
'slain by ffrancis ffreger; the I of June.' Marlowe's death, like
his life, remains mysterious. He represents a London hitherto
barely known, scarcely acknowledged, but slowly emerging
through hints, enigmatic references, revised research: perhaps
pagan, or atheist, certainly metaphysical, submerged by the
Tudor State.

Another writer, Dunstan Thompson, journeyed to
Deptford through a London tired and smashed by the Second
World War to lay violets on Marlowe's grave. He found
St Nicholas's Church ruined, the churchyard desolate, without
trace of Marlowe. Nobody knew or cared. He wandered about,
following the tram line to Greenwich:

> Was this, I wondered, Deptford Strand, and if so where
> had that tavern been which was kept by the Widow Bull?
> I found no answers. Some sailors from a foreign ship, who
> were wearing caps with long black streamers, passed by
> talking in a strange language. I came to a pub and went
> into part of it, for even here, far from the middle class,
> the distinctions between saloons and lounge and Private
> and Public were maintained by wooden partitions and
> separate doors . . .
> I sat drinking ale and listening to the voices of old
> women in the next bar talking against the Jews. I thought
> back to the swastika I had seen smeared on one of the
> tombs.

Soon he departed, for the Greenwich Royal Maritime
Museum:

Wandering about the Queen's House, that small heartless
box put up by Inigo Jones, going from one good plain
room to the next good plain room, remarking the pure
boredom of minor perfection, I looked listlessly at the
portraits of murderous royalties, their attendant gang-
sters, My Lord This and My Lord That, and went out
unimpressed except by the brutal butcher's face of the first
Defender of the Faith and the bejewelled dispassion of the
unsexed bastard queen called Gloriana. But there was
more to see farther on and dutifully I saw it: sextants and
quadrants and compasses and maps and astrolabes, miniature ships, miniature barges, miniature rowboats, gold
plate and silver plate and commemorative crystal, chunks
of the deck and bits off the bridge from various immortal
dreadnoughts, memorabilia of heroes, their swords, their
medals, their cocked hats, their brass buttons, and a whole
pantheon of knicknacks and junk belonging to Nelson,
including a chest of cheap presents given to him by Lady
Hamilton. I looked at statues of sexless admirals, paintings of meaningless battles, the absolute deadness of
history.

The old, vanished, peach-red Greenwich Palace was built
by Good Duke Humphrey of Gloucester, collector of one
of the finest fifteenth-century libraries. There Elizabeth
listened to the guns of the Armada; also to the Mayor of
Queenborough's congratulations, learning that, in meddling
with her, His Spanish Majesty 'had taken the wrong sow by
the ear'.
Charles II destroyed the old Palace, yet he had Wren
construct the great Naval Hospital. The populace continued
to enjoy the town's ancient pastimes. 'Boz' in 1837 visited
Greenwich Fair:

this immense booth, with a large stage in front, so
brightly illuminated with variegated lamps, and pots of
burning fat, is 'Richardson's'; where you have a melodrama (with three murders and a ghost), a pantomime, a
comic song, an overture, and some incidental music, all
done in five-and-twenty minutes.

The banks of the Thames today lack glamour for those apathetic to recent architectural developments and the unceasing standardization of river craft. But the sky remains, changing by the minute, reflected in cleaner waters and without need of history. Writers will create a new Thames.

In his 1974 essay on London, Alasdair Clayre summarizes:

As with gambling there can be good runs and bad runs in London. Good runs, for me, have generally been in alliance with the river. The river flows through London, without geometry, giving shape, making edges, dividing one quarter from the next; a new stanza begins when you cross from Chelsea to Battersea, a different paragraph when you tunnel from Rotherhithe to the Commercial Road. Doubling and looping, it closes off enclaves like Pimlico and the Isle of Dogs. You know where you are, and it is never where you could have predicted with a ruler or grid map, as in New York or the right bank of Paris.

2

PICCADILLY CIRCUS TO VICTORIA

A city should not only be commodious and serious,
but merrie and sportful.

William FitzStephen, secretary to Thomas Becket

PICCADILLY CIRCUS

London is too vast to possess a centre, being an aggregate of
villages and townlets, each with its own function, tradition,
style and speech. Many, particularly if they are not Londoners,
however, see Piccadilly Circus as London's centre, and it may
serve here as a focus. From it, streets radiate towards
Bayswater, Soho, Kensington, Charing Cross; around it lie
Pall Mall clubs, the Mall, Piccadilly hotels, St James's Park, the
Haymarket, Leicester Square, the theatres of Shaftesbury
Avenue. We owe it to the Regent, and originally it was 'The
Regent Circus', though its personality is no longer that of
Nash calm and proportion.

Here George Moore's Esther Waters and her escort saw the
mob of prostitutes and loafers outside the Criterion; Moore
himself, Henry Arthur Jones called 'a boiled ghost'. Beneath
the Circus, in the tube station, Virginia Woolf's Jinny, in *The
Waves*, momentarily had her vision of London as a ferment of
innumerable wheels, crushing and inexorable, the figures on
escalators like the pinioned and terrible descent of some army
of the dead, from which she cowered, seeking shelter. When
the nightmare faded she saw urban civilization overhead as

victory and banners: 'Those broad thoroughfares – Piccadilly, North Regent Street and the Haymarket – are sanded paths of victory driven through the jungle.'

H.M. Tomlinson witnessed Mafeking Night, in 1900, when

Piccadilly Circus was the volcanic crater of London. The converging channels poured suppressed fire from the subterranean city to its crater, and you could seethe there in the exultant outpouring of a capital's joy; though, once the vortex had got you, there was no escape. There were no citizens. There was a flux of elemental stuff, roaring and molten, of a weight and heat to consume a reluctant thought in a spark, and to burn and bury, if it overflowed, what the labour of centuries had built. Round the multitude stood the walls of the crater, echoing the roaring, lurid with reflections and shifting lights.

By the Regent Street exit of the Circus survives the Café Royal, possessed of much history, if not much present. Its royalty was always more suggestive of Napoleon III than of Prince Albert. Garish, raffish, smoky, loud, crowded, with lush ceilings of clouds and deities, Venetian chandeliers, private rooms and gilded recesses, it told lingering tales of Oscar Wilde, Frank Harris, George Bernard Shaw. Writing of Wilde, Philippe Jullian calls up others:

There was Simeon Solomon, who lived from hand to mouth on the proceeds of blackmail or the sale of pornographic drawings. Ernest Dowson, the charming poet, and his friend the artist Conder, who kept harking back to old stories of Montmartre. There were the failures on whom Max Beerbohm based the pathetic imaginary character Enoch Soames . . . Sometimes at a bar Oscar Wilde would get into conversation with a poor wretch who used to warm himself before the coals of a roast chestnut stall; his eyes dilated with hunger and with opium, he was dressed in an old caped box-coat. It was the poet Francis Thompson who slept among the down-and-outs under the arches of Charing Cross Station.

In a novel, *Caprice*, Ronald Firbank airily envisaged:

'The Café Royal'
Miss Sinquier fluttered in.
By the door the tables all proved to be taken.
Such a noise!
Everyone seemed to be chattering, smoking, lunching,
Casting dice or playing dominoes.
She advanced slowly through a veil of mist, feeling her
Way from side to side with her parasol.
    It was like penetrating deeper and deeper into a bath.

Kirsty McCleod surveys its later days:

Since the 1880's, the Café Royal . . . with its gilded walls
and unlikely decor of cherubs and caryatids, had been the
principal haunt of London's literary and artistic circles.
By 1914 sightseers, loud-voiced subalterns and impres-
sionable suburban bank-clerks almost outnumbered the
bohemian creative spirits they had come to see. As a result
the back entrance to the Café was a mecca for book-
makers, touts, moneylenders and conmen preying on the
naive or the unwary. But you could still buy paintings
'under the table' from penniless Chelsea set models or
artists with too many meals already 'on the slate'. The
Café, despite its rock-bottom prices, gave credit freely
and generously; its waiters even lent money at ten shillings 'danger' interest. Auguste Judah, the lanky,
distinguished manager, allowed his clients to sit from
opening to closing time over a beer and a six-penny plate
of chips.

On the last day of the Second World War, Philip Toynbee,
novelist, poet, critic, was hurrying round London, desperate
for news of the German surrender. He drank in El Vino's, Fleet
Street, in the Wheatsheaf and the Black Horse, Fitzrovia, and
in the Criterion, and finally staggered into the Café Royal,
where, perched at a bar, he recognized the novelist Peter de
Polnay.

'Ah! Philip! Good! Have you heard the news?'

'No. Thank God! What is it?'

'I'm surprised, Philip, and a little put out that you don't know the news.'

'But for Christ's sake, what is it?'

'I've gone back to Hutchinsons.'

Back in the Circus, one finds a sense of what Gibbon termed 'crowds without company, and dissipation without pleasure'. In his novel *Magog*, Andrew Sinclair reminds us that a circus used to mean a place where people moved around on their business, but today they merely sit in caftans and torn jeans, 'the survival experts of the urban frontier':

The wind blew the water from the jets of the fountain under the statue of Eros on high. The little silver god shot his stringless bow at the passing traffic and scored no hits. The street people sat to leeward, where the steps were dry that led up to the fountain; the old sailors, they knew which way the wind was blowing. The traffic roared and stopped and started in intermittent complaint on the other side of the grey barriers, while above them, the Edwardian buildings hung on until the next rebuilding scheme for the Circus which was never rebuilt. Foppish façades stood by, old dandies left out of this new happening where they were not invited. Four stone nymphs huddled under their conch shells over the All-Night Chemists where the registered addicts were waiting for their legal fixes, while the learners were blowing out their grass smoke in hopeless competition against the exhausts of the buses besieging them.

THE HAYMARKET AND TRAFALGAR SQUARE

A few yards from the Circus, separating it from Leicester Square, is the Haymarket, famous for its theatre, before which is John Nash's portico with six white columns, their gilt and red now vanished. Its fame in mid-Victorian London was less decorous. Dostoevsky observed:

Whoever has visited London must have seen the night-
time Haymarket at least once. An area where thousands
of whores swarm through the dark, down streets lit by
gas, itself unknown in Russia. On all sides are magnificent taverns, all mirrors and gilding, not only shelters
but places of assignment. To find oneself in that mob is
frightening, old women mixing with the beautiful before
whom you halt, astounded, for in all the world none are
so lovely as English women. The streets are scarcely large
enough for the packed, jostling crowds, a human army
fighting for spoils, assaulting the newcomer without
shame, wholly cynical. Clothes rich and shiny mingle
with tatters, all generations are seen. A drunken tramp
stumbling through this infernal horde is jostled by the
wealthy, the titled. Curses are heard, quarrels, entreaties,
and the furtive invitation of some beauty not yet wholly
brutalised. . . .

I noticed mothers who brought their little daughters to
the Haymarket to engage them in the same profession.
Little girls of about twelve grab your arm and urge you
to go with them. I have one memory of seeing in a crowd
of people there a small girl, not older than six, ragged,
dirty, without shoes, cheeks all hollows, body evidently
savagely thrashed. There she was, walking as if quite
alone, without any haste at all, dawdling in the crowd for
God knows why. Perhaps from hunger. None seemed
aware of her. However, I was mainly shocked by her
expression of such distress and hopeless desperation, so
that the sight of that small human waif was somehow
unnatural and fearful. Her tousled head constantly shook
as if in argument, her hands gestured, waved, came
together, pressing against her small, bare breast. I
returned, gave her a sixpence. She took the little silver
coin, gazed at me wildly, frightened and astonished, then
abruptly ran away, swift as possible, as though fearing I
would demand the money back. A merry sight!

A more cheerful story is told of the spectacular actor-
manager, Sir Herbert Beerbohm Tree, who had long association with the Haymarket Theatre. Crossing to enter it, he

allegedly saw a man carrying a grandfather clock. 'Ah, my dear fellow . . . some of us find it easier to wear a watch.'

The Haymarket remains crowded but outwardly more demure. It descends to Trafalgar Square, where large, potentially violent, political demonstrations still gather. These are traditional. William Morris, denouncing Victorianism as 'The Age of Shoddy', lost some of his trust in the future on Black Sunday, 13 November 1887, when 20,000 angry protestors in the Square were countered by 500 police and 300 Grenadiers with bayonets, later reinforced by 300 Life Guards. A socialist pamphleteer and public speaker, Bernard Shaw, amid fights, charges, uproar, was asked what was to be done, but went home to tea. Alfred Linnell was killed, at once prompting a poem, 'A Death Song', by William Morris.

> They will not learn; they have no ears to hearken.
> They turn their faces from the eyes of fate;
> Their gay-lit halls shut out the skies that darken.
> But lo! This dead man knocking at the gate.
> NOT ONE, NOT ONE NOR THOUSANDS MUST
>   THEY SLAY,
> BUT ONE AND ALL IF THEY WOULD DUSK THE
>   DAY.

A lover of London and an authority on its streets and buildings, Blake Ehrlich is nonetheless not enamoured of Trafalgar Square:

> a huge, sloping traffic bowl, its road junctions broadening into lakes of asphalt, and its surrounding buildings arguing fruitlessly with the wide open spaces. . . . It has seven major arteries radiating from it, it is girt with objects of interest and beauty, and from it there are several exciting vistas. It is stuffed with statuary, fitted with fountains, and endowed with the Nelson Column. But . . .
> There are the mendicant side-walk artists and mendicant pigeons, throngs of distraction-seekers and wheeling of heavy traffic, but nevertheless, it remains cheerless and curiously barren. A bizarre memorial for that great romantic hero, Horatio Nelson.

This seems drab, after the Square seen in *The Soul of London* by Ford Madox Ford: 'with the glint of straw blown from horses' feeds, the shimmer of wheel marks in the wood pavement, the shine of bits of harness, the blaze of gold lettering along the house fronts'.

Nelson on his column, high above the statues of generals and admirals, was, for Lawrence Durrell, less a romantic hero than a hero of romances. His witty, bawdy 'A Ballad of the Good Lord Nelson' ends:

> Now stiff on a pillar with a phallic air
> Nelson stylites in Trafalgar Square
> Remind the British of what once they were
>   Aboard the Victory, Victory O.
>
> If they'd treat their women in the Nelson way
> There'd be fewer frigid husbands every day
> And many more heroes in the Bay of Biscay
>   Aboard the Victory, Victory O.

On the north side of the square is James Gibbs' St Martin-in-the-Fields Church, rated by Sacheverell Sitwell the most aesthetically successful of all London churches, though Nikolaus Pevsner, disliking this architect's influence on London, deplored 'the painful illogicality . . . the uncomfortable position' of the tower above the portico of tall Corinthian pillars. The church's name is a reminder that fields had not, in 1726, been eliminated by brick and stone. In her novel *Young Jemmy* (1947), Elizabeth D'Oyley has Monmouth, some five decades previously, entering the earlier church for an instant of peace during the uproar about excluding from the throne his uncle, the future James II, and smelling the sweetness of hawthorn blowing in from St Martin's Lane.

Sometimes derided as 'The National Cruet Stand', facing Whitehall and Westminster, is William Wilkins' National Gallery. Its elevated entrance provides a stage-box for sightseers of the Square. Ehrlich commented in 1963 that most architects and historians imply they could have achieved a finer design – a view confirmed in the controversies kindled by the Gallery's later extension:

Wilkins was striving for one sole effect: that of keeping his job. He was told, incorporate the colonnade of dismantled Carlton House in your façade. He was told, don't distract from or impede the view of St Martin-in-the-Fields; leave plenty of room around the barracks behind the site, and don't forget we want a dome and cupolas and porticoes. He was told, don't spend more than £100,000, more like £95,000 (he spent £96,000). So he did as he was told.

Wilfrid Blunt, brother of Anthony, though warmer, considered that 'while scarcely comparable to Wren and Hawksmoor, Wilkins was a dignified architect, with a never-failing sense of space and proportion: forced to economise, he never became "cheap"; forced to simplify, he never became merely empty.'

The Gallery gleams with colours antique and new, rare and familiar, sustained above the grey spaces of the Square. It has long provided fictional characters with a meeting place. In Antonia White's *The Lost Traveller*, Nicole 'suggested that she should slip away from her chaperone and meet Clara in the National Gallery or the British Museum, *like guilty characters in Henry James*.'

In Iris Murdoch's novel *The Bell*, Dora, during a personal crisis, goes there to regather emotions, perhaps reach a decision:

Dora had been to the National Gallery a thousand times and the pictures were almost as familiar to her as her own face. Passing between them now, as through a well-loved grove, she felt a calm descending on her. She wandered a little, watching with compassion the poor visitors armed with guide-books who were peering anxiously at the masterpieces. Dora did not need to peer. She could look, as one can at last when one knows a great thing very well, confronting it with a dignity which it has itself conferred. She felt that the pictures belonged to her, and reflected ruefully that they were about the only thing that did. Vaguely, consoled by the presence of something welcoming and responding to the place, her footsteps took her to various shrines at which she had worshipped so often before: the great light spaces of Italian pictures, more vast and southern than any real South, the angels of Botticelli, radiant as birds, delighted as gods, and curling like the tendrils of a vine, the glorious carnal presence of Susanna Fourment, the tragic presence of Margarethe Trip, the solemn world of Piero della Francesca with its early-morning colours, the enclosed and gilded world of Crivelli. Dora stopped at last in front of Gainsborough's picture. 'You know I get to the National Gallery quite a bit?'

'Too much,' said Barbara, blowing her nose. 'Nobody needs to go that much. It is becoming an obsession with you.'

'Well, but you see, I am trying to decipher all those expressions. They are held up to one as standards of excellence, to be always admired, and yet there are many terrible lessons there. One realizes that even the Holy Family didn't have a lot of time for the rest of Creation. We will not even speak of the Crucifixion, if you don't mind. And all the martyrdoms. Those poor saints, throwing away their lives, the only possessions they could really call their own. And the cruelty of their tortures. All so that they could be shown in painting, resurrected in perfect form, with merely a tower or a key or a wheel as a dainty allusion to their sufferings. As if the realm of painting were taking its lead from the kingdom of heaven. I worry about that a lot.'

'Well, then, don't look at these things if they upset you.'

'There is actually worse to come, if you turn to the pagans. They recline on clouds absolutely impervious to everything and everyone. No kindness there. No begging for mercy from the ancient gods – they would laugh. They obey a different code, and it is exceedingly difficult to know what it is. It fascinates me. You are wrong to say that I shouldn't study these things. It is quite harmless, and it is very instructive. I am learning a lot. Only it is rather difficult at the moment to work out exactly what I am learning. That is why I keep going back.'

Siegfried Sassoon's 'In the National Gallery' traces a similar pattern, in a dissimilar tone:

> Faces irresolute and unperplexed,
> Unspeculative faces, bored and weak,
> Cruise past each patient victory of technique
> Dimly desiring to enjoy the next
> Yet never finding what they seem to seek.
>
> Here blooms, recedes, and glows before their eyes
> A quintessential world preserved in paint,
> Calm vistas of long-vanished Paradise,
> And ripe remembrances of sage and saint;
> The immortality of changeless skies,
> And all bright legendries of Time's creation . . .
>   Yet I observed no gestures of surprise
>   From those who struggle in to patronize
>   The Art Collection of the English Nation.

The Gallery can reach towards paradise. It can also be a graveyard. Winifred Gérin traces Branwell Brontë, all ambitions failing, in his hapless descent upon London:

> When after several days of desultory wandering through the streets and of dreaming upon the Embankment as he watched the great Indiamen come and go, he eventually visited the National Gallery and saw the work of the great masters after which he had yearned all his life, his reaction was one of despair. He saw their perfection and realized his own incapacity, in the same horrible and illuminating moment of truth.

WHITEHALL PALACE

Trafalgar Square debouches into Whitehall, passing Le Sueur's statue of Charles I, long celebrated in Lionel Johnson's poem, 'By the Statue of King Charles at Charing Cross', too lengthy to quote in full.

Comely and calm he rides
Hard by his own Whitehall.
Only the night wind glides:
No crowds, nor rebels brawl.

Gone, too, his Court: and yet,
The stars his courtiers are;
Stars in their stations set;
And every wandering star.

Alone he rides, alone,
The fair and fatal King;
Dark night is all his own,
That strange and solemn thing.

All that remains of Whitehall Palace, after the fire accidentally started by a Dutch menial in 1698, is Inigo Jones's
Banqueting Hall, its ceiling rated by Sir Roy Strong as 'the
greatest surviving baroque ceiling in northern Europe'. From
here the King stepped on to the scaffold. Hilaire Belloc
imagined the scene:

At two o'clock there was a break in the clouds and a
brilliant sun shone down upon all those uplifted faces, and
upon the stage whereon Charles Stuart was to die. The
populace could see figures passing rapidly behind the windows of the Banqueting Hall. They came the whole
length of it, and out through a door which had been made
by lowering a window at the extreme northern end. From
that door it was a step round the corner pilaster of the
building on to the scaffold itself, and thither, on this
scaffold, rapidly gathered somewhat more than a dozen
men. Among whom the King. In his hand was a paper,
from which he read. Standing by among the rest, but near
the block, were two masked men, dressed as sailors, and
grotesque in huge false wigs . . .
    For one second they saw the great axe lifted high in the
sight of all, then flashing down, and the thud of the blow.
One of those masked figures held up the severed head, and
immediately there rose from the vast multitude an awful
groan, such as those who heard it had never thought to

hear; and one of them (Pepys) prayed to God that he might never hear such a human sound again.

Charles I reappeared in a different tone of voice, that of Mr Jingle, in *The Pickwick Papers*.

'Heads, heads – take care of your heads,' cried the loquacious stranger as they came out under the low arch, which in those days formed the entrance to the coach-yard. 'Terrible place – dangerous work – other day – five children – crash – knock – children look round – mother's head off – sandwich in her hand – no mouth to put it in: head of a family off – shocking, shocking! Looking at Whitehall, Sir? – fine place – little window – somebody else's head off there, eh, Sir? – he didn't keep a sharp look-out enough either – eh, Sir, eh?

A German traveller, Paul Hentzner, visited Elizabeth's Whitehall Palace, observing the tapestried walls, the ceilings enriched with complex patterning, the floors strewn with rushes, even hay. He particularly admired

The Royal Library, well-stored with Greek, Latin, French and Italian books, bound in velvet of different colours, though chiefly red, with clasps of gold and silver and some with pearls and precious stones in their bindings.

Two little silver cabinets of exquisite work, in which the Queen keeps her papers.

The Queen's bed, made of woods of different colours, with quilts of silk, velvet, gold, silver and embroidery.

A little chest, ornamented all over with pearls, in which the Queen keeps her bracelets, ear-rings, and other very valuable objects.

The Palace was usually staffed, save under Charles I and the Lord Protector, not only by the lustful and the greedy, but also by the erratic, the quarrelsome and the arrogant, all three qualities uniting in the Jacobean, Philip Herbert, fourth Earl of Pembroke, Gentleman of the Bedchamber, disapproved of by

Clarendon, the seventeenth-century historian and statesman: 'There were few great persons in authority, who were not frequently offended by him by sharp and scandalous discourses, and invectives against them.'

Thomas Hinde adds, of this paragon:

At Croydon racecourse he was horse-whipped by William Ramsay, one of the King's pages. Three years later he and the Earl of Southampton struck at one another with tennis rackets in the Whitehall Palace court. During the next reign, he hit the poet Thomas May over the head with his staff of office. May accepted £50 in compensation.

Of the Palace itself, in its last days, Hinde continues:

For the most part Charles II and his court occupied the great rambling palace of Whitehall, which was less like a palace as the word is normally understood than a village, consisting of 'a heap of houses erected at diverse times and of different models, made continuous.' It had some two thousand rooms, stretched for half a mile along the Thames and reached inland as far as today's Downing Street and New Scotland Yard. Here the public could come and go with little restriction, watch the King pray in his chapel or eat in his banqueting hall, and meet him strolling about the lawns – trying to avoid the many royalist gentlemen who had come to London to claim rewards for their loyalty during the Civil War. Some he did reward. Above the official number of forty-eight Gentlemen of the Privy Chamber, he created four hundred and ninety Gentlemen and of the Privy Chamber in Extraordinary. Even his Bedchamber was open to visitors, and only the King's Closet, a smaller, upper room, was comparatively private. Here Keepers of the Closet like the brothers Chiffinch would bring only those who had been invited – including whores who entered by back stairs from the river and who were rewarded by payments of Secret Service money.

Pepys, of course, was often in the Palace. On 24 June 1664:

To White Hall; and Mr Pierce showed me the Queen's
bed-chamber, and her closet, where she had nothing but
some pretty pius pictures, and books of devotion; and her
holy water at her head as she sleeps, with a clock by her
bed-side, wherein a lamp burns that tells her the time of
the night at any time. Thence with him to the Park, and
there met the Queen coming from chapel, with her Maids
of Honour. Thence he carried me to the King's closet:
where such variety of pictures, and other things of value
and rarity, that I was properly confounded and enjoyed no
pleasure in the sight of them; which is the only time in
my life that ever I was so at a loss for pleasure, in the
greatest plenty of objects to give it me.

Victor Hugo in his novel, *L'Homme qui rit*, published in Paris
in 1869, allowed his fancy to roam freely through Stuart
Whitehall:

It was the custom of the Kings of England to have a sort
of watchman, who crowed like a cock. This watcher,
awake while all others slept, ranged the Palace, and raised
from hour to hour the cry of the farmyard . . . thus
supplying a clock. This man, promoted to be cock, had
in childhood undergone the operation of the pharynx.
Under Charles II, the salivation inseparable from the performance having disgusted the Duchess of Portsmouth,
the appointment was indeed continued, so that the
splendour of the crown should not be tarnished, but
they got an unmutilated man to represent the cock. A
retired officer was generally selected for this honourable
employment. Under James II the official was William
Sampson, Cock, and for his crow received £9 2s 6d
annually. . . .
    Barbara, Duchess of Cleveland and Countess of
Southampton, had a marmoset for a page. Francesca
Sutton, Baroness Dudley, eighth peeress in the bench of
barons, had tea served by a baboon clad in gold brocade,
which her ladyship called My Black. Catherine Sedley,
Countess of Dorchester, would watch Parliament, having
travelled therein a coach with armorial bearings, behind

which stood, their muzzles stuck upwards, three monkeys in grand livery.

THE HOUSES OF PARLIAMENT

Further down, past Ralegh's statue, stand the Houses of Parliament with another statue in the foreground, the solemn Lord Protector with Bible and sword. In Stuart days, Parliament produced virulence and ferocity. An adroit and unscrupulous opponent of Charles II, who nicknamed him 'Little Sincerity', was the first Earl of Shaftesbury, dominating Parliament and the London streets:

> One man in England never feared him. At the height of Shaftesbury's power, King Charles would stroll into the House of Lords and stand shaking with laughter while virulent abuse was being hurled against his ministers . . . The Parliament of 1679 passed . . . the Habeas Corpus Act. It was only passed by a practical joke, 'the best joke ever made in England.' The Lord who was counting the votes in the House of Lords in favour of passing the Bill, counted a very fat lord as ten by way of pleasantry. The joke was not noticed, but without the extra votes the Bill would not have been passed. (Carrington and Jackson)

Dickens's Mr Twemlow called Parliament the best club in London but Dickens himself, once a parliamentary reporter, had small respect for the Mother of Parliaments. In *Bleak House* he enjoys himself:

> Then there is my Lord Boodle, of considerable reputation with his party, who has known what office is, and who tells Sir Leicester Deadlock with much gravity, after dinner, that he really does not see to what the present age is tending. A debate is not what a debate used to be; the House is not what the House used to be; even a Cabinet is not what it formerly was. He perceives with astonishment, that supposing the present Government to be over-

thrown, the limited choice of the Crown in the formation
of a new ministry, would be between Lord Coodle and
Sir Thomas Boodle – supposing it to be impossible for
the Duke of Foodle to act upon Doodle, which may be
assumed to be the case of consequence of the breach
arising out of that affair with Hoodle. Then, giving
the Home Department and the leadership of the House
of Commons to Joodle, the Exchequer to Koodle, the
colonies to Loodle, and the Foreign Office to Moodle,
what are you to do with Noodle? You can't offer him the
Presidency of the Council; that is reserved for Poodle.
You can't put him in the Woods and Forests; that is
hardly good enough for Quoodle. What follows? That
the country is shipwrecked, lost, and gone to pieces (as
is made manifest to the patriotism of Sir Leicester
Deadlock), because you can't provide for Noodle.

Dickens might have been thoughtful had he been in Cabinet
and heard Lord Melbourne: 'Stop a minute, what did we
decide? Is it to lower the price of bread, or isn't it? It does not
matter what we say, but, mind, we must all say the same.'
   Trollope shows a new member, Phineas Finn, investigating
the Commons:

At two punctually Phineas was in the lobby at
Westminster, and then he found himself taken into the
House with a crowd of other men. The old and the
young, and they who were neither old nor young, were
mingled together, and there seemed to be very little
respect of persons. On three or four occasions there was
some cheering when a popular man or a great leader came
in; but the work of the day left but little clear impression
on the mind of the young member. He was confused, half
elated, half disappointed, and had not his wits about
him. He found himself constantly regretting that he was
there; and as constantly telling himself that he, hardly yet
twenty-five, without a shilling of his own, had achieved
an entrance into that assembly which by the consent of all
men is the greatest in the world, and which many of the
rich magnates of the country had in vain spent heaps of

treasure in their endeavours to open to their footsteps. He tried hard to realise what he had gained, but the dust and the noise and the crowds and the want of something august to the eye were almost too strong for him. He managed, however, to take the oath early among those who took it, and heard the Queen's speech read and the Address moved and seconded. He was seated very uncomfortably, high up on a back seat, between two men whom he did not know; and he found the speeches to be very long. He had been in the habit of seeing such speeches reported in about a column, and he thought that these speeches must take at least four columns each. He sat out the debate on the Address till the House was adjourned, and then he went away to dine at his club. He did go into the dining-room of the House, but there was a crowd there, and he found himself alone – and to tell the truth, he was afraid to order his dinner.

Lecturing to a literary society in 1896, Augustine Birrell, Secretary for Education, mentioned an ancient dandy in Bond Street encountering an acquaintance hurrying towards Westminster:

'Whither away so fast this hot day?'
'To the House of Commons.'
'What! Does that go on still?'

The dandy might have appreciated Saki's story, 'The Jesting of Arlington Stringham':

Arlington Stringham made a joke in the House of Commons, and a very thick joke; something about the Anglo-Saxons having a great many angles. It is possible that it was unintentional, but a fellow-member who did not wish it to be supposed that he was asleep because his eyes were shut, laughed. One or two of the papers noted 'a laugh' in brackets, and another, which was notorious for the carelessness of its political news, mentioned 'laughter.' Things often begin in this way.

In the shadow of Parliament is William Rufus's Westminster Hall which the royal mason, Henry Yevele, and the
carpenter, Hugh Herland, renewed between 1394 and 1400.
The historian John Harvey considers:

> Herland's oak roof remains as the greatest single work
> of art of the whole of the European Middle Ages. No
> such combined achievement in the fields of mechanics
> and aesthetics remains elsewhere, nor is there any evidence
> for such a feat having ever existed. This amazing work
> owes its existence to the taste and cultural energy of the
> King, Richard II, for whom the contemporary Wilton
> Diptych was painted, while Geoffrey Chaucer wrote his
> Canterbury Tales.

Here, ironically, Richard himself was deposed and, in
Shakespeare's play, laments:

> Alack, why am I sent for to a king
> Before I have shook off the royal thoughts
> Wherewith I reigned?

Here another king, Charles I, faced his judges. In his poem
'Westminster Hall', John Masefield observed:

> Here lit by this same window, sat the court.
> Pacing this very pavement, side to side,
> The sentries took tobacco and made sport,
> Keeping the rebels peace for regicide.

At Charles II's coronation banquet in the Hall, on 23 April
1661, Pepys was a guest:

> I went from table to table to see the Bishops and all others
> at their dinner, and was infinitely pleased with it. And
> at the Lords' table, I met with William Howe, and he
> spoke to my Lord for me, and he did give me four rabbits
> and a pullet, and so I got it, and Mr Creed and I got
> Mr Minshell to give us some bread, and so we at a stall
> eat it, as everybody else did what they could get. I took

a great deal of pleasure to go up and down, and look upon the ladies, and to hear the music of all sorts, but above all, the 24 violins.

Pepys was also there in July 1667:

One thing extraordinary was this day, a man, a Quaker, came naked through the Hall, only very civilly tied about the loins to avoid scandal, and with a chafing-dish of fire and brimstone burning upon his head, did pass through the Hall, crying, 'Repent! repent!'

By Pepys' time, the Hall, in normal days, was a jostling, scrawling place of geegaw stalls, cheapjack trestles and sweating crowds seeking bargains and easy thefts, all jostling with lawyers, whom Tom Brown, in his *Amusements Serious and Comical* (1700), described as:

the terrible approaches of a multitude of men in black gowns and round caps, that make betwixt 'em a most hideous and dreadful monster called 'Petty-fogging,' of which there is such a store in England, that the people think themselves obliged to pray for the Egyptian locusts and caterpillars, in exchange for this kind of vermin: and the monster bellows out so pernicious a language, that one word alone is sufficient to ruin whole families.

WESTMINSTER ABBEY

The Abbey has the grandeurs and platitudes and sententiousness of a national monument, best seen when it is empty and hushed. Amongst gaping, chattering, wearied sightseers, one realizes the truth of G.K. Chesterton's remark that a statue may be dignified but the absence of a statue is always dignified. The Jacobean Francis Beaumont's 'Ode on the Abbey Tombs' is appropriate:

Mortality, behold and fear,
What a change of flesh is here:

Think how many royal bones
Sleep within these heaps of stones;
Here they lie, had realms and lands,
Who now want strength to stir their hands,
When from their pulpits seal'd with dust
They preach, 'In greatness is no trust.'
Here's an acre sown indeed
With the richest royallest seed
That the earth did e'er suck in
Since the first man died for sin:
Here the bones of birth have cried
'Though gods they were, as men they died!'
Here are sands, ignoble things,
Dropt from the ruin'd sides of kings:
Here's a world of pomp and state
Buried in dust, once dead by fate.

When the Abbey was vandalized by republican troopers
during the Civil War, Major-General George Wither (1588–
1667), pastoral poet, seeking poetry in motion, strutted about
under the columns and gleaming effigies, arches and shadows,
with crown and sceptre stolen from the Chapel of the Pyx.
Arrested at the Restoration, he escaped death, according to
John Aubrey: 'Sir John Denham went to the king and desired
his Majesty not to hang him for that while George Wither
lived, he should not be the worst poet in England.'

Following the tone of Beaumont, Addison wrote in *The
Spectator*:

When I am in a serious humour I very often walk by
myself in Westminster Abbey; where the gloominess
of the place, and the use to which it is applied, with
the solemnity of the building and the condition of the
people who lie in it, are apt to fill the mind with a kind
of melancholy, or rather thoughtfulness, that is not
disagreeable. . . .
     When I look upon the tombs of the great, every
emotion of envy dies in me; when I read the epitaphs of
the beautiful, every inordinate desire goes out; when I
meet with the grief of parents upon a tomb-stone, my

heart melts with compassion; when I see the tomb of the parents themselves, I consider the vanity of grieving for those whom we must quickly follow. When I see kings lying by those who deposed them, when I consider rival wits placed side by side, or the holy men that divided the world with their contests and disputes, I reflect with sorrow and astonishment on the little competitions, factions, and debates of mankind.

Oliver Goldsmith, adopting the guise of a Chinese visitor in *The Citizen of the World*, notices 'a particularly fine monument, of exceptional workmanship and magnificence of design.' He assumes that it commemorates some statesman, hero, lawgiver or poet. A friendly native is informative:

'I suppose that the gentleman was rich, and his friends, as is usual in such a case, told him he was great. He readily believed them; the guardians of the temple, as they got by the self-delusion, were ready to believe him too; so he paid his money for a fine monument; and the workman, as you see, has made him one of the most beautiful. Think not, however, that this gentleman is singular in his desire of being buried among the great; there are several others in this temple, who, hated and shunned by the great when alive, have come here, fully resolved to keep them company now they are dead.'

The Chinese is further disconcerted by interminable demands for payment. Receiving his threepence, a gate-keeper explains:

'As for that there threepence, I farm it from one, – who rents it from another, – who hires it from a third, – who leases it from the guardians of the temple, and we all must live.'

I expected upon paying here, to see something extraordinary, since what I had seen for nothing filled me with so much surprise: but in this I was disappointed; there was little more within than black coffins, rusty armour, tattered standards, and some slovenly figures in wax. I was sorry I had paid, but I comforted myself by

considering it would be my last payment. A person
attended us, who, without blushing, told a hundred lies;
he talked of a lady who died by pricking her finger; of a
king with a golden head, and twenty such pieces of absurdity. 'Look ye there, gentlemen,' says he, pointing to an
old oak chair, 'there's a curiosity for ye; in that chair the
kings of England were crowned: you see also a stone
underneath, and that is Jacob's pillow.'

John Betjeman's 'In Westminster Abbey' extracts wartime
humour. In one verse an old lady prays:

> Gracious Lord, oh bomb the Germans
>   Spare their women for Thy sake.
> And if that is not too easy
>   We will pardon Thy mistake.
> But gracious Lord, what e'er shall be,
>   Don't let anyone bomb me.

Behind the Abbey, Westminster School retains a gateway in
Little Dean's Yard, allegedly designed by Inigo Jones. Here
studied, or at least attended, Ben Jonson, Dryden, Cleland,
Matthew Prior, Charles Churchill, Gibbon, Cowper and,
more recently, Angus Wilson. Cowper afterwards wrote that
a public school would be useful if:

> Would your son be a sot or a dunce
> Headstrong, lascivious or all three at once.

Gibbon was to write that 'school is a cavern of fear and
sorrow'. Westminster in his day was still rural. S.M. Brewer
relates that when Lord Chesterfield's son, Philip Stanhope,
with Churchill and Cowper,

went to play games 'Up Fields', they went down Tufton
Street. At the bottom, to the south of Dean's Yard, there
was a very large open space known as Tothill Fields,
where the boys used to play. This stretched south as far
as the river, and north-west to Castle Lane and Petty
France. Here was a fence, and a rough cart-track leading

to the river, which was known as Horse Ferry Road.
Beyond, the stems of poplar trees and some low-growing
willows could be seen, lazily dipping and swinging in the
breeze.

An earlier visitor to Tothill Fields had been Pepys, on 7 June
1666, though not for cricket, football or bird-nesting. He left
Westminster Hall in his new silk camlet coat, where he had
'picked up the fairest flower and by coach to Tothill Fields till
it was dark. I'light, and with the fairest flower to eat a cake
and there did do as much as was safe with my flower, and that
was enough on my part.'
Outside the Abbey Caxton established his printing press.
Print stabilized memory, promoted the authority of texts,
dogma, the State; helped standardize language and expose the
past. By Elizabeth's time, information was readily available to
an increasingly literate middle-class public. Books offered what
Marchette Chute, in *Shakespeare's London*, called 'the short cut'
to people wanting to know everything, very quickly. 'Books
poured forth from the presses to tell . . . how to keep accounts,
how to survey land, how to play the cittern without a teacher,
how to take spots off velvet, or cook, or ride . . . and what
to do "when the physician is not present".'

FROM THE ABBEY TO VICTORIA

Besides headmasters and deans in Westminster dwelt those like
Alfred Taylor, formerly wealthy, but now reduced to a small
shabby house in Little College Street. Amongst his visitors was
Oscar Wilde, in a despondent crossing of frontiers, a linking
of Chelsea with Westminster that did no full justice to either.
There, Philippe Jullian recounts, Wilde

> would hold forth in a little sitting-room, where the
> curtains were always drawn, surrounded by newspaper
> boys and messenger boys to whom he offered fairy stories
> and cigarette cases. Their cocky animation amused him,
> and their underworld activities had all the attraction of
> danger. All the boys knew who he was, some therefore

did not hesitate to importune him in his own home [Tite Street], or to encourage the flower-sellers to insult him when he crossed Piccadilly with their rival, Alfred Douglas. Neither they nor the street-walkers minced their words, because they complained that homosexuals took the bread out of their mouths. Sighing at the vulgarity of the lower orders, Oscar hailed a cab to take him to Taylor's house where a fancy-dress party was being held to celebrate the burlesque marriage of the master of the house with Charles Mason.

The last entry suggests less Westminster than nearby Victoria. A big London railway station perceptibly greys the atmosphere. Though Mozart, at eight, was composing his first symphony in Ebury Street, nothing Mozartian survives in this area of small private hotels, bus termini and pubs.

William Sansom's story, 'Various Temptations', absorbs some uneasy atmospherics:

His name unknown he had been strangling girls in the Victoria district. After talking no one knew what to them by the gleam of brass bedsteads; after lonely hours standing on pavements with people passing? After perhaps in those hot July streets, with blue sky blinding high above and hazed with burnt petrol, a dazzled head-aching hatred of some broad scarlet cinema poster and the black leather taxis? After sudden hopeless ecstasies at some rounded girl's figure passing in rubber and silk? After the hours of slow crumbs in the empty milk-bar and the balneal reek of grim-tiled lavatories? So that after all the day town's faceless hours the evening town might have whirled quicker on him with the death of the day, the yellow-painted lights of the night have caused the minutes to accelerate and his fears to recede and a cold courage then to arm itself – until the wink, the terrible soft girl smiling towards the night . . . the beer, the port, the meat-pies, the bedsteads?

In Ashley Gardens, on the south side of Victoria Street, is the Early Byzantine-styled Westminster Cathedral, its campanile soaring 270 feet above Victoria. A.N. Wilson, in his biography, reveals how Belloc attended a Requiem Mass there for his friend G.K. Chesterton. 'In the course of the Mass he managed to sell his exclusive obituary of Chesterton to no less than four different editors.'

Though a belligerent Catholic, Belloc's behaviour in churches was seldom ostentatiously devotional. When his son-in-law, Rex Jebb, was received into the Roman Catholic Church, Wilson writes that

the atmosphere which Belloc brought with him to church that day was one of restless social bustle rather than prolonged awe. While Rex Jebb recited the Apostles' Creed in Latin, Belloc leaned forward to Father Vincent McNabb, who was conducting the ceremony and said in a loud voice,

'Excuse me, Father, is there a telephone in the sacristy?'

3

PICCADILLY CIRCUS TO LUDGATE HILL

But tell me, when my mortal memories wane
As death draws near, and peace is mine and pardon,
When will it like an escaped dove repair?
To what Platonic happy heaven – where – where?

Untouchable by Fate and free of Time,
That one immortal moment of the mime
We saw Nijinski dance at Covent Garden.
                         Frances Cornford, 'Grand Ballet'

COVENT GARDEN

From the Circus, in Coventry Street J.B. Priestley, after the destruction of the Café de Paris during the Blitz, saw the rich laid out on the pavement, covered with sawdust 'like broken dolls'. Coventry Street leads to Leicester Square (where, in Leicester House, Spenser missed his chance to ingratiate himself with the magnificent if perplexing Earl of Leicester) and ends in the booklovers' centre, Charing Cross Road. Here, in 1926, Arnold Bennett paused, writing in his Journal:

> I went first of all to Charing Cross Road; but couldn't find any book that I really wanted to buy. I bought one or two little brochures on French and German painters, and a copy of the Calendar [a literary review edited by Edgell Rickword] with a grotesque article by D.H. Lawrence in dispraise of Wells's *Clissold*: a terrible revelation of Lawrence's childish and spiteful disposition.

A few streets away, southwards towards Charing Cross and the river, spreads Covent Garden. The area, for centuries a famous fruit and vegetable market, is dominated by the Covent Garden Opera and, close at hand, the Drury Lane Theatre, which houses the ghost of a murdered man; and St Paul's, 'the actors' church', designed, like the square itself, by Inigo Jones. Until quite recently, little of it was relished by the fastidious. Harold P. Clunn, after the Second World War, praised the theatre and noted the improvement of the streets:

A century ago Drury Lane contained numberless blind alleys, courts and passages on either side, and gin was sold in public-houses which from their size and splendour might almost have been mistaken for the mansions of noblemen, and this in neighbourhoods where poverty and misery abounded. They stood mostly in conspicuous places such as the corners and crossings of the various streets, and here mothers would leave their children to play whilst they went into the gin-palaces to enjoy a far-thing's-worth of gin. They could be seen from afar, and could properly be termed the lighthouses which guided the thirsty soul on the road to ruin, for not only were they resplendent with plate glass and gilt cornices, but each house displayed signs informing you that it sold the only real brandy in London, or that it offered the famous cor-dial medicated gin strongly recommended by the faculty.

Of the Garden in 1685, Macaulay deplores that there 'a filthy and noisy market was held close to the dwellings of the great. Fruit women screamed, carters fought, cabbage stalks and rotten apples accumulated in heaps at the thresholds of the Countess of Berkshire and of the Bishop of Durham.'

In *Humphry Clinker*, Tobias Smollett was even more explicit about the market a century later:

I saw a dirty barrow-bunter in the street, cleaning her dusty fruit with her own spittle and who knows but some fine lady of St James's parish might admit into her delicate mouth those very cherries, which had been rolled and moistened between the filthy, and perhaps ulcerated chops of a St Giles's huckster – I need not dwell upon the pallid, contaminated mash, which they call strawberries; soiled and tossed by greasy paws through twenty baskets crusted with dirt; and then presented with the worst milk, thickened with the worst flour, into a bad likeness of cream: but the milk itself should not pass unanalysed, the product of faded cabbage-leaves and sour draff, lowered with hot water, frothed with bruised snails, carried through the streets in open pails, exposed to foul rinsings, discharged from doors and windows, spittle, snot, and tobacco-quids from foot-passengers, overflowings from mud-carts, spatterings from coach-wheels, dirt and trash chucked into it by roguish boys for the joke's sake, the spewings of infants, who have slobbered in the tin-measure, which is thrown back in that condition among the milk, for the benefit of the next customer: and finally, the vermin that drops from the rags of the nasty drab that vends this precious mixture, under the respectable denomination of milk-maid.

In startling contrast to the market was the Opera, though this too sometimes caused rowdiness and fruit-flinging. Performances have attracted many writers. Thomas De Quincey often attended the famous theatre, as he relates in *Confessions of an English Opium Eater*:

I seldom drank laudanum at that time, more than once in three weeks: this was usually on a Tuesday or a Saturday night; my reason for which was this. In those days Grassini sang at the Opera; and her voice was delightful beyond all I had ever heard. I know not what may be the state of the Opera-house now . . . but at that time it was by much the most pleasant place of public resort in London for passing an evening. Five shillings admitted one to the gallery, which was subject to far less annoyance than the pit of the theatre: the orchestra was distinguished by its sweet and melodious grandeur from all English orchestras, the composition of which, I confess, is not acceptable to my ear, from the predominance of the clangorous instruments, and the absolute tyranny of the violin. The choruses were divine to hear; and when Grassini appeared in some interlude, as she often did, and poured forth her passionate soul as Andromache, at the tomb of Hector, etc., I question any Turk, of all that have ever entered the Paradise of opium-eaters, can have had half the pleasure I had.

In 1870, Disraeli's Lothair in the novel of the same name was less charmed, on his first visit: 'There were rival prima donnas, and they indulged in competitive screams; the choruses were coarse, and the orchestra much too noisy.'

Virginia Woolf, in *The Years*, felt the contrasts between Market and Opera House:

Men and women in full evening dress were walking along the pavement. They looked uncomfortable and self-conscious as they dodged between costers' barrows, with their high piled hair and their evening cloaks with their button holes and their white waistcoats, in the glare of the afternoon sun. The ladies tripped uncomfortably on their high-heeled shoes; now and then they put their hands to their heads. The gentlemen kept close beside them as though protecting them. It's absurd, Kitty thought; it's ridiculous to come out in full evening dress at this time of day. She leant back in her corner. Covent Garden porters, dingy little clerks in their ordinary working clothes, coarse-looking women in aprons stared in at her. The air smelt strongly of oranges and bananas. But the car was coming to a standstill. It drew up under the archway; she pushed through the glass doors and went in.

She felt a sense of relief. Now that the daylight was extinguished and the air glowed yellow and crimson, she no longer felt absurd. On the contrary, she felt appropriate. The ladies and gentlemen who were mounting the stairs were dressed exactly as she was. The smell of oranges and bananas had been replaced by another smell – a subtle mixture of clothes and gloves and flowers that affected her pleasantly. The carpet was thick beneath her feet. She went along the corridor till she came to her own box with the card on it. She went in and the whole Opera

House opened in front of her. She was not late after all. The orchestra was still tuning up; the players were laughing, talking and turning round in their seats as they fiddled busily with their instruments. She stood looking down at the stalls. The floor of the house was in a state of great agitation. People were passing to their seats; they were sitting down and getting up again; they were taking off their cloaks and signalling to friends. They were like birds settling on a field. In the boxes white figures were appearing here and there; white arms rested on the ledges of boxes; white shirt-fronts shone beside them. The whole house glowed – red, gold, cream-coloured, and smelt of clothes and flowers, and echoed with the squeaks and trills of the instruments and with the buzz and hum of voices.

The performances had improved as the century lengthened. Twenty-four years earlier, Covent Garden Opera had reached a dynamic pitch when, in June 1913, Lady Diana Manners (later Lady Diana Cooper) watched the Imperial Russian Opera Company's *Boris Godunov*. Years later she reflected:

Never since have we in England had our eyes so dazzled with new lights. The comets whizzed across the unfamiliar sky, the stars danced. The time-revered old Italian opera in its buskins and farthingales, its tights and its cap-doffing had wearied an audience older than me. Boxes at Covent Garden were hired for the season, but not for music. The darkness hid many sleepers. Wagner nights were more musically alert, because only enthusiasts could stand them. Now came a blast to awaken the dead, a blaze of blinding gold, the Kremlin bells clanged and clashed, and Boris was there, a humble giant on his way to be crowned.

The Covent Garden region compressed much of a London murky enough but memorable. Tavern and church vied with brothel and bookshop, slum with mansion. Long vanished, but remembered by readers, were the Piazza Coffee House, the Turk's Head Coffee House, the Bedford Coffee House, Will's

Coffee Rooms, the Shakespeare Tavern, the Rose Tavern and Davies's Bookshop.

Of booksellers, Dr Johnson asserted, rather surprisingly, that they were generous, liberal-minded men. Boswell recounts a fateful meeting at Mr Davies':

> I drank tea at Davies' in Russell Street, and about seven came in the great Mr Samuel Johnson, whom I have long wished to see. Mr Davies introduced me to him. As I know his mortal antipathy at the Scotch, I cried to Davies, 'Don't tell him where I come from.' However, he said, 'From Scotland?' 'Mr Johnson,' said I, 'indeed I come from Scotland, but I cannot help it.' 'Sir,' replied he, 'that, I find, is what a very great number of your countrymen cannot help.' Mr Johnson is a man of a most dreadful appearance. He is a very big man, is troubled with sore eyes, the palsy, and the king's evil. He is very slovenly in his dress and speaks with a most uncouth voice. Yet his great knowledge and strength of expression command vast respect and render him very excellent company. He has great humour and is a worthy man. But his dogmatical roughness of manners is disagreeable. I shall mark what I remember of his conversation.
>
> He said that people might be taken in once in imagining that an author is greater than other people in private life. 'Uncommon parts require uncommon opportunities for their exertion.'

By that time Johnson was no longer the impecunious hack, but 'Dictionary Johnson', the Great Cham of letters, presiding at informal gatherings at taverns, coffee-houses and literary clubs from Covent Garden to the Monument. He first met Goldsmith at Tom's Coffee House, Covent Garden:

> In a tavern, a club, a drawing-room, or a post-chaise, Johnson would argue, and have the best of the argument, on the institution of slavery or the choice of books for babies; on the government of India or the poetry of Gray; on the decline of free will or the points of a bull-dog; on the management of a university or the writing of a

good cookery book. In 1737 he came to London with twopence-halfpenny and a half-written tragedy in his pocket and for nearly twenty years did the work of an unknown literary drudge; for the last thirty years of his life he was the dominant figure in the educated society of London, laying down the law on politics to Edmund Burke, on literature to Oliver Goldsmith, on painting to Sir Joshua Reynolds, on history to Edward Gibbon, on acting to David Garrick, and on everything to James Boswell. (Carrington and Jackson)

Johnson himself remarked: 'I dogmatise, and I am contradicted, and in this conflict of opinions and sentiments I find delight.'

By 1720, nearly 500 London coffee-houses were rivalling the taverns and chop-houses, with their cliques and coteries, Londoners then, as now, delighting to form clubs, sporting 'Members Only', 'Private' or 'Reserved'. At the Cocoa Tree, St James's, Gibbon could notice 'Twenty or thirty, perhaps, of the first men of the kingdom in point of fashion and fortune, supping at little tables covered with a knapkin, in the middle of a coffee-room, upon a bit of cold meat, or a Sandwich, and drinking a glass of punch.'

Dryden predominated at Will's Coffee Rooms, Covent Garden. Pope and Gay attended the Scriblerus Club in St James's Palace, thanks to a fellow-member and royal physician, John Arbuthnot. The coffee itself is mentioned by the chronicler Tom Brown as 'Black as soot . . . which being soppishly sum'd into their noses, eyes and ears, has the virtue to make them talk and prattle together of everything but what they should do.'

Goldsmith's essay, 'Proceedings of the Club of Authors', is set in Islington, 'at the Sign of the Broom', but is as typical of any in Covent Garden, Holborn, the Strand or Fleet Street:

Upon our entrance, we found the members all assembled, and engaged in a loud debate.

The poet in shabby finery, holding a manuscript in his hand, was earnestly endeavouring to persuade the company to hear him read the first book of an heroic poem, which he had composed the day before. But against this all the members very warmly objected. They knew no reason why any member of the club should be indulged with a particular hearing, when many of them had published whole volumes which had never been looked in. They insisted that the law should be observed where reading in company was expressly noticed. It was in vain that the poet pleaded the peculiar merit of his piece; he spoke to an assembly insensible to all his remonstrances; the book of laws was opened, and read by the secretary, where it was expressly enacted, 'That whatsoever poet, speech-maker, critic, or historian, should presume to engage the company by reading his own works, he was to lay down sixpence previous to opening the manuscript, and should be charged one shilling an hour while he continued reading: the said shilling to be equally distributed among the company as recompense for their trouble.'

Our poet seemed at first to shrink at the penalty, hesitating for some time whether he should deposit the fine, or shut up the poem; but, looking round, and perceiving two strangers in the room, his love of fame outweighed his prudence.

The hapless author reads, too self-admiring to sense the nods, winks, shrugs and stifled laughter of his audience.

Lodging for a while off Covent Garden was John Cleland's Fanny Hill, amiable, hedonistic, gutsy. Her fellow-prostitutes once enjoyed an evening of the sort for which the neighbourhood was renowned:

Louisa and she went one night to a ball, the first in the habit of a shepherdess, Emily in that of a shepherd; I saw them in their dresses before they went, and nothing in nature could represent a prettier boy than this last did, being so fair and well limbed. They had kept together for some time, when Louisa, meeting an old acquaintance of her's, very cordially gives her companion the drop, and leaves her under the protection of her boy's habit, which was not much, and of her discretion, which was, it seems, still less. Emily, finding herself deserted,

sauntered thoughtless about a-while, and, as much for
coolness and air as anything else, at length pull'd off her
mask and went to the sideboard, where, eyed and mark'd
out by a gentleman in a very handsome domino, she was
accosted by, and fell into chat with him. The domino,
after a little discourse, in which Emily distinguish'd her
good nature and easiness more than her wit, began to
make violent love to her, and drawing her insensibly to
some benches at the lower end of the masquerade room,
for her to sit by him, where he squeez'd her hands,
pinch'd her cheeks, prais'd and played with her fine
hair, admired her complexion, and all in a style of court-
ship dash'd with a certain oddity, that not comprehending
the mystery of, poor Emily attributed to his falling in
with the humour of her disguise; and being naturally
not the cruellest of her profession, began to incline to a
parley on those essentials. But here was the stress of the
joke: he took her really for what she appear'd to be, a
shock-fac'd boy; and she, forgetting her dress, and of
course ranging quite wide of his ideas, took all those
addresses to be paid to herself as a woman, which she
precisely owed to his not thinking her one. However, this
double error was push'd to such a height on both sides,
that Emily, who saw nothing in him but a gentleman of
distinction by those points of dress to which his disguise
did not extend, warmed too by the wine he had ply'd
her with, and the caresses he had lavished upon her,
suffered herself to be persuaded to go to a bagnio with
him . . .

The Strand

Just south of Covent Garden, reaching towards Ludgate Hill
and St Paul's, from Trafalgar Square and Charing Cross, the
Strand is so called by virtue of its having been the river's shore.
On one side it is bounded by the Embankment and the Temple,
on the other by the Law Courts and, further back, the resonant
names of Lincoln's Inn Fields, Chancery Lane and Holborn.
Charing Cross Station lies at one end, Fleet Street and the

Savoy at the other, punctuated by a lengthy, once famous, sequence of taverns, coffee houses and eating-places: the Robin Hood Tavern, Essex Street; Robinson's Coffee House, Charing Cross; and the Essex Head, Strand, where Johnson and Fielding founded a literary club. With its lost Tivoli Music Hall, its theatres and hotels, the Strand has always been a street of movement, purpose, random encounters – lawyers, clerics, actors, medical students, prostitutes and con-men jostling with the famished, the opulent and the famous.

In his *London Journal*, Boswell experienced the Strand's low life:

I should have mentioned last night that I met a monstrous big whore in the Strand, whom I had a great curiosity to lubricate, as the saying is. I went into a tavern with her, where she displayed to me all the parts of her enormous carcass; but I found that her avarice was as large as her arse, for she would by no means take what I offered her. I therefore with all coolness pulled the bell and discharged the reckoning, to her no small surprise and mortification, who would fain have provoked me to talk harshly to her and so make a disturbance. But I walked off with the gravity of a Barcelonian bishop. I had the opportunity tonight of observing the rascality of the waiters in these infamous sort of taverns. They connive with the whores, and do what they can to fleece the gentlemen. I was on my guard, and got off pretty well. I was so much in the lewd humour that I felt myself restless and took a little girl into a court; but wanted vigour. So I went home, resolved against low street debauchery.

Boswell also describes Johnson's arrival in London:

He had little money when he came to town, and he knew how he could live in the cheapest manner. His first lodgings were at the house of Mr Norris, a stay-maker, in Exeter Street, in the Strand. 'I dined,' said he, 'very well for eightpence, with very good company at the Pine Apple in New Street, just by: several of them had travelled; they expected to meet every day, but did not

know one another's names. It used to cost the rest a shilling, for they drank wine; but I had a cut of meat for
sixpence, and bread for a penny, and gave the waiter a
penny; so that I was quite well served, nay, better than
the rest, for they gave the waiter nothing.'

In the next century, Crabbe Robinson dismissed William
Blake's apartment in Fountain Court, Strand, as 'a squalid place
of but two chairs and a bed', though Samuel Palmer, contemplating the same place reckoned that 'the millionaire's
upholsterer can furnish no enrichment like those in Blake's
enchanted room'. Blake himself claimed to have learnt his own
artistic technique from Joseph, husband of the Virgin Mary.
As for Boswell, he would have been at home in the Strand
as described by Thomas Burke a century later:

Covent Garden and Drury Lane were still noted as stews,
and the association was stressed by the kind of literature
being sold in Holywell Street. A sort of equivalent of the
snack-bar of to-day, to which young people went after the
theatre, was the Oyster Room. The Strand and its side
streets had numbers of these, and their note, since they
belonged to Victorian London, was a good deal stronger
than the note even of one of our underground night-
clubs. They were regularly filled with the girls from
Drury Lane, dressed out in the silks and feathers of the
establishment to which they belonged, and made up with
what was called 'slap', which it seems was ochre and
bismuth. The most notorious of these places was Jessop's,
in Catherine Street.

Illustrating another layer of the Strand, Burke cites Disraeli,
who deplored the tameness, insipidity and uniformity of
Marylebone and Paddington, Baker Street, Portman Square and
Belgravia – rapid creations of trade and colonialism:

Where London becomes interesting is Charing Cross.
Looking to Northumberland House, and turning your
back on Trafalgar Square, the Strand is perhaps the finest
street in Europe, blending the architecture of many

periods; and its river ways are a peculiar feature and rich
with associations. Fleet Street, with its Temple, is not
unworthy of being contiguous to the Strand. The Fire of
London has deprived us of the delight of a real old quarter
of the city; but some bits remain, and everywhere there
is a stirring multitude, and a great crush and crash of
carts and wains. The Inns of Court, and the quarters in
the vicinity of the port, Thames Street, Tower Hill,
Billingsgate, Wapping, Rotherhithe, are the best parts of
London; they are full of character; the buildings bear a
nearer relation to what the people are doing than in the
more polished quarters.

In *Little Dorrit*, Dickens gives a vivid inset: 'He was passing
at nightfall along the Strand, and the lamp-lighter was going
on before him, under whose hand the street-lamps, blurred
by the foggy air, burst out one after the other, like so many
blazing sunflowers into full-blow all at once.'
Kipling, living for a while in Villiers Street, would have seen
the twilight street-lamps which Richard le Gallienne, in 1895,
evoked:

> Lamp after lamp against the sky
> Opens a sudden beaming eye,
> Leaping alight on either hand
> The iron lilies of the Strand.

The iron lilies might have been overshadowed, in 1889, with
the opening of the Savoy Hotel. Its owner, D'Oyly Carte, the
theatrical backer of Gilbert and Sullivan, pioneered new hotel
grandeur, inducing a fashion for dining out, and installing not
only Cesar Ritz as chef but, to popular astonishment, seventy
bathrooms. The hotel, in all its manifold workings, relation-
ships and problems, is the theme of Arnold Bennett's novel,
Imperial Palace:

> The organisation of the hotel was divided into some
> thirty departments, and the head of each had a fixed
> conviction that his department was the corner-stone of
> the success of the hotel. Evelyn Orcham [the General

Manager], Machiavellian, impartially supported every one of these convictions, just as he consistently refrained from discouraging the weed of inter-departmental jealousies inevitably sprouting from time to time in the soil of strenuous emulation which he was always fertilising. Thus the head-waiter did not conceal his belief that the room-service was the basis of prosperity; the restaurant-manager knew that the restaurant was the life-blood of the place; the manager of the grill-room was not less sure that the grill, where at lunch and at supper the number of celebrities and notorieties far surpassed that of the restaurant (though it cost the hotel not a penny for bands), was the chief factor of prosperity; the audit-manager was aware that without his department the hotel would go to hell in six months; the bills manager had no need to emphasise his supremacy; head of the Reception, who could draw from memory a plan of every room with every piece of furniture in it, and who knew by sight and name and number every guest, and had a file record of each guest, including the dubious, with particulars of his sojourns, desires, eccentricities, rate of spending, payments – even to dishonoured cheques, who could be welcoming, non-committal, cool, cold and ever tactful in foreign languages – this marvel never had a doubt as to the identity of the one indis-pensable individual in the hierarchy of the hotel. And so on.

And there were others – especially their mightinesses the French, Italian and Viennese chefs. Evelyn always remembered the ingenious, sincere remark of the chief engineer, who passed his existence in the lower entrails of our revolving planet, where daylight was utterly unknown. 'You see these things,' the chief engineer had said to a visitor. 'If they shut up, the blessed hotel would have to shut right up.' *These things* were the boilers, which made the steam, which activated the engines, which drew the water from the artesian wells, made the electric light and the electric power, heated the halls, restaurants and rooms, froze or chilled perishable food, baked the bread, cooked the meat, boiled the vegetables, cleansed and dried the very air, did everything except roast the game over a wood fire.

In his Journal entry for 16 December 1928, Arnold Bennett jotted down a real-life episode which united the Savoy with Fleet Street:

Terrific day. The best I have done for years. Nearly 5000 words. I dined at the Savoy. The millionaire owner of a number of papers came up to me and I didn't know him. I asked him: 'Who are you?' He said he wanted some really good stuff for X. He said my article in the first issue had done them a great deal of harm, and asked why I had attacked Lloyd George, and Ll George wanted to know. Considering that I had not mentioned him, or indicated him in any way, or any other politician, I said that this was a bit thick. I said I didn't know whether I could think of any subjects; I had too much to do. He said he worked harder than I did. I said 'You don't!' 'Don't?' said he. 'Don't,' said I. I gazed at him. His eyes fell.

THE EMBANKMENT

Along the Embankment, towards St Paul's and the City, much of the Westminster élite and intellectual aristocracy trained at the Inns of Court, which virtually constituted England's third university. The Inns included Lincoln's Inn, the now vanished New Staple and Clifford's Inns, Gray's Inn, the Inner Temple, the Middle Temple, where *Twelfth Night* was performed before the Queen in 1602, and Clement's Inn, where Shakespeare's Justice Shallow trained, and from where, as he tells Sir John Falstaff, he fought Sampson Stockfish, fruiterer, behind Gray's Inn.

Of the Temple Gardens, overlooking the river, where Shakespeare's ill-tempered noblemen fatefully exchanged red and white roses, Charles Lamb wrote in a London essay: 'What a transition, the passing from the crowded Strand or Fleet Street by unexpected ways, into its unexpected avenues, into its magnificent ample squares, its classic green recesses!'

In 1810, Lamb was living in 4, Inner Temple Lane. Writing to Mr Manning, he described his lodgings:

I have two sitting-rooms: I call them so *par excellence*, for you may stand, or loll, or lean, or try any posture in them, but they are best for sitting; not squatting down, Japanese fashion, but the more decorous mode which European usage has now consecrated. I have two of these rooms on the third floor, and five sleeping, cooking, etc. rooms on the fourth floor. In my best room is a choice collection of the works of Hogarth, an English painter of some humour. In my next best are shelves containing a small but well-chosen library. My best room commands a court, in which there are trees and a pump, the water of which is excellent cold with brandy, and not very insipid without.

Here Johnson had walked, and Goldsmith lived and studied the habits of rooks while in neighbouring streets, Huguenot skills enriched libraries and lexicons. Hundreds of writers are indebted to Roget and his *Thesaurus*. The American writer Washington Irving loved London and its entertainments, and wrote a biography of Goldsmith:

Goldsmith's play, *The Good-Natured Man*, earned him £500, so that he emerged from near poverty to better rooms in the Middle Temple, furnishing them with mahogany sofas, card-tables, and bookcases, with curtains, mirrors, and Wilton carpets. His awkward person was also furnished in a style befitting his apartment; for, in addition to his suit of Tyrian bloom satin grain, we find another charged about this time in the books of Mr Filby, in no less gorgeous terms, being 'lined with silk and furnished with gold buttons.' Thus lodged and thus arranged, he invited the visits of his most aristocratic acquaintances, and no longer quailed beneath the courtly eye of Beauclerck. He gave dinners to Johnson, Percy, Reynolds, Bickerstaff, and other friends of note, and supper parties to young folks of both sexes.

Blackstone, whose chambers were immediately below,

and who was studiously occupied on his *Commentaries*, used to complain of the racket made by his 'revelling neighbour.'

Johnson too lived for some time in the Temple where, despite his bouts of melancholic guilt, friends hurried for his company. Though familiar, a Boswell story is difficult to omit.

One night when Beauclerk and Langton had supped at a tavern in London, and sat till about three in the morning, it came into their heads to go and knock up Johnson, and see if they could prevail on him to join them in a ramble. They rapped violently at the door of his chambers in the Temple, till at last he appeared in his shirt, with his little black wig on the top of his head, instead of a night-cap, and a poker in his hand, imagining, probably, that some ruffians were coming to attack him. When he discovered who they were, and was told their errand, he smiled, and with great good humour agreed to their proposal. 'What, is it you, you dogs! I'll have a frisk with you.' He was soon drest, and they sallied forth together into Covent-Garden, where the greengrocers and fruiterers were beginning to arrange their hampers, just come in from the country. Johnson made some attempts to help them; but the honest gardeners stared so at his figure and manner, and odd interference, that he soon saw his services were not relished. They then repaired to one of the neighbouring taverns, and made a bowl of that liquor called *Bishop*, which Johnson had always liked: while in joyous contempt of sleep, from which he had been roused, he repeated the festive line,
> 'Short, o short then be thy reign,
> And give us to the world again!'
They did not stay long, but walked down to the Thames, took a boat and rowed to Billingsgate.

From the north side, where the Strand merges with Fleet Street, Chancery Lane has the decorated gate through which Trollope's Phineas Finn passed from Lincoln's Inn Fields, largest of London squares, patterned with plane trees, roses, lunch-hour games players and statues. Lincoln's Inn Fields was not always so pleasing. Macaulay described it in the late seventeenth century:

> An open space where the rabble congregated every evening within a few yards of Cardigan House and Winchester House, to hear mountebanks harangue, to see bears dance, and to set dogs at oxen. Rubbish was shot in every part of the area. Horses were exercised there. The beggars were as noisy and importunate as in the worst governed cities of the Continent. A Lincoln's Inn mumper was a proverb. The whole fraternity knew the arms and liveries of every charitably disposed grandee in the neighbourhood, and, as soon as his lordship's coach and six appeared, came hopping and crawling in crowds to persecute him.

At the Inn, with its Inigo Jones chapel, Edward Gibbon attended a dinner in 1780 for Northumberland officers who had helped suppress the Gordon Riots. Not backward in talk Gibbon suffered a social mishap, described by Peter Quennell in his *Four Portraits*. He had just concluded

> one of his best foreign anecdotes, in which he had introduced some of the fashionable levities of political doctrine then prevalent, and, with his customary tap on the lid of his snuff-box, was looking round to receive our tribute of applause, when a deep-toned but clear voice, was heard from the bottom of the table, very calmly and civilly impugning the correctness of the narrative, and the propriety of the doctrines of which it had been made the vehicle. This voice proceeded from a tall, thin, rather ungainly-looking young man who, when Gibbon finally turned on him a surprised, disdainful stare, had relapsed into silence and was quietly eating some fruit. The historian undertook a reply; but the antagonist he had engaged was no less a personage than William Pitt the younger; and after a brilliant and protracted debate, Gibbon was obliged to give ground, excused himself, left the room, and was discovered by the solicitous narrator,

who had followed him, searching for his hat. Begged to
rejoin the company, he declined with emphasis, saying
that he did not doubt that the young gentleman who had
interrupted him was 'extremely ingenious and agreeable,
but I must acknowledge that his style of conversation is
not exactly what I am accustomed to, so you must
positively excuse me.'

FLEET STREET

As a preliminary to Fleet Street are the Law Courts – whose
eight acres of grey, fake-Gothic decorated façades Henry James
described as 'in a good stage of that dusky-silvering which is
the best that London buildings can look for in the operative,
so tormenting (no, find the right, kindly, affectionate word)
air'. The road is divided by two famous churches and Dr
Johnson's statue. Today, in Fleet Street, almost all the famous
journalists and authors have departed, but for three centuries
its fame depended on them. Here a Ben Jonson circle formed
the Apollo Club at the Devil Tavern, later frequented by
Addison who, with Steele, also enjoyed the neighbouring
Dick's Coffee House. Around Johnson's Fleet Street, literary
life, if not always literature itself, hummed and buzzed. Wit
abounded, often rather chilly. Attributed to Matthew Prior
was:

When Pontus wished an edict might be passed,
    That Cuckolds should into the sea be cast,
His wife, assenting, thus replied to him,
    'But first, my dear, I'd have you learn to swim.'

Fleet Street activities reflected the growing literacy of
London, and of the nation itself. The chief glory of a people,
Johnson maintained, arises from its literature. Not only in
Fleet Street but throughout Hanoverian London, diaries,
tracts, novels, moral tales and verses about Love, Envy, God,
Death, Failure, Climate, Mechanics, Physics and the short-
comings of other writers abounded. The clubmen at Dick's or
the Devil might have applauded the anti-Methodist, Joseph

Trapp, who in 1739 published *The Nature, Folly, Sin and Danger of Being Righteous Overmuch*. Even the rarefied St James's dandy, Beau Brummell, condescended to write verses – two, it is claimed, to a butterfly:

> The Butterfly was a gentleman,
>   which nobody can refute,
> He left his lady-love at home
>   and roamed in a velvet suit.
>
> I would be a butterfly,
>   born in a bower,
> Christened in a tea-pot
>   and dead in an hour.

Johnson himself, who lived some years in Gough Square, off Fleet Street, is inescapable; at 72, he jumped over a rail, twice: his assertions can have a startling ring. He fully realized man's need to conceal his unimportance from himself. Like the Greek and Jacobean dramatists, he could anticipate Freud.

> Anxiety wears a man out in schemes to obviate evils that never threatened him.
> Abundant charity is an atonement for imaginary sins.
> Nature has given women so much power that the law has very wisely given them little.
> It is better to LIVE rich than to DIE rich.
> A country governed by a despot is an inverted cone.

He defined a club as an assembly of good fellows, meeting under certain conditions.

Throughout the nineteenth and for most of the twentieth century, such taverns as El Vino's, the Cheshire Cheese in Wine Office Court, the Mitre in Mitre Court, the King and Keys, and Peele's at Fetter Lane Corner were bases for the exchanges, disputes and driftings of journalists. G.K. Chesterton was almost part of Fleet Street architecture. In his biography of Chesterton, Dudley Barker evokes the street in the era before 1914, before it became a jumble of brick and steel and glass of all heights and shapes, and when it still housed the bulk of the national and provincial press:

It was a life of taverns, of roaring discussions that went on for hour after hour, of articles scribbled on odd sheets of paper wedged on the pub table beside the tankard of beer or the bottle of wine, the printer's boy waiting patiently for the copy, and often the cab standing at the kerb outside, forgotten, the driver pulling the thick rug around his legs to keep warm, and the cab-horse's head dropping into its nosebag; and the gaslamps flaring over the presses bringing out the issues for that night.

Through such scenes moved the formidable figure of G.K. Chesterton, in a haze of talk and uproarious laughter. Sometimes he would break off for a while to cross the street to a newspaper office (quite often stopping in mid-traffic, holding it all up, for several minutes of oblivious pondering or a chance meeting, and an argument with his brother). Sometimes, on his way down the street, he would pull from his pocket a penny exercise book and a pencil, and write his essay against the support of the nearest wall. An American visitor to London noted that he had seen Chesterton standing in a shop doorway in Fleet Street, composing a poem, jotting it on a piece of paper and reading it aloud as he wrote.

For two centuries Fleet Street was the hub of the national press, crowded with famous and anonymous writers, almost all in a hurry to meet deadlines. H.M. Tomlinson knew it in 1900:

Fleet Street was waking up to its usual crisis. Midnight was coming. It was growing tense with the pressure of the knowledge of important things which twenty-four hours had engendered. The *Daily Telegraph* clock, which after dark takes over the influential duty of the cross of St Paul's – the cross stands over The Street by day – projected its round pale warning among us. Each narrow side turning of the street was filled with ranks of newspaper carts, waiting for the hour. Their horses, hysterical through a life of rush and excitement, snatched savagely at the elbows of wayfarers, but these were compositors, machine-men, and journalists, sauntering to the

Quill Club, or the 'Black Dog' or the 'Green Dragon' or the 'Clachan', and they knew what to expect of professional vice. From basements and walls came the rumble of machinery, already beginning, with the first revolutions of its heavy load of rumours and alarums, to communicate a tremor to the earth.

Wine Office Court is but a hole in the wall, a footpath out of Fleet Street, and then its narrow passage was unlighted at night except for the bright dabs of the Quill Club windows. It was a modest boast of the club that Goldsmith once wrote in its building, a fact which was never more curious than when you were in the rooms late at night. How did he manage it? Perhaps he had something to write about, and the distraction of good-fellowship could not thwart him.

The bar of the club was immediately within the door. The door mat led to the bar. Bentley, the club familiar, who had seen too much to be surprised by anything that could happen, presided in a white jacket behind the counter with his company of shining pewter pots and chromatic array of bottles. When a member crossed the mat and paused before him no word was passed. Bentley knew. He had been in the club longer than any of us. He understood. He never spoke except when, deferential though with a suggestion of malice, he whispered, 'You are wanted on the telephone, sir'; as though he were aware of the decrees of fate and but waited the predestined signal, of which we could know nothing, to strike a doomed member down. He had a bony aspect, sunken expressionless eyes, and polished his tumblers in ironic deliberation, as though sure of the appropriate hour when the club and its careless frequenters would receive the award of their merit. Then, for the first time, he might laugh.

The Edwardian *Morning Post* acquired for its Literary Editor Chesterton's friend, the pugnacious, careless-with-the-truth and unmistakeable Hilaire Belloc. An undemanding job, A.N. Wilson calls it, and Belloc rendered it more so:

One of the difficulties which always arose when Belloc took employment was that he could not tolerate having a superior; nor was it temperamentally possible for him (for all his prodigious energy, and power of hard work) to keep hours. He only ever took 'jobs' as a way of making money. What is nowadays called 'job satisfaction' is not something which he ever found in employment. He found satisfaction on his own farm; in his own boat and (very occasionally) writing his own books. But he could not be dictated to.

A row with the Editor, Sir Fabian Ware, became inevitable, as Belloc, leaving his work to underlings, seldom visited his office, save perhaps to collect his salary. A.N. Wilson cites a letter:

Dear Belloc.
I owe you an apology for the way I shouted at you this afternoon; but PLEASE don't, on your rare and unexpected visits to the office (about which I shall say more on another occasion), stand in my door and wag your finger at me when I am engaged on a private and difficult business.

As Belloc, for five years, ignored his own literary pages, he was, to his astonishment and wrath, finally dismissed.

Fleet Street ends at Ludgate Hill, on which looms St Paul's Cathedral. Here, until 1737, when it was built over, the river Fleet flowed above ground, stuffed with dead pigs and dead babies, and of which Pope wrote in *The Dunciad*:

Fleet Ditch with disemboguing stream
Rolls the large tribute of dead dogs to Thames,
The King of Dykes! than whom no sluice of mud
With deeper sable blots the silver flood.

In the Fleet Prison for debtors, between Farringdon Street and Fleet Lane, John Cleland wrote *Fanny Hill* during imprisonment, Mr Pickwick discovered another world, and prisoners coolly ran a market for smuggled goods.

THE OLD BAILEY AND NEWGATE

Beneath Ludgate Hill and facing the Cathedral, Farringdon
Street, turning up left towards Holborn Viaduct, has further
away on its right the Old Bailey. Its copper dome glimmers,
the blindfolded effigy of Justice holding her scales catches the
light. The novelist Norman Collins saw the Old Bailey in his
London Belongs to Me (1941):

> There is nothing in the least prepossessing about the
> Old Bailey, even from the outside. It has none of the
> complicated Gothic charm of the Law Courts – all
> Tennysonian turrets and arrow-slits and things – and
> none of the almost domestic friendliness of the better-
> class County Courts. It is just a large bleak factory of the
> Criminal Law with an enormous gilt doll, dressed up as
> Justice, standing on top of the dome, and a public lavatory
> and an A.B.C. tea-shop. Old Bailey itself is a miserable
> thoroughfare, narrowing down at the Ludgate Hill end
> until it looks as though you could scarcely get a horse
> and cart through it. The other frontage – on Cheapside –
> is better.

Here, in 1960, Sybille Bedford covered the *Lady Chatterley*
trial, in which Penguin Books faced a prosecution for obscenity
after publishing D.H. Lawrence's novel. Her account appears
in her book of essays, *As It Was*:

> The Old Bailey is very much a place of its own, a highly
> specialised place where (apart from the occasional sensa-
> tional trial) humdrum, shabby crime is dealt with day
> after day in a steady, drab, conscientious grind. The
> prisoner sits in the dock, the contests are fought between
> teams of professionals and their attendants. Of course,
> there are other people, but they don't count. They are
> there because they must: if the accused has partisans they
> are helpless people, frightened, involved; his wretched
> wife perhaps in a back row, a humbled father; or they are
> there out of some unengaged curiosity, or to do a job, law
> pupils, the regular crime reporters, a pack of Pavlov dogs

sitting in their pew waiting for their cues of sex and violence. This, then, was one of the rare occasions when the court was packed with outside people of conscience, heart and mind, people who were passionately concerned about the outcome, and who were not wholly – at least outside the actual court – mute and powerless: writers, poets, educators, Lawrence enthusiasts, literary journalists, English, American, Canadian . . .

The exchanges, Sybille Bedford reported, bounded between the serious and the ludicrous, the perplexed and the grotesque, the mean and the honest. Witnesses were numerous and famous, most of them dignified and articulate.

There came a most moving moment when counsel called:

'Edward Morgan Forster!' And in came Mr E.M. Forster – alone – he had been sitting on a bench in the hall the best part of the morning, waiting to be called. Now here he was, in a mackintosh, old only in years, looking very firm and calm.

The greatest living writer perhaps in the English language had come into this court, and of course there was no sign of recognition; that is not within the rules or spirit of the place. But Mr Jeremy Hutchinson, very likely seized by a desire to do something, chose the one gesture of favour or respect that can be made in a courtroom – he asked the judge if Mr E.M. Forster might be given a chair. His lordship said Certainly. But Mr Forster said no, no, he didn't want one, he didn't want a chair. Then he spoke.

'I knew Lawrence quite well. In nineteen hundred and fifteen . . .' And there came a sense of the past, and the years.

How would he place him in English literature, asked Mr Hutchinson.

'I would place him enormously high. The greatest imaginative writer of his generation . . . he is part of the great puritan stream of writers, Bunyan, Blake . . . though that may seem a bit paradoxical at first sight. A preacher . . .'

But Mr Forster's passage was all too brief. Mr Griffith-Jones said he had no question, and Mr Forster was gone.

Prosecution and defence, indeed the Old Bailey itself, suggest the proximity of a prison, and indeed to the right of Holborn Viaduct lies the site of Newgate Prison. The prison was designed by Charles Dance, rated by the architectural historian and critic Sir John Summerson as an artist of extraordinary power, often best with a grim theme:

Newgate was an extraordinary building. Far from being a mere dump for felons, a gigantic lock-up, it was splendid and costly architecture, a great Palace of Retribution. To the street it presented a façade of magnificent gloom, hung with chains and enriched with carved figures of horrible appropriateness, writhing in constricted, boulder-lined niches. Inside, though less theatrical, it was no less designedly grim.

Grimness did not cease with the architecture. 'Boz', visiting the prison in 1837, noticed, amongst some thirty condemned to hang, of all ages and appearances, 'a handsome boy, not fourteen years old'; also, a young man at a table, 'who appeared to be teaching the younger ones to write'.
Dickens indeed still dominates the vanished Newgate. He continues:

The prison chapel is situated at the back of the governor's house; the latter having no windows looking into the interior of the prison. Whether the associations connected with the place – the knowledge that here a portion of the burial service is, on some dreadful occasions, performed over the quick and not upon the dead – cast over it a still more gloomy and sombre air than art has imparted to it, we know not, but its appearance is very striking. There is something in a silent and deserted place of worship, solemn, and impressive at any time: and the very dissimilarity of this one from any we have been accustomed to, only enhances the impression. The meanness of its appointment – the bare and scanty pulpit, with the paltry painted pillars on either side – the women's gallery with its great heavy curtain – the men's with its unpainted benches and dingy front – the tottering little table at the altar, with the commandments on the wall above it, scarcely legible through lack of paint, and dust and damp – so unlike the velvet and gilding, the marble and wood, of a modern church – are strange and striking. There is one object, too, which rivets the attention and fascinates the gaze, and from which we may turn horror-stricken in vain, for the recollection of it will haunt us, waking and sleeping, for a long time afterwards. Immediately below the reading-desk, on the floor of the chapel, and forming the most conspicuous object in its area, is the *condemned pew*; a huge black pen, in which the wretched people, who are singled out for death, are placed on the Sunday preceding their execution, in sight of all their fellow-prisoners, from many of whom they may have been separated but a week before, to hear prayers for their own souls, to join in the responses of their own burial service, and to listen to an address, warning their recent companions to take example by their fate, and urging themselves, while there is yet time – nearly four-and-twenty hours – to 'turn and flee from the wrath to come!' Imagine what have been the feelings of the men whom that fearful pew has enclosed, and of whom, between the gallows and the knife, no mortal remnant may now remain! Think of the hopeless clinging to life to the last, and the wild despair, far exceeding in anguish the felon's death itself, by which they have heard the certainty of their speedy transmission to another world, with all their crimes upon their heads, rung into their ears by the officiating clergyman!

At one time – and at no distant period either – the coffins of the men about to be executed, were placed in that pew, upon the seat by their side during the whole service. It may seem incredible, but it is true.

The Gordon Rioters exacted savage revenge on Newgate, graphically depicted by Dickens himself in *Barnaby Rudge*.
Successive editions of the Newgate Calendar from 1774,

with contributions from George Borrow, excited both sensa-
tionalists and reformers. Jack Sheppard's escapes from Newgate
were romanced in a novel by Harrison Ainsworth, and
intrigued such men as Hogarth, Defoe, Sir James Thornhill,
and also Courvoisier, who murdered his employer after reading
a clutch of sensational novels glorifying the thief. Sheppard was
eventually hanged at Tyburn in 1724.

SMITHFIELD

North of Holborn, at the end of Charterhouse Street, lies
Smithfield, part of the medieval Smooth Field, where tour-
naments and executions were held. St Bartholomew's Fair also
took place here, revived in Ben Jonson's energetic, anti-Puritan
play of that name, ripe with ironic jollity, extravagant antics
and bad behaviour, as raucous and bawdy as the Fair itself,
which had been first promoted as a Cloth Fair in 1123 by
Henry II's jester Rahere, founder of nearby St Bartholomew's
Hospital.

In Ben Jonson's play, Mr Zeal-of-the-Land Busy deplores the
urge of Dame Purecraft's daughter Win-the-Fight Little-Wit
to visit the Fair: 'Sister let her fly the impurity of the place,
swiftly, lest she partake of the pitch thereof. Thou art the Seate
of the Beaste, O Smithfield, and I will leave thee. Idolatry
peepith out of every side of thee.'

In his diary for 1 September 1668, Pepys enscribed:

To Bartholomew Fair, and there saw several sights;
among others the mare that tells money, and many things
to admiration; and, among others, come to me when she
was bid to go to him of the company that most loved a
pretty wench in a corner. And this did cost me 12d to the
horse, which I had flung him before, and did give me
occasion to kiss a mighty 'belle fille' that was exceeding
plain, but 'fort belle.'

Three days later, having eaten a pig at the Fair, Pepys saw
Jonson's play acted by puppets. 'It is an excellent play: the more
I see it, the more I love the wit of it, only the business of

abusing the Puritans begins to grow stale and of no use, they being the people that, at last, will be found the wisest.' Earlier, in May 1652, Pepys' friend John Evelyn had noted: 'passing by Smithfield I saw a miserable woman burning, who had murdered her husband.'

Here, amid sights and memories of violence, animal flesh, hilarity and smoke, dwelt John Webster, master dramatist of Jacobean horror, black comedy, tortuous and sophisticated lusts, disconcerting tenderness, of bright words and noble phrases. In *The White Devil* he wrote:

> Call for the robin redbreast and the wren,
> Since o'er shady groves they hover,
> And with leaves and flowers do cover
> The friendless bodies of unburied men.

In Smithfield, E.M. Forster was reminded of Daniel Defoe. In his essay on that writer, he concludes:

> Moll Flanders is the apotheosis of the Cockney; not criminal, not law-abiding, not respectable, warm-hearted. Next time you go down the little passage which leads to St Bartholomew's, Smithfield, give a thought to Moll Flanders, for it was here she robbed of a gold necklace a little girl who was coming back from a dancing-class. She thought of killing the little girl too, but desisted, and conscious of the risk the child had run, she became indignant with the parents for 'leaving the poor little lamb to come home by itself, and it would teach them to take more care of it another time'.

In *Great Expectations*, Smithfield Meat Market – still with its green domes, carved dragons and arches – is 'a shameful place, being asmear with filth and fat and blood and foam', but by the twentieth century, the market had been cleansed and smartened. Arnold Bennett has a sight of it in his novel *Imperial Palace*:

> The ultimate interior had four chief colours: bright blue of the painted constructional ironwork, all columns and

arches; red-pink-ivories of meat; white of the salesmen's long coats; and yellow of electricity. Hundreds of bays, which might or might not be called shops, lined with thousands of great steel hooks from each of which hung a carcass, salesmen standing at the front of every bay, and far at the back of every bay a sort of shanty-office in which lurked, crouching and peering forth, clerks, pen in hand, like devilish accountants of some glittering, chill inferno.

One long avenue of bays stretched endless in part, and others on either hand, producing in the stranger a feeling of infinity. Many people in the avenues, loitering, chattering, chaffing, bickering! And at frequent intervals market-porters pushing trucks full of carcasses, sped with bent heads feverishly through the avenues, careless of whom they might throw down or maim or kill. An impression of intense, cheerful vitality, contrasting dramatically with the dark somnolence of the streets around! A dream, a vast magic, set in the midst of the prosaic reality of industrial sleep! You were dead; you stepped at one step into the dream; you were alive.

4

ST PAUL'S AND THE CITY

I got into the heart of City life. I saw and felt
London at last: I got into the Strand; I went into
Cornhill; I mixed with life passing along; I dared
the peril of crossings. To do this, and do it utterly
alone gave me, perhaps an irrational, but a real
pleasure. Since those days, I have seen the West-
end, the parks, the fine squares; but I love the
city far better. The City seems so much more in
earnest, its rush, its roar are such serious things,
sights, sounds. The City is getting its living – the
West-end but enjoying its pleasures. At the West-
end, you may be amused, but in the City you are
excited.

Charlotte Brontë, *Villette*

ST PAUL'S

For generations, the environs of St Paul's were a focus for
literary London. From stalls, booths, and sheds crammed
round the churchyard developed the dusty, muddled, magnificent acreage of bookshops, a gigantic attempt to withstand
time, in Paternoster Row and nearby streets, squares and
alleys.

For most of the City, the Cathedral, the old and the new,
was a dominating and inescapable shape, symbol less of religion
than of authority, ritual and opportunity, with shreds of belief
and superstition filtering through the cracks. Marchette Chute
recalls:

In Shakespeare's London, the Cathedral of St Paul's did what it could to supply the City's obvious need for the still non-existent daily newspaper. Its middle aisle was the meeting place for every news-monger in London, and not only was the news exchanged here but a great deal of informal business was transacted, especially by lawyers. Since the position of the building blocked the road that would otherwise have been used to reach Fleet Street, the Cathedral was used as a short-cut even by delivery men. So many people passed through it every day instead of using Carter Lane that it was treated as an advertising agency. Anyone who was out of work posted the information so that a prospective employer could write his name and address beneath, and the west door of the Cathedral was 'pasted and plastered up with serving-men's supplications'.

John Earle in *Micro-cosmographia* (1628) reconsidered the shrine of Old St Paul's, before the Great Fire. He found it

the general mint of all famous lies, which are here, like the legends of popery, first coined and stamped in the church. All inventions are emptied here, and not a few pockets. The best sign of a temple in it is that it is the thieves' sanctuary, which rob more safely in the crowd than a wilderness, whilst every searcher is a bush to hide them. It is the other expense of the day, after plays, taverns, and a bawdy-house; and men have still some oaths left to swear here. It is the ears' brothel and satisfies their lust and itch. The visitants are all men without exceptions, but the principal inhabitants and possessors are stale knights, and captains out of service, men of long rapiers and breeches, which after all turn merchants here, and traffic for news.

The Cathedral was littered with ornate national monuments, the inscriptions mostly in Latin, that of the Lord Chancellor Christopher Hatton, even in translation, not perhaps the worst of literary flourishes:

> A gift for worms I lie below,
> And in this way I try to show
> That, just as I am buried, so
> The glory of this world shall go.

Deans of St Paul's included John Donne, William Inge and Sydney Smith, whose wit once so convulsed Mrs Siddons that she had to be helped from the dinner table. Of Brighton Pavilion, he remarked that it was as if St Paul's had gone to the seaside and pupped. Much of his wit remains bright:

> Macaulay is like a book in breeches . . . he has occasional flashes of silence, that make his conversation perfectly delightful.

> Preaching has become a byword for long and dull conversation of any kind, and whoever wishes to imply, in any piece of writing, the absence of everything agreeable and inviting, calls it a sermon.

Sydney Smith, for his Cathedral duties, lived in Amen Corner, Paternoster Row, 'an awkward name on a card', he wrote, 'and an awkward annunciation to the coachman on leaving any fashionable mansion'. His death in 1845, according to a biographer, had

> plunged Jeffrey into an agony of grief, shaken Lord John Russell, silenced Macaulay, caused Lady Holland to forget her ailments, made Samuel Rogers sentimental, stopped the pen of Dickens, saddened the house of Grey, forced Brougham to think for a moment of someone beside himself, reddened the eyes of Thomas Moore, and upset Luttrell's dining arrangements.

Clustered round Old St Paul's were not only bookshops and prebendal homes but also stinking shanties, open sewers, stalls of tainted food and pyramids of dung – a reminder of Dickens' 'golden dustman' in *Our Mutual Friend*, two centuries later. Encircling it were the City's numerous Perpendicular churches – All-Hallows the More, St Mary Axe, St Andrew

Undershaft, St Nicholas Flee-Shambles, St Andrew-by-the-Wardrobe – from which sermons contributed substantially to the annual output of print. Preachers were listed in popularity stakes by congregations willing to acknowledge their own sins and eager to speculate on those of their neighbours.

Much of this was devastated in four days of high winds in 1666, when Pepys, looking up Ludgate Hill, saw that 'most horrid, malicious, bloody flame, not like the fine flame of an ordinary fire'. Amid spectacular horrors, with 'the whole heavens on fire', he noted, at the Exchange, a cat rescued from a hole 'with the hair burnt off the body, and yet alive'.

In the Cathedral, the monument to the poet Donne survived, while those of the politicians John of Gaunt and Francis Walsingham were destroyed. Towers crashed, porticoes crumbled, boiling lead flowed downhill in atrocious grandeur. John Evelyn, in his *Diary*, described how he walked

> from Whitehall as far as London Bridge, through the late Fleet Street, Ludgate Hill by St Paul's, Cheapside, Exchange, Bishopsgate, Aldersgate, and out to Moorfields, thence through Cornhill etc., with extraordinary difficulty, clambering over heaps of yet smoking rubbish, and frequently mistaking where I was: the ground under my feet so hot that it even burnt the soles of my shoes.

The shock of the Fire, which destroyed their home in Fleet Street, killed the dramatist James Shirley and his wife on the same day in the nearby village of St Giles-in-the Fields. Slightly happier is the thought of William Toswell watching the fire by night from Westminster, and in the glare perusing the Roman comic dramatist Terence.

Another literature was contributed by ranting preachers. After personal and courageous efforts to arrest the Fire, Charles II must have chuckled at the outburst of a Puritan zealot preaching in a London church:

> The calamity could not have been occasioned by the Sin of Blasphemy, for in that case it would have begun at Billingsgate; nor Lewdness, for Drury Lane would have

been first on the Fire; nor Lying, for then the flames would have reached the City from Westminster Hall [where the law courts were]. No, my beloved, it was occasioned by the Sin of Gluttony, for it began at Pudding Lane, and ended at Pie Corner.

Thousands of books placed for safety in St Faith's Church, and estimated by Pepys at a value of £150,000, vanished: 'All the great booksellers almost undone.' This devastation of books was repeated in 1940–1, when again the fire fell, as if indeed from heaven. The sudden confusion of classes, values, even identities, is netted in Henry Green's novel *Caught*, in which unprecedented and perilous visions overtake Londoners in crisis. *Caught* is set in the London of 1940 and the Battle of Britain, in the city of fires and bombs, agonies and resolution, haphazard encounters and the partial collapse of everyday habits, morals, values. At any instant the perilous, the grotesque, the unpredictable may emerge.

At that, so sudden it brought him up sharp, the tart stood back in a doorway, shone a copper beam, from the torch she carried, full on her left breast she held bared with the other hand. She murmured 'Hulloh love.' Longingly he ogled the dark purple nipple, the moon-full globe that was red Indian tinted by her bulb, with the whiff of scent. 'Jesus,' he moaned, but it was too near his sub-station. 'Don't you go hangin' around,' he added indistinctly and shambled off. She laughed into a cough and then, when she snapped down the light, was again, and at once, indigo, and the door against which she stood.

Not only in Yeats' Dublin was a terrible beauty born. After the Great Fire, strange and voluptuous growths and blossoms, queer hues and fantastic shapes surged in profusion almost tropical, barely natural, and, some thought, nourished by the Plague victims so recently buried. Something of this also emerged after the Blitz, and in *The World My Wilderness* Rose Macaulay shows a new barbarism thriving in the ruins around St Paul's. Under the Cathedral a jungle sprawls for a French boy to explore:

He slipped away into the ruinous twilight, treading lightly along broken walls above shadowed chasms and catacombs. Evening darkened over that long waste, where merchants and lawyers, clerks, typists, shop-keepers, tailors and chemists had their deserted lairs, now the dens of wolves and wild cats. A fine maquis, Rauel thought, in which to lurk and plot and hide from the Gestapo, lying in wait for them, tripping them up into brambled ravines, shooting at them from behind broken walls.

A cat – or was it a wolf? – leaped from beneath his feet and fled scuttering among rocks. He started, and hurried on, running down Monkwell Street, past Barber's Hall, past the Cooper's Arms at the corner of Silver Street, past St Olave's churchyard, past all the ruined halls, down the narrow alley of Noble Street, past the Church of St Anne and St Agnes with the gardens full of fig-trees, and the churchyard of St John Zachary, bright with dahlias and sunflowers, and so down Foster Lane into Cheapside, where streets were paved and buildings stood up, and a solid, improbable world began, less real, less natural than the waste land.

In another post-war novel, *Fireweed*, Jill Paton Walsh sees the wrecked City:

Grass grows there, covering, healing, and russet sorrel in tall spikes, and golden rod swaying beside broken walls, full of butterflies and purple loose-strife, and one plant, willow-herb, that some people call fireweed, grows wild in this stony place as plentifully as grass, though it used to be rare enough to be searched out and collected.

The bombing of the City is evoked by Stephen Spender, himself a wartime London fireman, in his poem 'Epilogue to a Human Drama':

The City burned with unsentimental dignity
Of resigned wisdom: those stores and churches
Which had glittered emptily in gold and silk,

Stood near the crowning dome of the cathedral
Like courtiers round the Royal Martyr.
August shadows of night
And bursting days of concentrated light
Dropped from the skies to paint a final scene –
Illuminated agony of frowning stone.
Who can wonder then that every word
In burning London seemed out of a play?
On the stage, there were heroes, maidens, fools,
Victims, a chorus. The heroes were brave,
The rescued appeared passively beautiful,
The fools spat jokes into the skull of death.
The victims waited with the humble patience
Of animals trapped behind a wall
For the pickaxes to break with sun and water.
The chorus assisted, bringing cups of tea,
Praising the heroes, discussing the habits of the wicked
Underlining the moral, explaining doom and death.

The bookshops round St Paul's revived after the Great
Fire. In the following century John Newbery was selling
books at the Bible and Sun, in St Paul's Churchyard, and it was
he who first popularized children's literature. He appears in
Goldsmith's *Vicar of Wakefield*. Goldsmith lived as his tenant,
Johnson rated him a friend. Austin Dobson, in an essay of
1925, cited his productions – *The Renowned History of Giles
Gingerbread: a little Boy who lived on Learning; Mrs Margery Two
Shoes afterwards Lady Jones; The Redoubtable Tommy Trip and
his Dog Jasper*; the *Lilliputian Magazine* – and 'a number of
other tiny masterpieces in that flowered and gilt Dutch paper
of which the art has been lost'.
    Dobson reveals more:

Gradually his indiscriminate activities narrowed themselves to two distinct branches of business, in these days
incongruous enough – the sale of books and the sale of
patent medicines. While at Reading, he had become part
owner . . . of Dr Hooper's Female Pills, and soon after
his settlement in London, he acquired the sole management of a more famous panacea, Dr James's Fever

Powders, which had in their time an extraordinary vogue. According to Mrs Delany, the King dosed the Princess Elizabeth with them, Gray and Cowper were both believers in their efficacy; and Horace Walpole declared he should take them if the house were on fire. Fielding especially praises them in *Amelia*, affirming that in almost any country but England they would have brought 'public Honours and Rewards' to his 'worthy and ingenious Friend Dr James'; while Goldsmith may be said to have laid down his life for them. With the sale of these and kindred species, John Newbery alternated his unwearied speculations as a bookseller. He was at the back of Smollett's venture of the *British Magazine*; it was for his *Universal Chronicle* that Johnson wrote his *Idler* and quizzed his proprietor as 'Jack Whirler'; he was the publisher of Goldsmith's *Traveller*; and he probably found part of the historical sixty guineas which somebody paid for *The Vicar of Wakefield*. He died at Canbury or Canonbury House, Islington, in the still existent tower.

THE ROYAL EXCHANGE AND CHEAPSIDE

Pepys, though frequently attending the royal brothers in Whitehall, was manifestly of the City. In 1663 he was living at the Navy Office in Crutched Friars, south of Leadenhall Street, already writing the Diary which, for Virginia Woolf, 'catches unfailing the butterflies and gnats and falling petals of the moment, which can deal with a day's outing or a merry-making or a brother's funeral'. His entry for 12 January is typical enough of a City day:

> With Mr Creed to the King's Head ordinary, but people being set down, we went to two or three places; at last found some meat at a Welsh cook's at Charing Cross, and here dined. After dinner to the 'Change to buy some linen for my wife, and going back met our two boys. Mine had struck down Creed's boy in the dirt, with his new suit on, and the boy taken by a gentlewoman into a house to make clean but the poor boy was in a pitiful taking and pickle,

but I basted my rogue soundly. Thence to my lord's lodgings. I found my lord within, and he and I went out through the garden toward the Duke's chamber, to sit upon the Tangier matters; but a lady called to my lord out of my Lady Castlemaine's lodging, telling him that the King was there and would speak with him. My lord could not tell me what to say at the Committee to excuse his absence, but that he was with the King; nor would suffer me to go into the Privy Garden, which is now a through passage and common, but bid me go through some other way, which I did; so that I see he is a servant of the King's pleasures too, as well as business. To my Lady Batten's, and sat with her awhile; but I did it out of design to get some oranges for my feast tomorrow of her, which I did. So home, and found my wife's new gown come home, and she mightily pleased with it. But I appeared very angry that there were no more things got ready against to-morrow's feast, and in that passion set up long, and went discontented to bed.

The Royal Exchange stands by Threadneedle Street, continuing east towards Leadenhall Street and Aldgate, from the Bank, linked to St Paul's by Cheapside, which, with its pageants and professions, shopkeepers and 'prentices, Chaucer knew so well. Pepys too knew the entire area better than most, through his official and unofficial journeys.

To the 'Change, and thence home, and took London Bridge in my way: walking down Fish Street, and Gracious Street, to see how very fine a descent they have made down the hill, that it is become very easy and pleasant. Going through Leadenhall, it being market-day, I did see a woman catched, that had stole a shoulder of mutton off a butcher's stall, and carrying it wrapped up in a cloth, in a basket. The jade was surprised, and did not deny it, and the woman so silly as to let her go that took it, only taking the meat.

The Royal Exchange, much burnt, decorated with campanile and Gresham's emblem of a golden grasshopper, was a

noisy, bustling centre of commercial dealings. Nearly a century
later, Addison reported in *The Spectator* that there 'I have been
pleased to hear disputes adjusted between an inhabitant of
Japan and an alderman of London, or to see a subject of the
Great Mogul with one of the Czar of Muscovy.'

Cheapside, Cornhill, Lombard Street, Gracechurch Street,
Eastcheap, Bishopsgate, Aldgate, Temple Bar, Mansion
House, Guildhall, Monument – in barely a square mile was
concentrated a financial and political ascendancy which was
soon to create a world power. Within the concourse of
magnates, bankers and merchants, the City kept a human
proportion. Ruthless ambitions, vast enterprises, stupendous
contracts abounded, but common life thrived: unruly, disrespectful, unpredictable, never still, certainly since Chaucer's
day, always vivid in Cheapside.

John Lydgate, monk and poet, in 'London Likpenny'
(*c*. 1410) includes:

> Then to the Chepe I began me drawne,
> Where mutch people I saw for to stande;
> One offered me velvet, sylke, and lawne,
> And other he taketh me by the hande,
> 'Here is Parys thred, the finest in the Lande.'

In Cheapside, wide and clamorous, Tudor and Jacobean
writers gathered in such nearby taverns as the Mermaid, in
Bread Street, Milton's birthplace, of which Francis Beaumont
wrote to Ben Jonson,

> What things have we seen
> Done at the Mermaid? Heard words that have been
> So nimble, and so full of subtle flame,
> As if that every one from whence they came,
> Had meant to put his whole wit in a jest,
> And had resolv'd to live a fool, the rest
>   of his dull life.

Here Ralegh could meet Marlowe and Donne, Drayton,
Fletcher and Shakespeare. Literary clubs were already forming,
where authors quarrelled, dissolved and began new clubs, after

some purges, a few streets away. At its best, which was probably seldom, the conversation must have anticipated Ezra Pound, in his *Cantos*:

> And they want to know what we talked about?
> Of letters and tragedies and music,
> Both of ancient times and our own,
> And men of unusual genius,
> Both of ancient times and our own,
> In short, the usual subjects of conversation between
>   intelligent men.

Outside, the common life struggled on, now gleeful, now angered by immigrants, debt-collectors, the press-gang, or the collapse of a favourite. Donald Lupton wrote of Cheapside in 1632:

> There are a great company of honest men in this place, if all be gold that glisters: their parcel-gilt plate is thought to resemble themselves, most of them have better faces than heart; their monies and coins are used as prisoners at sea, kept under hatches. One would think them to be good men, for they deal with the purest and best metals and every one strives to work best, and stout too, for they get muck by knocking and especially by leaning on their elbows.

London language was blossoming. In the Boar's Head, Eastcheap, close to the Monument and the river, Falstaff accosts the Hostess in language which reeks of crowded, quarrelsome, uninhibited City streets: 'There's no more faith in thee than a stewed prune nor no more truth in thee than in a drawn fox; and for womanhood, Maid Marion may be the deputy's wife of the ward to thee. Go, you thing, go!'

In another age, Coleridge related that as a daydreaming schoolboy, he was walking in Cheapside, fancying himself swimming the Hellespont, and making swimming gestures. Accidentally hitting a passing stranger, he was accused of attempted theft. Much agitated, he explained his fantasy and his accuser, moved, secured him entry to the library in nearby King Street.

THE MANSION HOUSE

Despite the power of its Livery Halls, the opulence of the Guildhall, the grandeur of the Mansion House, of the merchant in his counting-house and the magistrate on his bench, the seething, restless City was seldom demure. The Reformation had replaced extravagant religious processions with such spectacles as the Lord Mayor's Show, with mimes, dances, tableaux and songs, visually bawdy, often provoking violence and produced by such foremost dramatists as Dekker and Middleton. They were more than an excuse for carnival and orgy, they reminded Whitehall and Westminster of the City's status and privileges, and that frontiers were brittle.

In a letter of the 1720s, the Swiss traveller César de Saussure describes the City:

> The Lord Mayor's Day is a great holiday in the City. The populace on that day is particularly insolent and rowdy, turning into lawless freedom the great liberty it enjoys. At these times it is almost as dangerous for an honest man, and more particularly for a foreigner, if at all well-dressed, to walk in the streets, for he runs a great risk of being insulted by the vulgar populace, which is one of the most cursed brood in existence. He is sure of not only being jeered at and being bespattered with mud but, as likely as not, dead dogs and cats will be thrown at him, for the mob makes a provision beforehand of these playthings, so that they may amuse themselves with them on the great day.

Dr Johnson, though devout, was no pacifist in the City or out of it. In his *A Book for a Rainy Day* (1845), John Thomas Smith recalled a scene that once enlivened a street far from the City, but which must have occurred daily in all parts of London:

> I once saw him follow a sturdy thief who had stolen his handkerchief in Grosvenor Square, seize him by the collar with both hands, and shake him violently, after which he quickly let him loose; and then with his open hand, gave

him so powerful a smack on the face, that sent him off
the pavement, staggering.

The stately Lord Chesterfield was author of celebrated letters
on manners, deportment and courtesy, though his early indif-
ference to the indigent Johnson stung the latter into asserting
that his precepts taught the morals of a whore and the manners
of a dancing-master. Chesterfield once defined a gentleman as
one who knows how to play the trumpet, but refrains. He too
could face street violence, to be countered in a way more
fastidious than Johnson's. He was once accosted by a rough,
who snarled that he never made way for a scoundrel. 'Ah!'
Chesterfield stepped into the roadway, doubtless lifting his hat,
'I always do.'

In the crowded City, of small twisting streets, swarming
mazes, ill-lit cellars and dangerous roofs, hazards lurked in
every alley, at every corner. Cleland, in *Fanny Hill*, castigated
by moralists as 'that most licentious and inflaming book',
describes the gullible heroine's first arrival in London, a situation familiar to all generations. A waiter secures her a night's
lodging. Next day, she ventures to an 'intelligence office', seeking employment. An elderly lady examines her minutely:

'Sweet-heart, do you want a place?'
'Yes, and please you' (with a curtesy down to the
ground).
Upon this, she acquainted me that she was actually
come to the office herself to look out for a servant; that
she believed I might do, with a little of her instructions;
that she should take my very looks for a sufficient
character; that London was a very wicked, vile place; that
she hoped I would be tractable, and keep out of bad
company; in short, she said all to me that an old
experienced practitioner in town could think of, and
which was much more than was necessary to take in an
artless inexperienced country-maid, who was afraid of
becoming a wanderer about the streets, and therefore
gladly jump'd at the first offer of a shelter, especially from
so grave and matron-like a lady, for such my flattering
fancy assured me this new mistress of mine was; I was

being hired under the nose of the good woman who kept
the office, whose shrewd smiles and shrugs I could not
help observing, and innocently interpreted them as marks
of her being pleased at my getting into place so soon: but,
as I afterwards came to know, these BELDAMS understood one another very well, and this was a market where
'Mrs Brown', my mistress, frequently attended, on the
watch for any fresh goods that might offer there, for the
use of her customers and her own profit.

Another City personage, stamped on the imagination as
firmly as Hogarth's Moll Hackabout, was Jonathan Wild, a
real-life criminal, anti-hero of Fielding's *History of Jonathan
Wild the Great* and of whom Sherlock Holmes in 'The Valley
of Fear' informed young Inspector MacDonald:

Jonathan Wild was the hidden force of the London
criminals, to whom he sold his brains and his organisation
on a fifteen percent commission. The old wheel turns and
the same spoke comes up. It's all been done before and will
be done again.

In prison at the Compter, Wood Street, off Cheapside, Wild
met Mary Mulliner, thief and prostitute. On release, they ran
a tavern together in Cock Alley, opposite Cripplegate Church,
near Moorgate, birthplace of Keats. The affection of the
illustrious pair was later impaired when Wild sliced off his
partner's ear. Adopting gentility, abandoning the tavern, convinced that, as reported in the *Newgate Calendar*, 'all men are
knaves and fools, and much the greater number a composite of
both', he became the most powerful of London 'fences',
ingeniously pleasing the robbed by restoring their goods and
arranging, then pocketing, the reward, which he shared on
unequal terms with the felons. Variations of this skill secured
him wealth, reputation and authority, reinforced by blackmail,
threats, violence and the ability 'to foment eternal jealousies in
his gang'. In cold double-bluff he betrayed whoever queried his
conditions. Always resolved 'to maintain a constant gravity in
his countenance and behaviour and to affect wisdom on
all occasions', he blandly agitated for the reform of public

morals, in association with the City Marshal, carrying a silver staff which he passed off as an emblem of legal powers. The Marshal, however, at length disenchanted, began denouncing him as 'King of the Gypsies', 'Lying-Master-General of England', 'Captain-General of the Army of Plunderers' and 'Ambassador-Extraordinary of the Prince of the Air', 'amassing his Illicit Store in an Apartment fitted for Him by the Queen of Hell'. Public opinion enjoyed a rare chance of fulfilment and, over-reaching himself, Wild, after a strenuous legal battle, went to the gallows to the cheers of Londoners and the approval of the City Marshal.

BUNHILL FIELDS

Bunhill Row leads out of Moorgate towards Old Street and along it, between Clerkenwell and Shoreditch, lie Bunhill Fields. On his way to Old Street on a winter afternoon, through air chilled and leaden, the sky above the City a low ceiling of tarnished brass, J.B. Priestley's Mr Smeeth, average man, in *Angel Pavement*, finds himself in Bunhill Fields:

> He stared through the iron railings of the old graves there. He had been this way before, many a time, in fact, but he never remembered noticing before that the earth of the burying-ground was high above the street. The railings were fastened into a wall between two or three feet high, and the ground of the cemetery was as high as the top of this little wall. There was something very mournful about the sooty soil, through which only a few miserable blades of grass found their way. It was very untidy. There were bits of paper there, broken twigs, rope ends, squashed cigarettes, dried orange peel, and a battered tin that apparently had once contained Palm Chocolate Nougat. This dingy litter at the foot of the gravestones made him feel sad. It was as if the paper and cigarette ends and the empty tin, there in the old cemetery, only marked in their shabby fashion the passing of a later life, as if the

twentieth century was burying itself there too, and not
even doing it decently.

A passer-by, halting for a chat, tells Mr Smeeth that Daniel
Defoe is buried here.

'I tell yer, boy, there's some big men in there – what's
left of 'em.'
Mr Smeeth nodded and continued to stare idly through
the railings of Bunhill Fields, where the old nonconfor-
mists are buried in mouldering eighteenth-century elegance, to which they had at least conformed in death, if
not in life; and where, among the divines and elders, not
only Defoe, but also Bunyan and Blake, the two God-
haunted men, lie in the sooty earth, while their dreams
and ecstasies still light the world. As Mr Smeeth stared,
something floated down, touched the crumbled corner of
the meanest headstone, and perished there. A moment
later, on the curved top of the little wall beside him was
a fading white crystal. He looked up and saw against the
brassy sky a number of moving dark spots. He looked
down and saw the white flakes floating towards the black
pavement. In all his life he had never been so surprised by
the appearance of snow, and for one absurd moment he
found himself wondering who had made it and who was
responsible for tumbling it into the City.

GRUB STREET

Grub Street remains a symbol of a literary life linked by
Johnson with 'toil, envy, want, the garret, the jail'. Yet it was
also an actual place, which he describes in the *Dictionary* as
'originally the name of a street near Moorfields in London,
much inhabited by writers of small histories, dictionaries and
temporary poems, whence any mean production is called Grub
Street'.
Pope, in *The Dunciad*, gives forbidding portraits of Grub
Street dullness, mediocrity and vapidity.

> While pensive Poets painful vigil keep,
> Sleepless themselves, to give their readers sleep.

Goldsmith, like Johnson himself, struggled out of Grub Street to the larger London scene, but never lost sight of it. His 1765 essay contains its essence:

> the metaphysician, Doctor Nonentity: also the versatile Lawyer Squint; Doctor Syllabub is reckoned equally excellent at a rebus, a riddle, a bawdy song, and a hymn for the tabernacle. You will know him by a shabby finery, his powdered wig, dirty shirt and broken silk stockings . . . Mr Tibs, writes receipts for the bite of a mad dog, and throws off an Eastern tale to perfection: he understands the business of an author as well as any man, for no bookseller can cheat him. You may distinguish him by the peculiar clumsiness of his figure, and the coarseness of his coat; however, though it be coarse (as he frequently tells the company) he has paid for it.

Richard Savage, poet, bohemian, homicide, blackmailer and protégé of Pope – a typical inhabitant of Grub Street – was described by Dr Johnson as of 'a grave and manly deportment, a solemn dignity of mien, but which, upon a nearer acquaintance, softened into an engaging easiness of manner'. This did not prevent Savage, when drunk, from stabbing a man in a coffee-house brawl in 1727, though he escaped Tyburn. His play, *Sir Thomas Overbury*, produced posthumously in 1777 at Drury Lane, had a prologue by Sheridan:

> Ill-fated Savage, at whose birth was given
> No parents but the Muses, no friend but Heav'n.

Boswell mentioned that the poet's misfortunes and misconduct had reduced him to the lowest state and that he too died in a debtors' prison.

Savage remains a type familiar in literary London. He had charm and wit and was familiar with all classes, who forgave his scrounging in return for his talk. Robert Lynd wrote of him:

It was enough that he should be an author in distress and an entertaining conversationalist to make Johnson warm to him.

Savage was an extraordinary egotist. He regarded it as his right to live at the expense of others, like Shaw's artist in *The Doctor's Dilemma*. He was vain, disappointed, and a sponge. He thought that he ought to have been made Poet-Laureate after the death of Eusden, and, when the appointment was given to Colley Cibber instead he immediately assumed the title of Volunteer Laureate, though Cibber protested that he might as well have called himself a Volunteer Lord or Volunteer Baronet.

THE GUILDHALL

In contrast to tavern and coffee-house, bagnio and prison, Grub Street and beggaries, the Guildhall, the Mansion House and the Livery Halls stood ornate, resplendent and powerful between St Paul's and Leadenhall Street, London Wall and the river. Many, rebuilt after the Fire, finally perished in the Blitz. Ehrlich writes:

> Only the Merchant Taylors Hall at 30 Threadneedle Street retains in large part its fourteenth- and fifteenth-century rooms. Stationers Hall remains an essentially post-fire building of 1667, although several of its historic chambers had also to be reconstructed after bomb damage. The Hall is tucked away in an alley called Stationers' Hall Court, near Ave Maria Lane and Amen Corner in the precinct of St Paul's Cathedral.

These Halls entertained many grandees on ceremonial and commercial occasions, with the City populace, sharp-eyed, politically conscious, often subversive and always inclined towards disrespect, clamouring to be part of the show. The Bohemian Protestant, Baron Waldstein, first in London in 1602, noted in his Diary that the Lord Mayors 'kept open houses like princes' but that they spent £8,000 annually on expenses, receiving a mere £2,000 in payment. At Easter-tide the Lord Mayor was publicly honoured:

> Before him go 40 civil servants or public officials, followed by a group bearing a sword with its scabbard encrusted with pearls, and also a golden staff like a scep-tre. Two youths then follow in fine robes and wearing gold chains. After these comes my Lord Mayor himself, mounted on a white horse, with the Bishop of London at his side. The Mayor wears a crimson robe, its collar lined with black silk. Over his shoulders hangs a great chain, such as the Knights of the Garter wear. His horse is caparisoned with trappings and a bridle of black silk, all tipped with silver gilt. Two Aldermen are always in attendance on the Mayor and both wear robes of the same colour as his own; after these come secretaries and clerks on foot. The wives of these men, gorgeously dressed in red gowns and wearing gold chains, go on foot to the place, which is outside the City walls, where the service is held, and they return in procession to the City in the same way. The City is said to have 120 churches, in all of which they hold services; there are even churches where they have services in French, Italian and Flemish.

With the Guildhall, Pepys, of course, was very familiar. His entry for 29 October 1663 records:

> We went up and down to see the tables; where under every salt there was a bill of fare, and at the end of the table the persons proper for the table. Many were the tables, but none in the Hall, but the Mayor's and the Lords of the Privy Council, that had knapkins or knives, which was very strange. We went into the Buttery, and there stayed and talked, and then into the Hall again, and there wine was offered, and they drunk, I only drinking some hippocras, which do not break my vow, it being, to the best of my present judgment, only a mixed com-pound drink, and not any wine. If I am mistaken, God forgive me! but I hope and do think I am not. By and by met with Creed: and we, with the others, went within

the several Courts, and there saw the tables prepared for the Ladies, and Judges, and Bishops: all great sign of a great dinner to come. By and by, about one o'clock, before the Lord Mayor came, come into the Hall, from the room where they were first led into, the Lord Chancellor, Archbishop before him, with the Lords of the Council, and other Bishops and they to dinner. Anon comes the Lord Mayor, who went up to the Lords, and then to the other tables to bid welcome; and so all to dinner. I sat near Proby, Baron and Creed at the Merchant Strangers' Table; where ten good dishes to a mess, with plenty of wine of all sorts, of which I drunk none; but it was very unpleasing that we had no knapkins nor change of trenches, and drunk out of earthen pitchers, and wooden dishes. It happened that after the Lords had half dined, come the French Ambassador up to the Lords' table, where he was to have sat; but finding the table set, he would not sit down nor dine with the Lord Mayor, who was not yet come, nor have a table to himself, which was offered; but in a discontent went away again. After I had dined I and Creed rose and went up and down the house, and up to the Ladies' room, and there stayed gazing upon them. But though there were many and fine, both young and old, yet I could not discern one handsome face there; which was very strange. I expected music, but there was none but only trumpets and drums, which displeased me.

Worse could be experienced on such formal occasions. Following Allied victories over Napoleon, Alexander I of Russia paid a State Visit to London in 1814 as the guest of the Prince Regent – an unfortunate conjunction, not lost on the City crowds swarming around the Guildhall, as Sir Arthur Bryant relates:

The climax of this contest of pinpricks between the two vainest men in Europe occurred on June 18th when the two monarchs dined with the Lord Mayor. Knowing that if he went to the Guildhall unaccompanied, he would be insulted by the mob, the Regent had arranged to drive

with the Czar. But at the last moment the Grand Duchess
decided to come too. In vain it was pointed out that the
arrangements had all been made and that women were
excluded from civic feasts. Argument merely strength-
ened her resolution. All day frantic letters passed between
the Pulteney and Carlton House. The Czar was adamant;
unless the Grand Duchess drove with him by his side, he
would not go to the Guildhall at all. As it was impossible
for all three to occupy the same seat, and none could sit
with dignity on the opposite one, there was nothing for
the Regent to do but resign his state coach to the Czar
and proceed in a separate one. His reception in the City
streets was such as to make him vow he would never visit
it again. Despite the two Prussian princes hastily requisi-
tioned to sit opposite him, the Lord Mayor riding ahead
with the sword of state, the Yeomen of the Guard and the
massed escort of cavalry, the Regent was greeted with
hisses, groans and shouts of 'Where's your wife? Love
your wife!'

Nor did his humiliation end at the Guildhall. In the
presence of the Ministers, the King of Prussia and the
foreign princes, the head of the British State was forced
to await the arrival of the Russians for a whole hour, the
end of which was rendered the more agonising by the
frantic cheering which greeted them in the streets outside.
And as the royal procession at last entered the banqueting
hall to the strains of 'The Roast Beef of Old England', the
Czar deliberately stopped to talk to Lord Grey and Lord
Holland, two of the Regent's bitterest enemies. The
enraged Prince had to wait behind him under the gaze of
thousands. For the rest of the evening he preserved a
haughty and chilly silence . . . while the Lord Mayor
stood majestic behind, while the traditional baron of beef,
surmounted by the royal standard and attended by
sergeant carvers, was borne with musical honours to the
table, and toast followed toast, the Regent said not one
word to the imperial barbarian at his side.

But the Russians had not finished with him. When
after the toasts and 'Hip! Hip! Hurrahs,' at which the
Grand Duchess laughed deliciously, the fiddlers and

opera-singers in the gallery struck up the time-honoured songs appropriate to each sentiment – 'Rule Britannia!' 'Hail, Star of Brunswick,' 'To Arms, to Arms!' – she began to make signals of distress. If the caterwauling went on, she declared, she would be sick.

Today, the Halls are used, but becalmed, often surrounded by architecture miscellaneous but seldom arresting. Moreover, a newcomer insensitive to the depths and resonances of names – London Wall, St Peter-upon-Cornhill, St Katherine Cree, Ropemaker Street, St Lawrence Jewry, Ely Place, Stonecutter Street – might remain unstirred, though here Jonson argued, Swift drank coffee and Savage raged and collapsed. Seen on a weekend, the busy, polyglot crowds and purposeful aura dispersed, the City itself can be dispiriting in nakedness, the soaring offices featureless, ready to crush the surviving church, garden and old-style tavern. Alasdair Clayre, the poet and composer, analyses it:

> What is the peculiar feature of London architecture that tends to depress, and can drive to melancholy? Not merely the grime; though that is significant, the word being linked with 'grim' and so with anger, hostility, which is just what I sense – hostility directed at me and returned – when I walk through the streets north of London Bridge . . .
>
> Behind the grime, there is the density and confusion of decent blatancy, the drab opportunism of the buildings; of those buildings which stretch from Trafalgar Square east to the Tower. They are buildings like the headlines and newspaper columns that mask the faces on rush-hour trains; each one calls attention to itself, but the self-advertisement is kept within the strict limits of economy; each building has a commercial purpose, but neither this, nor any excess of interest in living, has driven the inventor to dazzle or attract with any especial ingenuity of either proportion or design. We may see nature in this mood when, early on wet mornings, she lays on the slabs of our fishmongers, slabs of her own wet cod. Otherwise nature scarcely reaches these levels of uniformity and dejection.

Only in the more undifferentiated rock strata, such as are quarried in Blaenau Festiniog, is nature in harmony with man in London, who goes busily burying under shovel-loads of newsprint, serge, soot, umbrella silk and competition the inward body of his senses' life.

A walk along Holborn Viaduct, through Cheapside, to Fenchurch Street, or from Ludgate Hill to the Barbican, St Giles and then Liverpool Street, will test the validity of this. He adds further:

The reason the City of London does not become beautiful, I suppose, is because it is not loved much; and those who could make it beautiful pay to live elsewhere. They give London the waste hours of their lives, the hours spent moving between office and train, between boardroom and restaurant. The City has the look, therefore, of a lumber room, where those who do not notice have stacked the suitcases of their unwanted moments; suitcase-shaped buildings, dirt and confusion, like lumber-room dust.

THE MONUMENT

Opposite London Bridge, backed by Eastcheap, stands the Monument, Wren's grey commemoration of the Great Fire, which formerly had an inscription attributing the disaster to a blameless Roman Catholic. Pope wrote of it, and of the inscription:

Where London's column, pointing to the skies,
Like a tall bully, lifts the head and dies.

Boswell climbed it, in 1763.

This is a most amazing building. It is a pillar two hundred feet high. In the inside, a turnpike stair runs up all the way. When I was about halfway up, I grew frightened. I would have come down again, but thought I would despise myself for my timidity. Thus does the spirit of pride get the better of fear. I mounted to the top and got upon the balcony. It was horrid to find myself so monstrous a way up in the air, so far above London and all its spires. I durst not look around me. There is no real danger, as there is a strong rail both on the stair and balcony. But I shuddered, and as every heavy wagon passed down Gracechurch Street, dreaded that the shaking of the earth would make the tremendous pile tumble to the foundation.

5

THE EAST END

They waited: soon the others would be through,
   they'd be admitted to the hall,
Served with bread and vegetables, the soup in the
                cups and all.
Oh, and then they'd grow sleepy and their twisted
              limbs would be untied.
And night and good sleep would bring them to
            rocking horses, to
Soldiers, the rooms of marvellous dolls' houses
                open wide.

Ernest Stadler, 'Children in Front of a London
              Soup Kitchen', 1913

The East End, beyond Ludgate and the Monument, was for centuries sickened by want and grimed by smoke, lively, thronged with immigrants, some gaudy and exotic, many anxious, beset by racial intolerance. It is associated, sometimes misleadingly, with *Cockney*, Old English for 'Cock's Egg', an absurdity which somehow became related to the fabulous Land of Cockaigne, where dislike of toil was marvellously indulged. Chaucer then used it for a spoilt or foolish child. Shakespeare's Fool, addressing Lear, meant a foolish woman – 'Cry to it, nuncle, as the cockney did to the eels, when she put them into the pail alive.'

Applied to Londoners, all this suggests rustic contempt for the debauched and turbulent town.

East Enders certainly contributed a fair share of London's immense vocabulary, with a humour at once stoical, independent, ribald, disrespectful and observant. When, in the eighteenth century, the Duc de Chartres visited London, he was at once dubbed the 'Duke of Burgundy' for his drinking habits. Colloquialisms were bright with the unexpected. As a young medico at St Thomas's Hospital, above Westminster Bridge, Somerset Maugham listed some, in *A Writer's Notebook*:

'A 'andsome young man with a Roman shiped eye an' a cast in 'is nose.'

'You are a 'andsome woman.'
'Yes, abaht the feet.'
'You said that before.'
'Well, I say it be'ind now.'

'I've 'ad fifteen children, 'an only two 'usbands ter do it on.'

Maugham once lodged in Vincent Square, Westminster, but his landlady probably came from further east. She appears briefly in *Cakes and Ale*.

'Such an aristocratic word, you know; why, it sounded as if it would break your jaw coming out.'

'He does look bad: I think he's going home soon.'

'Oh, it'll all come right in the end when we get four balls of worsted for a penny.'

This is somewhat in the style of the Cockney bus-conductor, a Sam Weller replica, reported by the American political commentator, Max Eastman, remarking of an MP, as he alighted: ''e's so mean 'e wouldn't pay a tanner to see St Paul piss on a duck.'

Professor J.F.C. Harrison describes how the East End suffered particularly badly in the Blitz: 'in Stepney two-fifths of the houses were destroyed or damaged by 11 November 1940'. He cites the memories of a young Hackney housewife, Nellie Priest, and her almost nightly descents to the shelter during the air raids:

V'e didn't get cold – there were too many of us down there. By the time you'd all packed in at night and you'd got your slacks and jumpers on over your pyjamas, you couldn't really feel the cold. When the bombing first started we only had wooden kitchen chairs in the shelter. We used to sit up all night, with a door on the floor to put our feet on. When we went to sleep, we used to lean on one another. But at 7 in the morning you'd got to come out, wash yourself and go to work, day after day. In the finish you would just lay down on the dirt at night because you couldn't keep awake . . . But it was ridiculous down there. It was work and shelter, work and shelter – no life, really.

Willy Goldman, Stepney docker, engineer and writer, reported on the effect of the bombs on Londoners, and found that it enabled them to discover things about each other:

I wish to consider my own native East London [where] . . . it is the distinctive cultural and recreational life that has built up its special 'character'; the sights and sounds that help the native feel its intimacy and the stranger its strangeness. It had a 'night life' all its own: the endless monkey parade of sexually precocious adolescents along the broad Whitechapel pavement; the pretentiously glittering pin-table saloons; the late cinema crowds pouring into the fish-and-chips shops for 'a last penn' worth' before bed; the street corner political arguments and oratory; the noisy pubs where babes in arms got their initiation into the delights of alcohol; the dim reeking cafés of the 'international' dock quarter, where violence was apt to break out and die away with the surprise of a thunderstorm; the enveloping rich smell of the Yiddish restaurants with their equally rich sounds of Yiddish chatter; the little corner sweetshops on whose shutters cynically lounging adolescents discussed girls and 'dogs'. Now, in 1941, even where you will not find the sweetshop demolished or 'evacuated', its young clientele are no longer present to make it a centre of social interest: they are in the Army. The streets, which were perhaps the main social centre, are deserted – by day as well as by night. It is rare to encounter a gossiping group of housewives: there is too great a danger of a marauding German 'plane spoiling the party . . .

There is something very sad about these back-streets. (A stranger might well believe he has stumbled into a partly sacked city.) The silence does not suit them as it does the widely terraced and richly foliaged streets. It is the gossiping, the street cries, the children, the dogs, that give a slum the 'life' it has. Without these, it might be a desert.

The 'East End' with its multiple associations, some moving, even sentimental, many gaunt, haggard, terrifying, survives today mostly in legends, faded sociological tracts and the barely remembered writings of Arthur Morrison, Israel Zangwill, W.W. Jacobs, W. Pett Ridge and H.M. Tomlinson. By 1968, before the Docklands development and much else, though long after the Blitz, Blake Ehrlich was writing of distinctions between the various East End 'villages':

> The rumbustious East End boroughs of Stepney, Bethnal Green and Poplar have vanished to bloom anew as Tower Hamlets. In the district, the old neighbourhoods of Limehouse, Isle of Dogs, Whitechapel, Mile End and Shadwell long ago ceased to exist except in the minds of the inhabitants.

In a region devastated by the Blitz, but rotting and over-crowded long before, lives, livelihoods and architecture have now been transformed. Ehrlich continues, on the grimmer aspect of the East End:

> Behind the street frontages were alleys and courtyards crammed with smaller buildings and sheds. Back doors, area ways and passages led from one warren to another. There were 63 brothels, 1,200 full-time prostitutes, 233 common lodging houses capable of sheltering 8,600 persons in this district. There is no record of the number of grogshops and cellar dives. Notorious gangs of thieves were headquartered here. Sailors from all over the world came through. There were the tough butchers and porters

from Spitalfields Market. There were 'good' shops where the merchants lived and kept shop, and there were thousands of Jewish refugees from Polish and Russian pogroms. Cholera was not infrequent. Brutality was banal. Poverty was universal.

As late as 1890, over a thousand brothels existed in Ratcliffe Highway, Shadwell. For his novel *Fanny by Gaslight*, Michael Sadleir researched the habits of West and East London:

A direct outcome of the misery in which a large part of the population lived, the sale of little girls was a regular proceeding in slum districts of every large city. In Hackney and Dalston and about the Mile End Road, were recognised buyers who would give three to five hundred pounds for a likely 'mark' of ten or twelve years of age, and arrange for her transfer to one of the West End houses. There were also men who, through a network of agents, drew up lists of prostitutes, and by threats rather than money, obtained options on any female children who might be born to these luckless women.

Visitors, on whatever errand, could make bizarre discoveries. Osborn Street, opposite Whitechapel Church, extends to Brick Lane, itself touching Bethnal Green Road. In Brick Lane, now a sumptuous and colourful shopping precinct, 'a kind of East End Bond Street' as Clunn has described it, Peter Ackroyd's novel *The Last Testament of Oscar Wilde* gives the ruined Oscar Wilde a phantasmagoric vision, yet one which Mayhew and Dr William Acton, authorities on London prostitution, would have confirmed:

I remember once, some years ago in London, being taken by an angel of the streets to Brick Lane, to one of those houses of shame where opium is bought and sold. I was led to an upstairs room – it was large and unhealthy, a lime pit where the diseased are buried – and I saw there only grinning phantoms, men who neither woke nor slept; they lived somewhere out of the world, and the

looks they cast were terrible. I had been thrown among
blind men who had put out each other's eyes.

Whitechapel Road still links with Mile End Road and then
Bow Road, dividing Stepney, Whitechapel and Limehouse,
nearer the river, from Bethnal Green, Hackney and Bow.
H.M. Tomlinson, in *All Our Yesterdays*, remembered standing,
as a young man in 1900, as night spread over the latter:

> Bow Bridge, over which kings with gay retinues once
> went to hunt the deer at Hainault, was as though change
> had crossed it for the last time. And Stratford-
> atte-Bow, where grisly walls enclosed backwaters of the
> industrial Lea as inky as creeks of Lethe, smelling of
> the dregs of time, had evidently worked through all its
> elegant deer. No more would its serfs and villeins, when
> they were overpressed by hard taskmasters, dive for
> defiant billhooks and fare forth; they had lost that
> impulse. And the last highwayman had passed through
> it; and no more outside its parish church would it shirt
> the martyrs in fire. Its life in the green was done. Never-
> theless, possibly it was only waiting in the pause at mid-
> night, for nobody knew what. It surrendered no secret.
> The shadow of masses of its factories stood dark and
> spectral over the sleepers of another age, who made no
> sign, for they had submitted, perhaps, to the incubus.
> But if ever those sleepers awakened, and girded them-
> selves, and went hunting again . . . there were many
> of them now. Had they better not sleep on, as things
> were?

The pre-1939 East End as a whole was rough, polyglot,
noisy, in parts criminal. Courage, toughness, sometimes
aggression were needed to survive. It never lacked vitality,
even exuberance. Poverty undermined people but did not
extinguish their spirit, nor the colour and variety of ethnic
groups. In 1902, S. Gelburg described it:

> Its denizens are a complicated piece of human patchwork
> with the ringleted Pole at one point, the Dutch Jew at

another, the English Hebrew in his own corner, and the Gentile Coster running like a strange thin thread through the whole design . . .

Its beshawled women, with their pinched faces, its long coated men with two thousand years of persecution stamped in their manner, its chaffering and its huckstering, its hunger, its humour, the very Yiddish jargon itself which is scrawled on its walls and shop windows, are part of the grand passion of the chosen people.

This now seems as dated as the barrel-organ, the messenger boy and the Blue Hungarian band, though many can still remember it.

Arthur Morrison, in his novels, set the 'Jago' district in an angle between Shoreditch High Street and Bethnal Green Road. His *A Child of the Jago* (1897) describes varied features of its personality, often genial and co-operative, sometimes less so:

That night fighting was sporadic and desultory in the Jago. Bob the Bender was reported to have a smashed nose, and Sam Cash had his head bandaged at the hospital. At the Bag of Nails in Edge Lane, Snob Spicer was knocked out of knowledge with a quart pot, and Cocko Harnwell's Missis had a piece bitten off of one ear. As the night wore on, taunts and defiances were bandied from window to door, and from door to window, between those who intended to begin fighting tomorrow; and shouts from divers corners gave notice of isolated scuffles. Once a succession of piercing screams seemed to betoken that Sally Green had begun. There was a note in the screams of Sally Green's opposites which the Jago had learned to recognise. Sally Green, though of the weaker faction, was the female champion of the Old Jago: an eminence won and kept by fighting tactics peculiar to herself. For it was her way, reserving teeth and nails, to wrestle closely with her antagonist, throw her by a dexterous twist on her face, and fall on her, instantly seizing the victim's nape in her teeth, gnawing and worrying. The sufferer's screams were audible afar, and

beyond their invariable eccentricity of quality – a quality
vaguely suggestive of dire surprise – they had mechanical
persistence, a pump-like regularity, that distinguished
them, in the accustomed ear, from other screams.

Board school children, particularly if assisted by a 'fence',
a Hoxton publican, did not meekly resign themselves to abject
poverty:

Dicky practised that petty larceny which is possible in
every street in London; and at odd times he would play
the scout among the practitioners of the 'fat's a-running'
industry. If he crossed Meakin Street by way of Luck
Row and kept his way among the courts ahead, he
presently reached the main Bethnal Green Road, at the
end whereof stood the great goods depot of a railway
company. Here carts and vans went to and fro all day,
laden with goods from the depot, and certain gangs
among the Jagos preyed on these continually. A quick-
witted scout stood on the look-out for such vehicles as
went with unguarded tailboards. At the approach of one
such he sent the shout 'Fat's a-running!' up the Luck
Row, and, quick at the signal, a gang scuttled down, by
the court or passage which his waved hand might hint at,
seized whatever might be snatched from the cart, and
melted away into the courts, sometimes leaving a few
hands behind to hinder and misdirect the pursuit. Taking
one capture with another, the thing paid very well . . .
His father took no heed of what he did, and even his
mother has so far accepted destiny as to ask if he had a
copper or two, when there was a scarcity.

V.S. Pritchett's *Collected Essays* includes his assessment of
Arthur Morrison and the East London he had known:

East of Aldgate, another city begins, London flattens
and sinks into its clay. Over those lower dwellings the
London sky, always like a dirty window, is larger; the
eyes and hands of people are quicker, the skins yellower,
the voices are as sharp as scissors. Every part of London

has its smell, and this region smells of rabid little shops, bloated factories, sub-let workrooms and warehouse floors; there is also the smell of slums, a smell of poverty, racy but oftener sour; and mingling with those working odours, there arises an exhalation of the dirty river which, somewhere behind these streets and warehouses and dock walls, is oozing towards the flats of the Thames estuary like a worm. The senses and the imagination of the stranger are so pricked by this neighbourhood that he quickly gets a fevered impression of it; it will seem dingier or more exotic than it really is. And when we turn to literature for guidance, we are even less sure of what we see. For the literature of the East End is very largely a stranger's literature. It lies under the melodramatic murk and the smear of sentimental pathos, which, in the nineteenth century, were generated by the guilty conscience of the middle classes. They were terrified by the poor who seethed in an abyss just beyond their back door.

Post-war developments have erased much of what Sir Victor calls 'the awful Gothic spectacle of hunger, squalor and crime', or transferred it to a different plane, but the literature of Morrison, Zangwill, Tomlinson, Gissing, Pett Ridge and Edwin Pugh remain.

Years after Morrison, and the Bethnal Green novelist and dramatist Israel Zangwill, of Russian-Jewish lineage and friend of Hardy and Shaw, Emanuel Litvinoff revived their lost world in *Journey Through a Small Planet* (1972).

Until I was sixteen I lived in the East London borough of Bethnal Green, in a small street that is now just a name on the map. Almost every house in it has gone, and it exists, if at all, only in the pages of this book. It was part of a district populated by the persecuted Jews of the Russian Empire and transformed into a crowded East European ghetto full of synagogues, back room factories and little grocery stores reeking of pickled herring, garlic sausage and onion bread. The vitality compressed into that one square mile generated explosive tensions. We were all dreamers, each convinced that it was his destiny

to grow rich, or famous, or change the world into a
marvellous place of freedom and justice. No wonder so
many of us were haunted by bitterness, failure, despair.

In the same book Litvinoff, now the author of twenty-one
books and plays, records his return for a glimpse of his native
Bethnal Green:

The place seemed faded, nondescript, much like any other
poor district of London at first sight. But as we proceeded
on foot through the once familiar streets the change was
startling. Clumps of Muslim men stood aimlessly on corners and there was a curious absence of women. Shrill,
eerie music wailed in the heat of the afternoon. The odour
of spices mingled with the stench of drains. Skinny little
girls with enormous, solemn black eyes sat on doorways
nursing babies. Outside a cinema crudely painted posters
of veiled ladies and jewelled rajahs advertised a film from
the sub-continent of India. Stubborn survivals of the
past existed in the form of one or two small Jewish
bakeries, or shops selling cigarettes, lemonade and long-
forgotten brands of boiled sweets; but instead of the
old Yiddish newspapers on the counters there were others
printed in Urdu. In Old Montague Street, the very heart
of the original Jewish quarter, nothing was left of the
synagogue but a broken wooden door carved with the
Lion of Judah.
    The tenement I grew up in had somehow survived
shrunken by time but otherwise unchanged – the same
broken tiles in the passage, the same rickety stairs, the
pervasive smell of cats. I took my friend up to the first-
floor landing window to show him the small yard with
its overflowing dustbin. That, too, had not changed.
Quite suddenly, a vivid memory returned. I was twelve
years old: the news had come that once again I had failed
the scholarship. Outside it was raining. I sat on the
window-ledge and carved my initials on the ledge. When
I looked they were still there, jagged and irregular,
'E.L.'

Henry Mayhew's *London Labour and the London Poor* (1851) startled many genteel readers and indeed can still do so, notably in his pictures of East London, the world not only of small houses and tired housewives, but also of Rope Dancers, Bearded Women, Fire-Eaters and Springheeled Acrobats, and its avenues of street markets, little fairs and barrows:

> One man shows off his yellow haddock with a candle stuck in a bundle of firewood; his neighbour makes a candlestick of a huge turnip, and the tallow gutters over its sides; whilst the boy shouting 'Eight a penny, stunning pears' has rolled his dip in a thick coat of brown paper, that flares away with the candle. Some stalls are crimson with the fire shining through the holes beneath the Baked Chestnut stove; others have handsome octahedral lamps, while a few have a candle shining through a sieve; these, with the sparkling ground-glass of globes of the tea dealers' shops, and the butchers' gaslights streaming and fluttering in the wind, like flags of flame, pour forth such a flood of light, that at a distance the atmosphere immediately above the spot is as lurid as if the street were on fire.

Likewise – further out from Bethnal Green and neighbour to Stoke Newington, Tottenham and Islington – is Hackney, with ancient associations with the medieval Templars, and a famous latter-day music-hall, the Empire and another in nearby Hoxton. The area possessed a culture of music, gardens, drama, religion, sport and reading which reached back long before the Victorian immigrants. A.S. Jasper in *A Hoxton Childhood* gives the flavour of it, when his sister Jo, around 1905, would take him for a night out:

> Sometimes on a Monday night she would come home from work and if she had a few coppers left over from the week-end she would say to Mum, 'Get yourself and the kids ready, we're going up to the Brit.' This was the old Britannia Theatre in Hoxton. Jo loved the dramas that were performed there. If Mum could afford it we had a bag of peanuts or a ha'penny bag of sweets. We went

in the 'gallery' for two pence – half price for us kids.
Among the dramas I remember was 'The Face at the
Window' – real horrible. Others were 'Sweeny Todd',
'Maria Marten', 'Why Girls Leave Home'. Many times
I have lain awake after going to the Brit, terrified to
open my eyes for fear of seeing the murdered lying next
to me. Sometimes we went to Collins Music Hall or
the Islington Empire. That was different. They always
had variety shows. We saw Harry Champion, Vesta
Tilley, the two Bobs, Hetty King, comedians of all
sorts and stars of the day.

People, however poor, were seldom passive spectators.
J.F.C. Harrison quotes Minnie Ferrie, a Hackney laundress,
who married in 1927:

We made our own life. A lot of it revolved round the
pub. You'd go in 'The Ren' [Rendlesham Arms] and
have a drink. Then you'd all get together and have a
sing-song 'Who's Sorry Now', 'Jealous of You', 'Nellie
Dean', 'Old County Down' and so on. Somebody would
say, 'Let's take a couple of bottles' and you'd all go home.
It was a happy place all the time. I used to be the life
and soul of the party, singing and all that. My brothers
and I used to sing in the pub. We enjoyed life.

Movement is constant, advance is never absolute. Somerset
Maugham had known Bermondsey, Hoxton, Hackney, before
the First World War, and revisited his old haunts after the
Second. A charwoman told him: 'They've cleaned up the
slums and the dirt, and all the happiness and joy have gone
with it.'
    Whitechapel, east of Aldgate and part of the borough of
Stepney, though with its own distinctiveness, is delineated
by Jean Liddiard:

Whitechapel Road, which runs into Mile End Road, was
the old Roman highway into the City. The market,
which has been there for centuries, is still there, spilling
noisily across the broad pavements. At the beginning of

the nineteenth century the great docks were built to deal
with the increasing imperial trade and a second road from
the East India docks, the aptly named Commercial Road,
scythed ruthlessly through the maze of crowded courts
and little streets to intersect, scissor-like, Whitechapel
Road.

Here, as throughout the post-war East End and Docklands,
amid high-rise developments and housing estates lurk lost
communities, each with its legend – off Whitechapel Road
Mr John Harrydaunce once sermonized on the Bible, from
a window, with the impressive authority of total illiteracy.
Names point towards the North Sea – Stepney, Limehouse,
Poplar, Blackwall, Canning Town, West Ham, Barking . . .
William Pett Ridge's street-gangster girls so vigorous in
his novel *Mord Em'ly* (1898) rampaged through Whitechapel
with an enterprise that Jonathan Wild would have noted and
Fagin resented. Here too were music-hall and gaming-house,
temperance hall and grog-shop, church and synagogue, night
school and boxing booth.
The journalist J. Hall Richardson knew the whole district
for fifty years, before retiring in 1926:

I recall a visit to Bird Fair, in Schaler Street, nearer to
Bethnal Green than to Whitechapel. It still [1927] retains
its popularity on Sunday morning as a mart for flying
pigeons, canaries, chaffinches, rabbits, poultry, geese,
goats and dogs, and this street itself, with all the streets
in the neighbourhood are thronged with bird fanciers,
and fanciers of every kind. At the corner of one of the
streets a missionary who accompanied us suddenly asked
me 'to say a word', and before I knew what I was in
for I was in the middle of a ring haranguing the crowd
much as the Salvation Army officer does today, and I
had a patient hearing.

Richardson knew the saintly George Holland, who headed
a Victorian Mission in George Yard, Whitechapel. Asked to
supply some local material,

FLEET STREET

Each narrow side turning of the street was filled with ranks of newspaper carts, waiting for the hour . . . From basements and walls came the rumble of machinery, already beginning, with the first revolutions of its heavy load of rumours and alarums, to communicate a tremor to the earth.

H. M. Tomlinson, *All Our Yesterdays*

LONDON FOG

Look out of this window, Watson. See how the figures loom up, are dimly seen, and then blend once more into the cloud-bank. The thief or the murderer could roam London on such a day as the tiger does the jungle, unseen until he pounces, and then evident only to his victim.

Sir Arthur Conan Doyle, 'The Bruce Partington Plans'

Sometimes on a Monday night she would come home from work and if she had
a few coppers left over from the week-end she would say to Mum, 'Get yourself
and the kids ready, we're going up the Brit.' This was the old Britannia Theatre
in Hoxton . . . We went into the 'gallery' for two pence – half price for us kids.

A. S. Jasper, *A Hoxton Childhood*

THE FROZEN THAMES

[I] viewed with a pleasing horror the rude and terrible appearance of the river, partly froze up, partly covered with enormous shoals of floating ice which often crashed against each other.

James Boswell, *London Journal*

THE BANK UNDER BOMBS

And bursting days of concentrated light
Dropped from the skies to paint a final scene –
Illuminated agony of frowning stone.

Stephen Spender, 'Epilogue to a Human Drama'

WHITEHALL

Looking at Whitehall, Sir? – fine place – little window – somebody else's head
off there, eh, Sir? – he didn't keep a sharp look-out enough either – eh, Sir, eh?

Charles Dickens, *The Pickwick Papers*

BYRON AND SCOTT AT NO. 50 ALBEMARLE STREET

And they want to know what we talked about?
Of letters and tragedies and music,
Both of ancient times and our own,
And men of unusual genius,
Both of ancient times and our own,
In short, the usual subjects of conversation between
      intelligent men.

Ezra Pound, *Cantos*

ST JAMES'S PARK

So I to the Park, and there walk an hour or two; and in the King's garden, and
saw the Queen and ladies walk, and there I did steal some apples off the trees;
and there did see my Lady Richmond, who is of a noble person as ever I did see,
but her face worse than it was considerably by the small-pox.

Samuel Pepys, *Diary*

COVENT GARDEN

Men and women in full evening dress were walking along the pavement. They looked uncomfortable and self-conscious as they dodged between costers' barrows, with their high piled hair and their evening cloaks, with their button holes and their white waistcoats, in the glare of the afternoon sun.

Virginia Woolf, *The Years*

BLOOMSBURY

All this rubbish about Bloomsbury . . . I don't feel Bloomsbury; do you feel
Marylebone (or Chelsea, Kensington or Hampstead)?

Rose Macaulay quoting Virginia Woolf

Athwart the Victorian dykes the waters were falling on property, manners and morals, on melody and the old forms of art – waters bringing to his mouth a salt taste as of blood lapping to the foot of the Highgate Hill where Victorianism laid buried.

John Galsworthy, *The Forsyte Saga*

SUBURBIA

In front of our house in Golders Green
the lawn like a cliché mutters 'Rose bushes'.
The whole suburb is very respectable.

Dannie Abse, 'Odd'

To my horror and astonishment [Holland] took me
with him, a stone's throw away, into a cellar-like room,
opening from a dingy court. There was no fire, scarcely
any light, and no ventilation; the atmosphere was foetid.
And in that room – how it was possible for human beings
to exist without the knowledge of the authorities in
that deplorable state I cannot imagine – neither father,
nor mother, nor children had a stitch of clothing.

Like Morrison and Zangwill, Pett Ridge and Isaac
Rosenberg, Richardson would have seen the second-hand
clothes trestles, cheap jewel trays and trotter stalls of Petticoat
Lane, seen, too, the Pudding Man and the Eyeglass Seller and
heard the slang, 'Bristol' (breast), 'the Artful' (lodger), 'Tea'
(thief). They would all have known the Loose-Tea man and his
ware:

Tea, until comparatively recent times, was sold by the
ounce by street traders and shops. Usually heavily adul-
terated with copper and other dangerous additives, the
tea was the dregs collected from the big houses and
hotels in the better quarters. (Roy Curtis)

Richardson's journalism included the so-called Whitechapel
Murders of 1888. Jack the Ripper, together with East End
poverty, Mosley riots and fictional opium dens, has remained
better known than the achievements of the London Hospital,
Toynbee Hall, the People's Palace, the fifteenth-century St
Dunstan's Church, the Great Synagogue, or the Whitechapel
Art Gallery. In a few lines, Richardson touches one East End
nerve, sensitive before 1939, and viciously preyed upon by
outsiders. Of the Ripper case:

It would scarcely be believed that the Metropolitan Police
held the clue to the identification of the murderer in their
hands and deliberately threw it away under the personal
direction of the then Commissioner of Police, Sir Charles
Warren, who acted in the belief that an anti-semitic riot
would take place if a certain damning piece of writing

were permitted to remain on the walls. Following the
murder in Mitre Square . . . the murderer threw away
a portion of the apron of the murdered woman, upon
which he had wiped his bloodstained hands, in the doorway of some model dwellings in Goulstone Street, not
far from Petticoat Lane, and then some freak of fancy
had led him to write upon the wall this sentence: 'The
Jewes are not the men to be blamed for nothing.'

These words, Richardson claimed, were erased.

In a Stepney and Whitechapel of gin palace and thieves'
kitchen, pawnbroker, doss-house and back-alley kitchen-table
abortionist, from what Tennyson called 'the crowded couch
of incest in the warrens of the poor', and Ruskin castigated
as an industrial slavery a thousand times more bitter and
degrading than that of the scourged African or the helot Greek,
Londoners survived. Moreover, while poverty, like censorship,
can muffle literature, it does not extinguish it. East End Jews
in particular maintained a zest for story telling, racial sagas
and rabbinical wisdom, so strong in Zangwill and Cyril Kersh.
Cyril Connolly saw Whitechapel in 1928 and in his essay,
'One of My Londons', noticed a society very different from
that in Kensington and Belgravia:

> Much of the best part of East End, especially side streets
> off Commercial Road (markets) and Leman Street,
> Wentworth, Old Montague Streets, on the Stepney side.
> Here is Latin gaiety, crowds and music and colour, rows
> of cars standing outside obscure cafés, and an excellent
> band and a tiny dance-hall. The Jewesses are amazingly
> attractive, a mass bloom seems to emanate from them
> in large quantities and they appear to walk up and down
> the street all night. Men dingy and undersized. Even
> when English themselves, these girls all deeply dislike the
> English, and the foreigners' good manners and capacity
> for passion are everywhere well-spoken of.

In the late nineteenth century a Jewish Lithuanian family
of seven inhabited one room in Cable Street near Sidney Street,
between Whitechapel Road and Commercial Road, where,

in 1910, the siege of the anarchist 'Peter the Painter' entered
London folklore and motivated Emanuel Litvinoff's novel,
A Death out of Season (1973). From this room came a poet
and painter, Isaac Rosenberg, killed in the First World
War, hailed by many as a genius. Ian Parsons, introducing
Rosenberg's *Collected Works*, mentions that the youth reached
the Slade School of Art with David Bomberg and Mark
Gertler. 'He formed part of that extraordinary cultural explo-
sion which took place between 1900 and 1914 in London's
East End, and gave currency to the appellation "The White-
chapel Boys".'
Two verses from Rosenberg's 'A Ballad of Whitechapel'
give tentative glimpses of future masterpieces:

> I stood where glowed
> The merry glare of golden whirring lights
> Above the monstrous mass that seethed and flowed
> Through one of London's nights.
>
> I watched the gleam
> Of jagged warm lights on shrunk faces pale:
> I heard mad laughter as one hears in dreams,
> Or Hell's harsh lurid tale.

Another part of the district, Limehouse, often called
'Chinatown', was, in popular fiction at least, shown as the
haunt of Lascar opium-seekers, gullible sailors, smugglers and,
more recently, Triad protection gangs. Arnold Bennett went
slumming there on a Tuesday in 1925:

> I went to Chinatown last night with Beaverbrook and
> Ashfield. Pennyfields is the name of the chief street, Lime-
> house. We went to Limehouse Police Station first. It
> took us exactly fifteen minutes (from the West End)
> to drive from Ciro's. Great change in a short time. We
> saw some 'curios' (as the Chief Inspector called them)
> first. Explanation of 'Fantan' and 'Pluck Pigeons'. The
> first seems a purely childish game in which the bank
> pays 2 to 1 winnings on a 5 to 1 chance. Then out with
> the Inspector to Pennyfields. No gambling after 8 o'clock,

he said, usually not later than 7. We entered two Chinese
restaurants (11 pm) where lots of people were drinking
tea. Humble people. All very clean and tidy indeed,
and the people looked decent. A few nice-looking
prostitutes – chiefly Jewesses. Nearly all houses closed.
Some windows, said the Chief Inspector, were always
shuttered. 'They don't like the light.' Glimpses of cur-
tained bedrooms higher up. We went into a Chinese
Music Club, where four men were playing Mah Jong
and one strumming a sort of Chinese guitar, with very
long string-pegs. Their singing nights were Wednesday
and Saturday. A suggestion that they should sing was
not well received. They were very polite but didn't want
us. We were to have seen the Chinese Chapel, where
the religion of Confucius is practised; but it was locked
up. Then we went to a club (closed) and found one or
two old topers (friends of the proprietor's) drinking stout
after hours. We were taken upstairs and there saw a
wonderful collection of Chinese carving of all sorts –
chiefly picked up from sailors. Lastly, return to police
station. No prisoners. Cells marvellously clean and sanitary. Steam heating. Temp. must be 63 at least. Plank
bed, white as a yacht's forecastle, but a pretty comfortable
pillow; one rug. On the whole a rather flat night. Still
we saw the facts. We saw no vice whatsoever. Inspector
gave the Chinese an exceedingly good character.

Three years later, Cyril Connolly, in Limehouse, found,
'Gambling dens suppressed. Met a Chinaman in Pennyfields
who offered to show me round, he was reading a book on
psychology.'
Nevertheless, in our own time, in his novel about Chinese
in contemporary London, *Sour Sweet*, Timothy Mo offers
a forbidding insight into a Triad gang which, behind an outwardly respectable screen of restaurants and small businesses,
organizes a methodical empire of drug imports, protection
levies, blackmail and murder:

White Paper Fan's gaze now ran down each man in
the lines. His cold inspection took three minutes. Only

two men met his gaze: a big, muscular fellow in the
front row, who was a boxing instructor, and a young
fellow at the back, gold watch and pens, who cockily
stared back at him. White Paper Fan was familiar with
this type: petty aspirant gangster, all show and big talk.
Had it been up to him he would never have accepted
that sort for membership. He knew this one had been
a street-runner and vendor and had gained favour by
recruiting several others for this risky and menial
job. He had also specialised in blackmail of illegal
immigrants. Night-brother had better keep him super-
vised. White Paper Fan made a note before dismissing
the men.

'Understand: you will remain silent about this meeting,
even though it is not an official ceremony. Leave now
in small groups and avoid attention.'

He pulled out his abacus and began work on accounts.

Despite new Dockland emporiums, newspaper fortresses
and commercial developments, older lives persist, with their
dreams and grievances, fantasies, hopes and myths, as they
have always done. In *Downriver*, Iain Sinclair concocts from
past and present East London a heightened, sometimes sur-
realist vision, a troll country of lazar-houses, six-in-a-bed drug
dens, every Stygian set of alleys an arsonist's delight, with
derelicts, dotty evangelists, ghouls and monsters, nastily contemporary yet timeless, merging in urban metaphor the
mythical, the fictional and the historical – Dickens's Magwitch,
Jack the Ripper, Oscar Wilde – making explicit Kipling's
belief that Fiction is Truth's elder sister.

The Council had taken power by offering an era to every
valium-gobbling fanatic. They put themselves forward
as the shock-absorbers of disenfranchised anguish; then
dutifully dissipated the pain by identifying the most
popular scapegoats. And passing out the brickbats. Rene-
gade socialists muttered in pubs that these scoundrels
were the barely acceptable face of skinhead fascism in
'liberal' drag. The party championed 'local' issues; when,
in truth, there was no locality left. Employment was a

sentimental memory: the whole corridor from Tower Bridge to the Isle of Dogs was in limbo. It was waiting to be called up. A cold wind ruffled the drowning pools, the labyrinthine walkways, the dumping pits. A few sponsored artists kept a window on the riverfront polished for the developers.

6

LONDON BRIDGE TO
SYDENHAM

Whoever goes into Marshalsea Place, turning out
of Angel Court, leading to Bermondsey, will find
his feet on the very paving stones of the extinct
Marshalsea jail; will see its narrow yard to the left
and to the right, very little altered if at all, except
that the walls were lowered when the place got
free; will look upon rooms in which the debtors
lived; and will stand among the crowded ghosts of
many miserable years.

Charles Dickens, Preface to *Little Dorrit*

SOUTHWARK

The Australian poet Peter Porter settled in London in 1951.
In an essay of 1974, he reflected:

I get lost south of the river immediately, especially as
I don't drive a car. This is the land of the juggernaut –
one look at the Tube Map tells you that. The south may
be more authentic than the north; it certainly is the
poor relation of the transport system. A peculiarity of
the area I live in (Paddington) is the immediate juxtaposition of slums with opulent houses, especially in the
Westbourne Park and Ladbroke Grove precincts. The
same is true of many parts of North London – Fulham,
Hammersmith, Turnham Green, Islington, Canonbury,
West Hampstead, Muswell Hill etc. It seems quite otherwise south of the river, which appears to me a uniformly

dim wilderness relieved only by disturbingly lush enclaves such as Dulwich, Denmark Hill, Greenwich, Blackheath, and parts of Clapham.

The oldest crossing of the river into the south was London Bridge which of all the sights of Elizabethan London, Baron Waldstein admired perhaps above all else. (It was demolished and replaced, in 1831, after centuries of use.)

This is an amazingly skilful construction of solid stone-work with nineteen arches; it has extremely fine buildings all along it like a street, making it easily one of the finest bridges in the whole of Europe, both for size and beauty.

A modern novel, *Firedrake's Eye* by Patricia Finney, visualized it as it was in 1583:

In all of England is no stranger nor finer sight than London Bridge, the glory of the City, with its serried fleet of piers against the onrush of the Thames. The best draper's shops in the land are on it, arching across it, enclosing those who care not that they get their cloth good cheap, but only that it be fine. There may be bought silks of Cathay and cottons of India, velvets and damasks of buttercup and viridion and violet and crimson and strange fancy colours like Dead Spaniard that was begun as a putty shade. There may you also find lawn that will pass on its entirety through a wedding ring and tissue of cloth of gold, cloth of silver and delicate leathers made to a buttery softness by the tanner's art. And all the colours and the textures are heaped up and arrayed by the great drapers in mountains of white samite and deep valleys of cramoisie and forest green so it be pleasing to the eyes of the folk that pass up and down and hither and yon beneath the Drawbridge Gate and the Stone Gate with its traitors' heads upon it and their attending ravens. The people choke Gracechurch and New Fish Street and Long Southwark as they bend their paths to the bridge, and slow at the old Drawbridge to gaze east upon the

lower side at the sturdy Hansa cogs and the graceful
ships of Venice and the brave and beautiful English ships.

From here, Boswell in 1763 'viewed with a pleasing horror
the rude and terrible appearance of the river, partly froze up,
partly covered with enormous shoals of floating ice which
often crashed against each other.'

The Bridge leads directly into Southwark. Here, travellers
arrived from the south, expecting, and receiving, hospitality
from inns and lodging houses, in the shadow of Southwark
Cathedral, which still sports memorials to Gower, Fletcher,
Massinger, Lancelot Andrews and Shakespeare, and where
John Harvard was christened.

From the Tabard Inn, Chaucer's pilgrims started:

> Bifil that in a seson on a day,
> In Southwark at the Tabard as I lay,
> Redy to wenden on my pilgrimage
> To Caunterbury with ful devout corage . . .

The area was always crowded and noisy, not only with
pilgrims and taverners, but also seamen, felons, madmen,
theatre-goers, pleasure-lovers, loafers, respectable citizens,
card-sharpers, beggars and racketeers, all exchanging a lively
local patois, quite distinct from that across the river. Thomas
Burke lists some of it:

> Five hundred years ago a drunken man was 'boozy', a
> companion was a 'cove', a group of friends was 'the
> bunch', clothes were 'duds' or 'stops', stealing from shops
> was 'lifting', a swindler was a 'shark', a madman was
> 'cranky', a beggar was a 'ragamuffin', the leader of a gang
> was an 'upright cove' and when a man was sent in the
> hangman's cart to Tyburn he was said to have 'gone
> Westward'.

In Southwark, Dickens, ever rummaging in London, found
for *Oliver Twist* the filthiest, the strangest, the most extraordinary of the many localities that are hidden in London,
wholly unknown, even by name, to the great mass of its
inhabitants.

Beyond Dockhead in the Borough of Southwark, stands
Jacob's Island, surrounded by a muddy ditch, six or eight
feet deep and fifteen or twenty wide when the tide is in,
once called Mill Pond, but known (now) as Folly Ditch.
It is a creek or inlet from the Thames, and can always
be filled at high water by opening the sluices at the lead
mills from which it took its old name. At such times, a
stranger, looking from one of the wooden bridges thrown
across it at Mill Lane, will see the inhabitants on either
side lowering from their back doors and windows,
buckets, pails, domestic utensils of all kinds, in which to
haul the water up; and when his eye is turned from these
operations to the houses themselves, his utmost astonishment will be excited by the scene before him. Crazy
wooden galleries common to the backs of half-a-dozen
houses, with holes from which to look upon the slime
beneath; windows, broken and patched, with poles thrust
out, on which to dry the linen that is never there; rooms
so small, so filthy, so confined, that the air would seem
too tainted even for the dirt and squalor which they
shelter; wooden chambers thrusting themselves out above
the mud, and threatening to fall into it – as some have
done; dirt-besmeared walls and decaying foundations;
every repulsive lineament of poverty, every loathsome
indication of filth, rot, and garbage; all these ornament
the banks of Jacob's Island.

And on the Southwark side of Blackfriars Bridge, on the
landing steps beneath the bridge, dogged by her murderer,
fatally thinking herself unseen, Nancy meets Rose Maylie
and Mr Brownlow:

A mist hung over the river, deepening the red glare of
the fires that burnt upon the small craft moored off distant
wharfs, and rendering darker and more indistinct the
murky buildings on the banks. The old smoke-stained
storehouses on either side, rose heavy and dull from the
dense mass of roofs and gables, and frowned sternly upon
water too black to reflect even their lumbering shapes.
The tower of old Saint Sepulchre's Church and the spire

of Saint Magnus, so long the giant-warders of the ancient
bridge, were visible in the gloom; but the forest of
shipping below the bridge, and the thickly-scattered
spires of churches above, were nearly all hidden from
the sight.

The girl had taken a few restless turns to and fro –
closely watched meanwhile by her hidden observer –
when the heavy bell of St Paul's tolled for the death of
another day. Midnight had come upon the crowded city.
The palace, the night-cellar, the jail, the madhouse; the
chambers of birth and death, of health and sickness, the
rigid face of the corpse and the calm sleep of the child:
midnight was upon them all.

Poets and painters both, Dante Gabriel Rossetti and the
ill-fated Elizabeth Siddal lived in a house near Blackfriars
Bridge, Rossetti writing to William Allingham in 1861:

We have got our rooms quite jolly now. Our drawing-
room is a beauty, I assure you, already, and on the first
country trip we make we shall have it newly papered from
a design of mine which I have an opportunity of getting
made by a paper-manufacturer . . . I shall have it printed
on common-brown packing-paper and on blue grocer's
paper, to try which is best.

The (printed) trees are to stand the whole height of
the room . . . the stems and fruit will be Venetian red,
the leaves black – the fruit, however, will have a line of
yellow to indicate roundness and distinguish it from the
stem; the lines of the ground black, and the stars yellow
with a white ring around them. The red and black will
be made of the same key as the brown or blue of the
ground, so that the effect of the whole will be rather
sombre, but I think rich, also. When we get the paper up,
we shall have the doors and wainscoting painted summer-
house green.

THE BOROUGH

Further south from Southwark, away from the river stretches the Borough, and here too Dickens is incessantly recalled, particularly in shabby, out-of-the-way alleys and courtyards, within sound of the traffic but often hushed and still, hinting at the secretive and the old. Despite its squalor, the area held fascinations for him. In *The Pickwick Papers*, he wrote that in the Borough survived 'several ancient inns; great rambling queer old places with galleries and passages and staircases wide enough and antiquated enough to furnish material for a hundred ghost stories'.

Here, off Borough High Street, is Lant Street where Bob Sawyer's party was ended by a wrathful landlady. Around lie Copperfield Street, Little Dorrit Court, Dickens Square, Marshalsea Road. Mr Dickens, senior, had been imprisoned in the Marshalsea for debt, to be remembered by his son in *Little Dorrit*.

> It was an oblong pile of barrack buildings, partitioned into squalid houses standing back to back, so that there were no back rooms; environed by a narrow paved yard, hemmed in by high walls duly spiked at the top. Itself a close and confined prison for debtors, it contained within it a much closer and more confined jail for smugglers. Offenders against the revenue laws, and defaulters to excise or customs who had incurred fines which they were unable to pay, were supposed to be incarcerated behind an iron-plated door closing up a second prison, consisting of a strong cell or two, and a blind alley some yard and a half wide, which formed the mysterious termination of the very limited skittle-ground in which the Marshalsea debtors bowled down their troubles.
>
> Supposed to be incarcerated there, because the time had rather overgrown the strong cells and the blind alley. In practice they had come to be considered a little too bad, though in theory they were quite as good as ever; which may be observed to be the case at the present day with other cells that are not at all strong, and with other blind alleys that are stone-blind. Hence the smugglers

habitually consorted with the debtors (who received them with open arms), except at certain constitutional moments when somebody came from some Office, to go through some form of overlooking something, which neither he nor anybody else knew anything about. On these truly British occasions, the smugglers, if any, made a feint of walking into the strong cells and the blind alley, while this somebody pretended to do his something: and made a reality of walking out again as soon as he hadn't done it – neatly epitomising the administration of most of the public affairs in our right little, tight little, island.

Today, a high aged wall above gardens, on the site of the old Marshalsea, is sufficiently blackened to suggest still the strange old prison. Of another sort of criminal of the period Mayhew made discouraging reports:

Child stripping is generally done by females, old debauched drunken hags who watch their opportunity to accost children in the streets, tidily dressed with good boots and clothes. They entice them away to a low or quiet neighbourhood for the purpose, as they say, of buying them sweets, or with some other pretext. When they get into a convenient place, they give them a halfpenny or some sweets, and take off the articles of dress, and tell them to remain till they return, when they go away with the booty.

This is done most frequently in the mews in the West End, and in Clerkenwell, Westminster, the Borough, and other similar localities . . . In most cases, it is done at dusk in the winter evenings.

Within the Borough district lies the Elephant and Castle, the subject of R.C. Hutchinson's novel of that name (1937) which brings into high relief the complexities of class, race and environment underlying the metropolitan scene.

A West End girl, Armorel, encounters the son of Italian immigrants in the Borough. A relationship flickers in uncertainty, perplexity, even mystery, rising into uncomprehending love and then marriage. She, and the Italian, will be the victims of a socially and racially divided London. The stir of Hutchinson's South London crowds, the social gulfs and nuances, relate tellingly to the world of Dickens, Gissing, H.G. Wells and V.S. Pritchett. From West London, well-servanted and well-laundered, the distance is not great, but, crossing it, Armorel accidentally discovers an unsuspected world, at odds with Bayswater and Portman Square, Cavendish Square and Regent Street:

> The English do not care, as a rule, to have their policemen murdered in the street, and the second, unnecessary blow had not been overlooked by the brewery men, who were accustomed to consider fighting with some discrimination.

This brings together Armorel and the young Italian. The girl crosses more than one frontier, the first and most obvious that of the Borough itself:

> This city was not made for summer. It is plaited with machinery that cannot repose. The trains pass at the height of bedroom windows, or a little below your garden fence; with the doors and the sideboard constantly trembling from their violence you cannot feel that the year has reached fulfilment. In high, overhead light the river itself loses nobility. The odour that follows people coming out of the Tube is one that should belong to winter, like the smell of a bakery; it joins the odours of exhaust and benzine, which the heat makes fatiguing, and when there is little wind the close, high cliffs of dirty brick will keep these bilious airs as an inverted tank would. If the sky is hazed, which is natural with the London sky, and there are no hard shadows, you have the sensation not of summer but of November noon cooked with an oilstove.

Exploring further, deeper, she at last reaches her goal, Bidault's Place:

> It is neither a street nor a square. The space was occupied, till about the middle of the last century, by Mr Bidault's

jobbing stables, which lay behind the old Queen of
Hungary and included a small riding school. The inn,
together with Bidault's house, gave place to Kinwick's
tailoring factory, and the new road leading to Southwark
yards, with its margin of workmen's houses, sliced off
one bank of stables and perhaps a fifth of the stable-yard,
leaving the riding-school intact in an open space where
grass and dandelions returned and where, as late as 1904,
a few scraggy goats lived tranquilly behind a row of
hoardings. The hoardings made way for the high, shallow
barrack now called Coronation Building; the marshy
waste remained littered with sections of drainpipe and
old tyres, a chicken or two and the Coronation urchins,
till a go-ahead butler realized he could make the riding-
school into cottages and squeeze a few more on to the
vacant land. . . .

The drab street she was leaving, remote and self-
occupied, its pulse enfeebled by the dead weight of the
sultry day, was still connected with the known world:
a sweeper's barrow with the Borough arms stood there,
at the far end you could just see the red flash of a bus
passing. To enter the passage was to cross a last border.
Sounds changed, as when a tuning-knob is turned; the
air, cooler here, fetid and still, closed in upon her like
an anaesthetist's mask. For one instant she hesitated,
turning to look back at the street, and her eye caught
its title, Mickett Lane.

The marriage is splintered by forces barely within their
control, psychological perhaps as much as social. Life itself
ends; the husband kills her: it is an accident, but the jury cannot
believe it and send him to the South London gallows:

Yes, it is to-day, eight o'clock they said, it must be that
soon. 'Can you tell me the time? Give me time, please?
Tell me the time?' I suppose it don't hurt long, bad
but not very long, only it'd be better if you knew before
what sort of hurt it was. And then nothing after that,
only it might not be nothing, depend if what they say
is right . . .

No, this ain't it, this can't be it, they can't be goin'
to do it now. Not a day like this, they can't do it a day
like this, decent blokes, they can't do it a day like this.
Exercise it is, mornin' exercise. Can't be nothing else.
Not a day like this. Decent blokes. . . .

Terror naked, the endless moment of terror like sky
splitting, like a sword of ice driven upwards from bowels
to throat.

SOUTH BANK

South London possessed not only prisons but also, some
distance removed from the direct authority of Whitehall
and Mansion House, brothels, cock-pits and theatres which
flourished, catering for a huge, though fickle public, periodically interrupted by fire and plague. Between Southwark
Cathedral and Blackfriars, distrusted by the City Fathers,
but often supported by the royal court and the Inns, Tudor
and Jacobean theatres rose, were destroyed by accident, often
revived: the Rose, the Curtain, the Swan, the Globe, the
Hope. Ancient names – Bear Garden Lane, Cardinal's Cap
Alley, Clink Street – survive from Shakespeare's London:
while a black rotting barge, a row of worn steps into murky
water, an iron lamp, a rusting chain, hint at Victoria's.

Tudor audiences on the South bank were galvanized by
new words and visions from lands half-fabulous; shoals of
colour tempered by dry observations recognized by most
Londoners. They would certainly have applauded Robert
Greene's line, 'These lawyers drink me dry as a sieve.'
Marlowe's resonant evocation of Persepolis could be balanced
by Shakespeare's workaday reflection, as true in Eastcheap or
Bankside as in Rome or Verona:

> War is no strife
> To the dark house and the detested wife.

Dr Johnson's estimate remains pertinent: 'He who will
understand Shakespeare must not be content to study him in
the closet, he must look for his meaning sometimes among

the sports of the field, and sometimes among the manufactures
of the shop.'

City Puritans regularly denounced the riverside theatres
as Chapels of Satan, centres of 'theft and whoredom, pride
and prodigality, villainy and blasphemy', though only Plague
would close them for long. Individual dramatists suffered
more. Ben Jonson was imprisoned for his outspoken play,
The Isle of Dogges, and his share in the Jacobean *Eastward hoe*
was deemed insulting to Scots, the monarch's compatriots.

Audiences assembled not only for spirited language and
intricate plots. Nearby the Globe was a rival enterprise, of
which Thomas Dekker wrote, in his pamphlet 'The Infection
of the Suburbs' (*c.* 1608):

> No sooner was I entered, but the very noyse of that place
> put me in mind of Hell; the beare (dragt to the stake)
> shewed like a black ragged soule, that was Damned, and
> newly committed to the infernall Churle, the Dogges
> like so many Divels inflicting torments upon it.

Not only the poor revelled in such sports. Orwell underlined
the penchant of intellectuals for cruelty, and Elizabeth I herself,
prodigious scholar, enjoyed cutting the throats of deer and once
removed a live hart's ear.

Continuing the ripe tradition of Bear Garden and Cock Pit,
our ancestors found the antics of lunatics amusing. Successively
at Bishopsgate and Moorfields and then south of the river
stood St Bethlehem Hospital, 'Bedlam', first lunatic asylum in
England, second in Europe, of which Shakespeare wrote in
King Lear:

> Of Bedlam beggars, who, with roaring voices,
> Strike in their numb'd and mortified bare arms
> Pins, wooden pricks, nailes, sprigs of rosemary . . .

By the mid-eighteenth century, 'Bedlam' had moved to
St George's Fields, Lambeth, where water violets once grew.
In *The Man of Feeling* (1771), Henry Mackenzie disclosed
'the dismal mansions of those who are in the most horrid state
of incurable madness. The clanking of chains, the wildness

of their cries, and the imprecations which some of them uttered, formed a scene impressibly shocking.'

A smiling, decent-looking man offers himself as a guide to Mr Harley and his party. One maniac has been a celebrated mathematician; another, a formerly wealthy habitué of the Royal Exchange. A third appears:

'It is like a spondee, and I will maintain it,' interrupted a voice on his left hand. This assertion was followed by a very rapid recital of some verses from Homer. 'That figure,' said the gentleman, 'whose clothes are so bedaubed with snuff, was a schoolmaster of some reputation: he came here to be resolved of some doubts concerning the genuine pronunciation of the Greek vowels. In his highest fits, he makes frequent mention of one Mr Bentley. But delusive ideas, Sir, are the motives of the greatest part of mankind, and a heated imagination the power by which their actions are incited: the world, in the eye of a philosopher, may be said to be a large madhouse.'

'It is true,' answered Harley, 'the passions of men are temporary madnesses; and sometimes very fatal in their effects, *From Macedonia's madman to the Swede.*'

'It was indeed,' said the stranger, 'a very mad thing in Charles to think of adding so vast a country as Russia to his dominations; that would have been fatal indeed; the balance of the North would have been lost; but the Sultan and I would never have allowed it.'

'Sir!' said Harley, with no small surprise in his countenance.

'Why, yes,' answered the other, 'the Sultan and I: do you know me? I am the Cham of Tartary.'

LAMBETH

From Westminster Bridge and Borough Road, Lambeth spread towards Kennington, with its wide and dangerous Common, and Vauxhall with its cheerful Gardens. In 1600, the tireless Baron Waldstein visited Lambeth Palace, the

London residence of the Archbishop of Canterbury since 1179, and saw in the garden

> its most interesting object – an English girl done in topiary. Indoors were portraits of Edward the Sixth and Prince William of Orange; a very large map of Germany; a complete life of Christ in pictures; the Spanish Inquisition in Belgium; and a picture of Queen Elizabeth when she was young. On a panel is written:
>
> These, according to the Angel, are the reasons why the Britons were driven out of their country:
>
> 'Among the prelates, idleness and evil-living; among the powerful, extortion; among the judges, greed; there was the fierce fury of desperate men; there was detestable licentiousness and shameless fashion of dress.'

One Lambeth resident, William Blake, who lived there from 1793 to 1800, would have agreed with the Angel, who had added that identical sins had tainted the conquering Saxons. Blake considered organized religion an empty fraud, government a contamination of vital human potential, fashion and dress a violation of beautiful nakedness. 'Damn braces,' he said. A mighty apostle of feelings, scourge of the limp and the tepid, he was convinced that London had lost the essential connection with 'Albion', 'Jerusalem', the pure England of freshness, impulse, inspiration, intuition. From successive London homes he saw

> Babes reduced to misery,
> Fed with a cold usurious hand

and castigated the grim, overgrown metropolis as deprived, by false sophistications, spiritual blindness, dry education and mechanization of tools, of feelings. London was a casualty in the duel between giants of mystical light and dark. Lambeth gardens could console him, and inspire sudden shafts of insight and illumination, displayed in his 'Holy Thursday':

> 'Twas on a Holy Thursday, their innocent faces clean,
> The children walking two and two in red and blue and
> > green,

Grey-headed beadles walk'd before, with wands as white
as snow,
Till into the high dome of Paul's they like Thames' waters
flow.

O what a multitude they seem'd, these flowers of London
town!
Seated in companies, they sit with radiance all their own.
The hum of multitudes was there, but multitudes of
lambs,
Thousands of little boys and girls raised their innocent
hands.

Now like a mighty wind they raise to heaven the voice
of song,
Or like harmonious thunderings the seats of heaven
among.
Beneath them sit the age'd men, wise guardians of the
poor;
Then cherish pity, lest you drive an angel from your door.

For Blake, angels too frequently ignored Lambeth or were
driven off by evils slow and inexorable as rot.

I wander through each charter'd street,
    Near where the charter'd Thames does flow
And mark in every face I meet,
    Marks of weakness, marks of woe.

In every cry of every man,
    In every infant's cry of fear,
In every voice, in every ban
    The mind-forged manacles I hear

How the chimney-sweeper's cry
    Every blackening church appals,
And the hapless soldier's sign
    Runs in blood down palace walls

But most, through midnight streets I hear
    How the youthful harlot's curse

Blasts the new-born infant's tear
And blasts with plague the marriage hearse.

In Lambeth, as in most London districts, different classes
worked alongside each other, too often aloof save in menial
services seldom very generously rewarded. Yet humane feelings
could transcend human conflicts. At St Thomas's Hospital as
a medical student W. Somerset Maugham felt more than he
probably disclosed. His recollections may well have been true
of most London districts, but for him they were directly of
Lambeth, and he never lost them.

> The directness of contact with men and women gave a
> thrill of power which he had never known. He found an
> endless excitement in looking at their faces and hearing
> them speak; they came in each with his peculiarity, some
> shuffling uncouthly, some with a little trip, others with
> heavy, slow tread, some shyly. Often you could guess
> their trades by the look of them. You learnt in what
> way to put your questions so that they should be under-
> stood, you discovered on what subjects nearly all lied,
> and by what inquiries you could extort the truth notwith-
> standing. You saw the different way people took the
> same things. . . .
> Joy was there and despair; the love of mothers for
> their children and of men for women; lust had trailed
> itself through the rooms with leaden feet, punishing the
> guilty and the innocent, helpless wives and wretched
> children; drink seized men and women and cost its
> inevitable price; death sighed in these rooms; and the
> beginning of life, filling some poor girl with terror and
> shame, was diagnosed there. There was neither good
> nor bad there. There were just facts. It was life.

George Gissing knew South London as thoroughly as
most. His novel *Thyrza* (1887) recreates an atmosphere which
could still be found until a few years ago, and which, on
Saturday, off the main streets, still lingers. He describes
Lambeth through the eyes of his character Gilbert Grail:

Lambeth Walk is a long, narrow street and at this hour [8 p.m.] was so thronged with people that an occasional vehicle with difficulty made slow passage. On the outer edges of the pavement, in front of the busy shops, were rows of booths, stalls, and barrows, whereon meat, vegetables, fish and household requirements of indescribable variety were exposed for sale. The vendors vied with one another in uproarious advertisement of their goods. In vociferation the butchers doubtless excelled; their 'Lovely, lovely, lovely!' and their reiterated 'Buy, buy, buy!' rang clangerous above the hoarse roaring of costermongers and the din of those who clattered pots and pans. Here and there meat was being sold by Dutch auction, a brisk business. Umbrellas, articles of clothing, quack medicines, were disposed of in the same way, giving occasion for much coarse humour. The market-night is the sole out-of-door amusement regularly at hand for London working people, the only one in truth, for which they show any real capacity. Everywhere was laughter and interchange of good-fellowship. Women sauntered the length of the street and back again for the pleasure of picking out the best and cheapest bundle of rhubarb, or lettuce, the biggest and hardest cabbage, the most appetising rasher; they compared notes, and bantered each other on purchases. The hot air reeked with odours. From stalls where whelks were sold rose the pungency of vinegar; decaying vegetables trodden under foot blended their putridness with the musty smell of second-hand garments; the grocer's shops were aromatic; above all was distinguishable the acrid exhalation from the shops where fried fish and potatoes hissed in boiling grease. There Lambeth's supper was preparing, to be eaten on the spot; or taken away wrapped in newspaper. Stewed eels and baked meat pies were discoverable through the steam of other windows, but the fried fish and potatoes appealed irresistibly to the palate through the nostrils, and stood first in popularity.

Very soon, Gilbert

turned towards Lambeth Walk. The market of Christmas
Eve was flaring and clamorous; the odours of burning
naphtha and fried fish were pungent on the wind. He
walked a short distance among the crowd, then found
the noise oppressive and turned into a by-way. As he did
so, a street organ began to play in front of a public house
close by. Grail drew near; there were children forming
a dance, and he stood to watch them.

Do you know that music of the obscure ways, to which
children dance? Not if you have only heard it ground to
your ears' affliction beneath your windows in the square.
To hear it aright you must stand in the darkness of
such a by-street as this, and for the moment be at one
with those who dwell around, in the blear-eyed houses,
in the dim burrows of poverty, in the unmapped haunts
of the semi-human. Then you will know the significance
of that vulgar clanging of melody; a pathos of which
you did not dream will touch you, and therein the secret
of hidden London will be half revealed. The life of men
who toil without hope, yet with the hunger of an
unshaped desire; of women in whom the sweetness of
their sex is perishing under labour and misery; the laugh,
the song of the girl who strives to enjoy her year or
two of youthful vigour, knowing the darkness of the
years to come; the careless defiance of the youth who
feels his blood and revolts against the lot which would
tame it; all that is purely human in these darkened
multitudes speaks to you as you listen. It is the half-
conscious striving of a nature which knows not what
it would attain, which deforms a true thought by gross
expression, which clutches at the beautiful and soils it
with foul hands.

The children were dirty and ragged, several of them
bare-footed, nearly all bare-headed, but they danced with
noisy merriment. One there was, a little girl, on crutches;
incapable of taking a partner, she stumped round and
round, circling upon the pavement till giddiness came
upon her and she had to fall back and lean against the
wall, laughing aloud at her weakness.

Gissing knew that one London disease, as powerful as cholera, typhoid or the pox, was loneliness, which hit him like paralysis. Confronting this, together with poverty and rebuffs, some self-induced, he lacked the exuberance of his friend H.G. Wells which could transform set-backs to assets. Gillian Tindall, in her biography *The Born Exile*, quotes a passage from a Gissing story, 'A Poor Gentleman', which reveals much of him in the character Mr Tymperley, and his lonely 'brethren', and reiterates a terrible truth about London, which perhaps never changes:

> All this time he was of course living in absolute solitude. Poverty is the great secluder – unless one belongs to the rank which is born to it; a sensitive man who no longer finds himself on equal terms with his natural associates, shrinks into loneliness, and learns with some surprise how very willing people are to forget his existence. London is a wilderness abounding in anchorites – voluntary or constrained. As he wandered about the streets and parks, or killed time in museums and galleries (where nothing had to be paid), Mr Tymperley often recognised brethren in seclusion; he understood the furtive glance which met his own, he read the peaked visage, marked with understanding sympathy, the shabby-genteel apparel.

BATTERSEA AND CLAPHAM

Further south, London has retained space, individuality and colour. In the mid-nineteenth century Thomas Carlyle noticed how, by crossing the river from Chelsea, he could in a few minutes enter new and unexpected territories. In *Letters from Chelsea* he continued:

> I went along Battersea Bridge, and thence by a wondrous path across cow fields, mud ditches, river embankments, over a waste expanse of what attempted to pass for country, wondrous enough in the darkening dusk, especially as I had never been there before, and the very road was uncertain. I had left my watch and my purse. I had a good

stick in my hand. Boat people sate drinking about the Red House; steamers snorting about the river, each with a lantern at its nose. Old women sate in strange cottages, trimming their evening fire. Bewildered-looking coke furnaces (with a very bad smell) glowed at one place, I know not why. Windmills stood silent. Blackguards, improper females and miscellanies sauntered, harmless all. Chelsea lights burnt many-hued, bright over the water in the distance – under the great sky of silver, under the great still twilight.

Arnold Bennett's Journal reveals that he too was in Battersea, on 22 January 1928. He mentions none of the market gardens, famed since the sixteenth century and owing much to Huguenot enterprise, and gained less than Carlyle, though likewise commenting on a frontier, and an unpleasant one:

Battersea is a different world. I saw on a *Sunday Express* poster: 'Hardy's last novel, by Sir Edmund Gosse.' It seemed terribly absurd there. How many people in Battersea Bridge had heard of Hardy, or of Gosse, or could get up any interest whatever in a last novel though it were written by God himself? It is a gloomy drab street, with most repulsive tenements, a big technical institute, an open gramophone shop (with a machine grinding out a tune and a song) and an open 'Fun Fair' sort of place (a shop with the front door taken out) and a few small boys therein amusing themselves with penny-in-the-slot machines.

Bennett would not have rated Clapham much higher, despite its trees and common. For Bennett, and perhaps for most, Clapham was little more than a district to rush through in trains for the West.

In *Mike*, a very early book published before the First World War, P.G. Wodehouse has the youthful patrician Psmith and his friend Mike Jackson accepting an invitation to Clapham from the earnest left-winger, Mr Waller:

'The first thing to do,' said Psmith, 'is to ascertain that such a place as Clapham Common really exists. One has heard of it, of course, but has its existence ever been proved? I think not. Having accomplished that, we must then try and find out how to get to it. I should say at a venture that it would necessitate a sea-voyage. On the other hand, Comrade Waller, who is a native of the spot, seems to find no difficulty in rolling to the office every morning. Therefore – you follow me, Jackson? – it must be in England. In that case, we will take a taximeter cab, and go out into the unknown, hand in hand, trusting to luck.'

'I expect you could get there by tram,' said Mike.

Psmith suppressed a slight shudder.

'I fear, Comrade Jackson,' he said, 'that the old *noblesse oblige* traditions of the Psmiths would not allow me to do that. No. We will stroll gently, after a light lunch, to Trafalgar Square, and hail a taxi.'

Oscar Wilde, however, came to realize that Clapham did indeed exist. His account in *De Profundis* has been queried, but must have substance:

Everything about my tragedy has been hideous, mean, repellant, lacking in style; our very dress makes us grotesque. We are the zanies of sorrow. We are clowns whose hearts are broken. We are especially designed to appeal to the sense of humour. On November 13th, 1895, I was brought down here from London. From two o'clock till half-past two on that day I had to stand on the centre platform of Clapham Junction in convict dress, and handcuffed, for the world to look at. I had been taken out of the hospital ward without a moment's notice being given to me. Of all possible objects I was the most grotesque. When people saw me they laughed. Each train as it came up swelled the audience. Nothing could exceed their amusement. That was, of course, before they knew who I was. As soon as they had been informed they laughed still more.

Tooting and Dulwich

A few miles further south, Tooting remained an independent village almost to within living memory before being absorbed into Wandsworth. In an autobiography *Tooting Corner*, Eric Bligh recounts his childhood in a late Victorian family of dissenters. They lived in a Tooting of old mellow walls and hayfields, fine trees and ancient vines, and country lanes crowded only on Derby Day. Still distant was smoky London, Cobbett's 'Great Wen'. In the Bligh household, and many others, volumes of Swinburne were concealed down the sides of respectable chairs, Tennyson's *Idylls* stood alongside the massive family Bible, and, between heavy meals, school and chapel, and jaunts to the Crystal Palace, verses were written, sometimes discovered years later in old drawers and grandfather clocks. Grandfather Bligh wrote:

> And never can my heart forget the chapel old and square,
> For twice on every Sabbath our mother took us there.
> And never will my ear forget my father's heavy bass,
> With full-toned sonorous depth and strength – it shook
>   the very place.

Faith gave significance to life. Little was really trivial. Most could be fearful but exciting: relatives, servants, rooms, furniture, toys, all possessed mystery, legend, infinite possibility, and each deserved consideration:

> The roller stood by the summer-house but was so old and heavy that it was not often used. Besides, it might have rolled down and destroyed something that looked very well as it was. For even the paths had their ascensions and declensions, and their small accretions of personality. One winter a small portion of one of them heaved itself up as if a spring were going to break forth. We were not the people to interfere with such natural behaviour.

Bligh's father was a doctor of strong religious convictions, by later standards almost manic. Like many outsize coevals he could see to the ends of the universe but not to the end of his nose. His generous intellect helped Eric develop a distinctive personality, his lack of imagination may have prolonged the son's stammer for years. He strode between the consulting room and the Sunday School, inescapable, awesome, pitiable, finally broken by theological obsessions: 'Draught of New Lease arrived. It contains new and oppressive conditions. I have committed the outcome of the negotiations to God that I may give and receive just consideration in the matter.'

Virtually parallel with Tooting is Dulwich. In his biography of 1863, Alexander Gilchrist related how at Peckham Rye, near Dulwich Hill, Blake, when a child, looked up and saw 'a tree filled with angels, bright angelic wings bespangling every bough like stars'. Once home he related this and only by his mother's intercession 'escaped a thrashing from his honest father, for telling a lie. Another time, one summer morn, he saw the haymakers at work and, amid them, angelic figures walking.'

Another temperament, dissimilar in much, though sharing some of Blake's freshness, was P.G. Wodehouse. Like Raymond Chandler and A.E.W. Mason, he attended Dulwich College, grateful memories of which formed the gist of his earliest work, conventional tales of public schoolboys competing on perfect lawns under Dulwich trees, from which his imagination, even during long years on Long Island, never permanently strayed.

A.E.W. Mason, novelist, author of *The Four Feathers*, marine, secret service agent, actor and Liberal MP, had a mother who, as disclosed in Roger Lancelyn Green's biography, was obsessed not with her son, nor with Dulwich, but with her house.

> On entering the front door you must wait upon the doormat until you had been brushed carefully by Holley, Mrs Mason's personal servant; if on a visit, you were kept awake until a late hour by your hostess who would knock on your door again and again with words of warning or command – 'You must not place your suitcase upon the cabinet in case you should scratch it;' 'Your bedroom candle must be on the table to the left of the

bed and not upon the chair to the right where it would
be dangerously near the curtains.'

Mason's autobiographical novel, *The Summons*, further re-
created the Dulwich home:

Between him and his parents there was little sympathy
and understanding. He saw them at meals, and fled from
the table to his own room, where he read voraciously.
'You never heard of such a jumble of books,' he said.
'Matthew Arnold, Helps' *Companions of My Solitude
and Other Essays*, *Paradise Lost*, *Ten Thousand a Year*,
The Revolt of Islam, Tennyson. I knew the whole of
In Memoriam by heart – absolutely every line of it, and
pages of Browning. . . . there were two red-letter days;
one when I first bought the two volumes of Herrick,
the second when I tumbled upon De Quincey. That's
the author to bowl a boy over. 'The Stage Coach', 'The
Autobiography', *The Confessions* – I could never get tired
of them. I remember buying an ounce of laudanum at
a chemist's on London Bridge and taking it home, with
the intention of following in the steps of my hero and
qualifying to drink it out of a decanter. The taste was
too unpleasant. I drank about half an ounce and threw
the rest away. I was saved from that folly.'

It was when walking among the Dulwich trees that
Browning received the first gleam of 'Pippa Passes', but a far
more substantial writer of London manners and outlooks,
perhaps the most original since Dickens, is V.S. Pritchett,
born in 1900. No modern writer, not even Henry Green and
William Sansom, has observed the capital more acutely, with
phrases apt, often startling: 'Whenever I come back from
abroad, I am always struck by the calm of the London face.
It reposes on its worry like a turnip in imperfect soil, and
positively fattens on self-control.'

When a child, he suffered frequent changes of address,
entailed by his father's lively but unorthodox business habits.
One address was at Dulwich, recalled in his autobiography,
A Cab at the Door, the title referring to those enforced changes:

The centre of Dulwich is still a Georgian village of fine houses and stately trees. There was the College and the old College chapel; and near it the small and famous Art Gallery. Everywhere one saw notice-boards reading Alleyn's College of God's Gift. College boys in their blue striped caps were in the streets. Ruskin, always dogging me, had often visited the Gallery; Browning had walked in the woods that overhung the village; and the Crystal Palace, built for the exhibition of 1851 and moved to Sydenham Hill, dominated all with its strange glass dome, like a sad and empty conservatory. From the Parade, at the top, one could see the dome of St Paul's only a few miles away, and a distant slit of the Thames.

Here, aged eleven, at Rosendale Road School near Herne Hill where Ruskin had wandered amongst grass and almond blossom, Sir Victor, largely influenced by a liberal, intelligent and energetic schoolmaster, decided to become a writer.

Throughout all London, from Westminster to Dulwich, Mansion House to Golders Green, the Pritchetts, Masons and Blighs pursued their imaginative lives, followed the dictates of impulse and intuition, exploring precarious kingdoms, experimenting with the future, embellishing the past, clutching the incessant *now*. The imagination could, even in abominable poverty or suffocating wealth, criminal neglect or indifferent flunkeydom, flourish on a few sticks, stones, bits of string, a crack in the ceiling, a dream, a rhyme:

> Sally go round the Sun,
> 　Sally go round the Moon,
> 　　Sally go round the Chimney Pot
> On a Sunday afternoon.

KENNINGTON AND SYDENHAM

Edith Nesbit, an early Fabian with an unreturned passion for Bernard Shaw, was a much-loved children's writer. Nesbit remembered her childhood home in Kennington during the 1860s:

with its big garden and a meadow and a cottage and a laundry, stables and cow-house and pig-styes, elm trees and vines, tiger lilies and flags in the garden, and chrysanthemums that smelt like earth and hyacinths that smelt like heaven. Our nursery was at the top of the house, a big room with a pillar in the middle to support the roof. 'The post' we called it: it was excellent for playing Mulberry Bush, or for being martyrs at. The skipping rope did to bind the martyrs to the stake.

She praised the Victorians' 'sense of romance that furnished the Crystal Palace at Sydenham, notably in their siting of replicas of prehistoric monsters amongst the rocks, plants, trees, of its lake'. Her biographer, Julia Briggs, expands on this:

Like the children of today, the little Nesbits were simultaneously terrified, intrigued and delighted by these mysterious dragons of the past, and not least because the great stone statues seemed so nearly alive. Their strange names and even stranger shapes exerted a powerful fascination – the giant sloth, clasping its tree, was remembered into middle age and put into *The Magic City* (1910); but best of all was the great stone Iguanodon, so large that an inaugural dinner for twenty-one scientists had been held inside its nearly completed shell. These vast sculptures had been built by Benjamin Waterhouse Hawkins to the (thoroughly inaccurate) specifications of Richard Owen, a professor at the Royal College of Surgeons. The dinosaur park, opened by the Queen and the Prince Consort in 1854, caught and gripped the Victorian imagination as a whole . . . In *The Enchanted Garden*, Edith was to recreate the dinosaur park with its hollow Iguanodon, but she endowed it with the magic of imagination: after dark the stone monsters came to life and lumbered about the park.

Removed to Sydenham from Hyde Park in 1854, the Crystal Palace was mocked by Leigh Hunt as being neither crystal nor a palace. For Ruskin it had 'no more sublimity than a cucumber frame between two chimneys, yet, by its stupidity of hollow bulk, dwarfs the hills'. In his Ode for the opening of the International Exhibition, 1862, Tennyson, who believed that industrialism could create both beauty and progress if bolstered by social and moral conscience, applauded the 'universal exhibition' the Palace housed:

> . . . the long laborious miles
> Of Palace; lo! the giant aisles,
> Rich in model and design;
> Harvest-tool and husbandry,
> Loom and wheel and engin'ry,
> Secrets of the sullen mine,
> Steel and gold, and corn and wine,
> Sunny tokens of the line,
> Polar marvels, and a feast
> Of wonder, out of West and East,
> And shapes and hives of Art divine!
> All of beauty, all of use,
> That one fair planet can produce,
> Brought from over every main,
> And mixt, as life's mixt with pain,
> The works of peace with works of war.

Here too, in the same spirit, Disraeli spoke of the choice before the nation: between a comfortable England imitating European models, or an imperial England whose sons would 'rise to paramount positions, and obtain not merely the esteem of their countrymen, but command the respect of the world'.

7

PICCADILLY CIRCUS TO KENSINGTON AND CHELSEA

There stands the noble hostess, nor shall sink
  With the three-thousandth curtsey. There with
                                        waltz,
The only dance which teaches girls to think,
  Makes one in love even with its very faults.
Saloon, room o'erflow beyond their brink,
  And long the latest arrival halts,
'Midst royal dukes and dames condemned to climb
  And gain an inch of staircase at a time.

Lord Byron, *Don Juan*

PICCADILLY

This area is perhaps the one most familiar to the world at large. It suggests a wealthy and elegant past, notable personages, famous clubs and hotels. In a wartime radio talk, Sir Max Beerbohm remembered the Piccadilly of his boyhood:

St James's Park seemed a natural appanage of St James's Street; and the two milkmaids who milked two cows there, and sold the milk, did not seem strangely romantic. The Green Park seemed not out of keeping with the houses of Piccadilly. Nor did the Piccadilly goat strike one as more than a little odd in Piccadilly.
   I don't know much about him, though I often saw him and liked him so much. He lived in a large mews

in a side-street opposite to Gloucester House, the home
of the venerable Duke of Cambridge. At about ten o'clock
in the morning, he would come treading forth with a
delicately clumsy gait down the side-street – come very
slowly, as though not quite sure there mightn't be some
grass for him to nibble at between the paving-stones.
Then he would pause at the corner of Piccadilly and flop
down against the railings of the nearest house. He would
remain there till luncheon-time and return in the early
afternoon. He was a large, handsome creature, with great
intelligence in his amber eyes. He never slept. He was
always interested in the passing scene. I think nothing
escaped him. I wish he could have written his memoirs
when he finally retired. He had seen, day by day, much
that was worth seeing.

He had seen a constant procession of the best-built
vehicles in the world, drawn by very beautifully bred and
beautifully-groomed and beautifully-harnessed horses,
and containing very ornate people. Vehicles of the most
diverse kinds. High-swung barouches, with immense
armorial bearings on their panels, driven by fat, white-
wigged coachmen, and having powdered footmen up
behind them; signorial phaetons; daring tandems; discreet
little broughams, brown or yellow; flippant high dog-
carts; low but flippant Ralli-carts; very frivolous private
hansoms shaming the more serious public ones.

Beerbohm was contemporary with many famous Londoners:
Wilde, Shaw, James, Virginia Woolf, Wells. Another, Arnold
Bennett, in his Journal for 1896, was less indulgent of the
gracious thoroughfare:

At ten o'clock, Piccadilly pavements were loosely
thronged with women in light summer attire – cool,
energetic, merry, inquisitive, and having an air of being
out for the day. Their restless eyes were on everything
at once: on each other; on the great houses of Piccadilly
decorated with bunting (for a royal wedding), where
workmen even then were erecting stands and gas pipes
curved into monogrammatic designs, and nailing festoons

of gold fringe upon red cloth; on the patient vendors of elevated standing room behind the railings of the Green Park; on the mounted police who, disposed in companies, dismounted like automata at the word of command.

Happy, infantile faces, most of them had faces expressive of a childish intention to enjoy; faces unmarked by thought and showing but slight traces of care; the faces of those to whom life is a simple, orderly affair, presenting few problems. Here and there was a family group – husband, wife, and tall young girls with long loose hair. And how transparently naive these last! Essentially as untutored as the veriest village maid, and offering a sharp contrast to the men of business, young and old, who in cabs and omnibuses and on foot were wending to the city just as though this had been a common day! Judging from the ordinary occupants of the streets, one is apt to think of London as a city solely made up of the acute, the knowing, the worldly, the blasé. But, hidden away behind sunblinds in quiet squares and crescents, there dwells another vast population, seen in large numbers only at such times as this, an army of the Ignorantly Innocent, in whose sheltered seclusion a bus-ride is an event, and a day spent among the traffic of the West End is an occasion long to be remembered.

Piccadilly for many, together with adjoining St James's, Bond Street and Mayfair, is less a thoroughfare than a synonym for opulence, pleasure, languid authority, privileged silence, for space, grace, smart lights, historical echoes. The actual street periodically loses grandiose landmarks. Near the Ritz Hotel once stood Devonshire House. Siegfried Sassoon ended his 'Monody' on its demolition:

> Where stood the low-built mansion, once so great,
> Ducal, demure, secure in its estate –
> Where Byron rang the bell and limped upstairs,
> And Lord knows what political affairs
> Got muddled and remodelled while Their Graces
> Manned unperturbed Elizabethan faces –
> There, blankly overlooked by wintry strange

Frontage of houses rawly-lit by change,
Industrious workmen reconstructed quite
The lumbered, pegged and excavated site,
And not one nook survived to screen a mouse
In what was Devonshire (God rest it) House.

The colonnaded mass of the Ritz itself dates only from 1906. Its associations, unlike those of the Café Royal and Wellington's nearby Apsley House, are mostly monied and trivial, though a story exists of Hilaire Belloc and G.K. Chesterton riding into the foyer on donkeys and, citing a medieval law, demanding provender for man and beast. More typical is Cynthia Asquith, daughter-in-law of the deposed Prime Minister, writing in her diary of a 'huge party' at the Ritz during grim 1917:

> Enjoyed my conversation with Duff [Cooper] very much. Felt tremendous reinforcement of mutual appreciation. We agreed that his friends were loose talkers and low livers, and that the blushing, shockable, formal, elder generation had been the ones for living and loving. He deplored this. I said it was always an alternative, and quoted the classic example of Swinburne. He told a delicious example of Margot's inconsequence. Talking to him of Venetia [Stanley] she said, 'Of course, she's a Jew. Both Lord Sheffield and Lord Carlisle are Jews.' Duff asked which was her father, and Margot said, 'Neither.'

Across the road, Burlington House survives, completed in 1872 in Italian Renaissance style and replacing the original mansion of 1668. The glittering shopping arcade to one side of it was originally a device erected by a Lord Burlington to protect his property from rubbish thrown over the wall. Its planner, Samuel Ware, advertised it, at its inception in 1815, as 'A Piazza for all Hardware, wearing Apparel and Articles not offensive in appearance or smell.' As home of the Royal Academy and several academic societies, Burlington House contains thirteen halls and a theatre, and its art exhibitions, like those of the National Gallery, attract novelists. In her novel *Still Life*, A.S. Byatt describes 'the pale grey, classical

quiet place where the bright light shone and sang off pig-
ment so that the phrase, miraculous stuff, seemed merely
accurate'.

Here Frederica Potter, as art critic, ascends the Palladian
marble stairway and looks around:

> An old woman, armed with a Sound Guide, became
> quite excited and pulled at the arm of another. 'Hey –
> look at that – WINSTON CHURCHILL painted that,
> the . . .' – carefully – 'Cap d'Antibes.'
>   Frederica dipped round her to stare: Claude Monet:
> 'Au Cap d'Antibes par vent de Mistral.' A whirl of blue
> and rose, formless, formed plungings of water and wind.
> 'To paint,' she remembered from Proust's description of
> fictive Elstir, 'that one does not see what one sees.' To
> paint light and air between ourselves and objects. 'I said,
> dear, WINSTON CHURCHILL' – The second woman
> tugged free of the clutching fingers; 'Not to be mentioned
> in the same breath with . . .' she said, looking nervously
> from Frederica to painted signature. The arrested water
> shone and danced.

The Piccadilly environs include Jermyn Street, the Mall
and Carlton House Terrace, St James's Street, two royal
parks and two palaces. The buildings are wide-windowed,
often pillared, sedate in tone, with suggestions of powers taken
for granted. The sentry outside St James's Palace is a mere
decoration. Here Thackeray, in his *The Four Georges*, gazed
at the acreage and saw behind it ghosts of older houses and
vanished personages. The Prince Regent's Carlton House,
the work of Henry Holland, a long, colonnaded palace with
Corinthian portico, was, like St James's Palace, more graceful
than authoritarian. It was pulled down in 1829, in an era of
massive replanning, leaving Thackeray to recall

> peeping through the colonnade at Carlton House, and
> seeing the abode of the great Prince Regent. I can yet
> see the Guards pacing before the gates of the palace. The
> palace? What palace? The palace exists no more than
> the palace of Nebuchadnezzar. It is but a name now.

Where be the sentries who used to salute as the Royal chariots drove in and out? The chariots, with the kings inside, have driven to the realms of Pluto; the tall Guards have marched into darkness, and the echoes of their drums are rolling in Hades. Where the palace once stood, a hundred little children are paddling up and down the steps to St James's Park. A score of grave gentlemen are taking their tea at the Athenaeum Club; as many grisly warriors are garrisoning the United Service Club opposite. Pall Mall is the great social Exchange of London now – the mart of news, of politics, of scandal, of rumour – the English forum, so to speak, where men discuss the last despatch from the Crimea . . .

Look! About this spot, Tom of Ten Thousand was killed by Konigsmarck's gang. In that great red house Gainsborough lived, and Culloden Cumberland, George III's uncle. Yonder is Sarah Marlborough's palace, just as it stood when that termagent occupied it. At 25, Walter Scott used to live; at the house, now no. 79, and occupied by the Society for the Propagation of the Gospel in Foreign Parts, resided Mrs Eleanor Gwyn, comedian. How often has Queen Caroline's chair issued from under yonder arch! All the men of the Georges have passed up and down the street. It has seen Walpole's chariot and Chatham's sedan; and Fox, Gibbon, Sheridan, on their way to Brooks's; and stately William Pitt stalking on the arm of Dundas; and Hangar and Tom Sheridan reeling out of Raggett's; and Byron limping into Watier's; and Swift striding out of Bury Street; and Mr Addison and Dick Steele, both perhaps a little the better for liquor; and the Prince of Wales and the Duke of York clattering over the pavement; and Johnson counting the posts along the streets, after dawdling before Dodsley's window; and Horry Walpole hobbling into his carriage, with a gimcrack just brought out at Christie's; and George Selwyn sauntering into White's.

Carlton House, with what Walpole termed its 'august simplicity', was replaced by Nash's Carlton House Terrace and the Duke of York's Steps, but some of the Regency atmosphere survived into the present century: extravagant, selfish, an easy mingling of taste and coarseness. Jermyn Street alongside Piccadilly and, like parallel Pall Mall, meeting St James's Street, is where Rosa Lewis, the 'Lottie Crump' in Evelyn Waugh's fictional London, managed the famous Cavendish Hotel, and where clubmen repaired to Turkish Baths for repairs. In *Laughter in the Next Room*, Sir Osbert Sitwell delineated pre-1914 Jermyn Street:

Who could wonder that foreigners loved London? Though as different from Vienna or Paris as Pekin, it was no less essentially a capital, with all the attractions of the centre of an Empire. It remained unique in being a masculine city, as it had been throughout its history, created to the same degree for men as Paris for women. The luxury shops were unrivalled in their appeal to male tastes, were full of cigarettes and objects made in leather, glass or silver, better than those to be seen anywhere in foreign capitals; solid, plain, unimaginative but showing the English feeling for material, the English sobriety. As for suits, shirts, shoes, ties, London was acknowledged throughout the world, by all races, of all colours, to set the fashion for men. And the years, 1913 and 1914 were the last when there was a successor to the long line of fops, macaronis, dandies, beaux, dudes, bucks, blades, swells and mashers, who for so many centuries had given life to the London world of pleasure; to these was now added the 'nut', or, more jocularly, the 'k-nut', as personified by a young actor, Mr Basil Hallam, who in this respect both summed up and set the tone in a song entitled 'Gilbert the Filbert, the Colonel of the Nuts!' The refrain ran –
    I'm Gilbert the Filbert, the Nut with a K,
    The pride of Piccadilly, the blasé roué.
    Oh, Hades, the ladies all leave their wooden huts
    For Gilbert the Filbert, the Colonel of the Nuts.'

Sir Osbert ignored a post-1945 development, when sartorial dandyism revived, though in East and South London, touched with faded, almost 'folk' memories of swells and dudes, with violence added. Bill Naughton has a knowledgeable passage about the elegant post-war, cocky layabout, the spiv:

> See his spivy coat – the width of the lapels, the padded-out shoulders . . . Notice how his hair was parted in the middle, and the wave at either side? And how it was long at the back, with the four-noughts clippers brought up to meet it? Regular Spivy touch is that; not one barber in ten knows it.

West End Clubs

Spivs, teddy-boys and mods would have been unacceptable in the St James's Street clubs and ménages of the Regency: Brooks's, White's, Watier's and the rest.

Max Beerbohm's goat

> was accustomed to what was called the man-about-town – a now extinct species, a lost relic of the eighteenth century and of the days before the great Reform Bill of 1832; a leisurely personage, attired with great elaboration on his way to one of his many clubs; not necessarily interesting in himself; but fraught with external character and point.

Such figures clustered on both sides of Piccadilly. Doubtless with feeling, Rosina Bulwer, in her Victorian novel *Cheverley*, defined 'Home' as 'a pen in which to keep women and children'.

The most famous of men-about-town were the dandies. For Anne Cliff:

> Dandyism was a decorative art, and the Dandies exhibited themselves freely to their audience whenever they set foot out of doors. Whenever curious Londoners wanted a free show, they had but to stroll down St James's Street to watch the elegant dandies sauntering from one club to another, or to see the four dandies-in-chief (Brummell,

Alvanley, Pierrepoint, Mildmay) sitting in the bow window at White's and quizzing the passers-by.

Lord Byron, himself a member of Watier's, the dandies' club, rated that the age had produced three great men: Brummell, Napoleon and himself, in that order. Brummell's triumphs were not those of the field or the pen. A biographer, Lewis Melville, suggested:

Brummell's greatest triumph was his neckcloth. The neckcloth was then a huge clinging wrap, worn without stiffening of any kind, and so bagging out in the front: Brummell, in a moment of inspiration such as rarely comes to a man in a lifetime, decided to have his starched. The conception was, indeed, a stroke of genius. But genius, in this case, had to be backed by infinite pains. What labour must Brummell and his valet, Robinson, have expended on experiments to discover the exact amount of stiffening to produce the best result. . . .

The sensation that Brummell made when he first appeared in his starched neckcloth was tremendous. It must have rewarded him amply for all the toil and moil. What was a shoe-buckle five inches wide to a stiffened cravat? Nothing else was talked about for a few days in polite circles. The clubs were sparsely occupied, all the members were at home practising before the looking glass.

The Regent is said to have wept when Brummell deplored the line of his cravat or the cut of his coat, but eventually the Beau's ascendancy of tone and deportment, his deft insolence of wit and behaviour, seem to have led to a permanent estrangement, the process doubtless accelerated by an incident related by another, earlier biographer, William Jesse.

His Royal Highness was going to the Picture Gallery in Pall Mall, and Brummell, who was watching with some other men about ten yards in front of me, was exactly opposite the door of the Exhibition as the Regent's low, dark red carriage stopped. Brummell evidently saw it, and saw who was in it, although he pretended not to do so, and when the two sentinels presented arms, he, with an air of pretended surprise and mock dignity which was most amusing, gravely raised his hat, turning his head very graciously towards the sentries and his back to the carriage window.

The Pall Mall, St James's and Piccadilly clubs – the Athenaeum, the Reform, the Travellers – with their Italianate façades preserved an atmosphere very singular, slow to change, recognized throughout much of Europe and America, with occasional attempts at imitation.

From the Reform Club, modelled on the Farnese Palace in Rome, with a double layer of columns, lavish ceilings and a massive central chandelier, Jules Verne sent his hero, Phileas Fogg, to encompass the world in eighty days:

Phileas Fogg was English to the backbone. He was never seen on the Stock Exchange, nor at the Bank, nor in any City House. No vessel consigned to Phileas Fogg ever entered the London Docks; he held no position under the Government; he was not a lawyer at any of the Inns; he had never pleaded at the Queen's Bench, the Chancery Bar, the Exchequer, nor the Ecclesiastical Courts; he was not a manufacturer, nor a merchant, nor a farmer; he was not a member of any of the learned societies of the metropolis. He was simply a member of the Reform Club.

At the Athenaeum, with its strict neo-classical outlines and decor, Lord Palmerston stole the chef, and Trollope, after overhearing disparaging comments from two unknown clerics, decided to eliminate Mrs Proudie forever. Here, too, Henry James heard the voice of Modernism, Ezra Pound, who wrote in 1918, after James's death:

The massive head, the slow uplift of the hand . . . the long sentences piling themselves up in elaborate phrase after phrase, the lightning incision, the pauses, the slightly shaking admonitory gesture with its 'wu-a-wait a little, wait a little, something will come,' blague and benignity and the weight of so many years' careful, incessant labour of minute observation always there to enrich the talk. I heard it but seldom, yet it is all unforgettable.

The traditional atmosphere of London clubs is preserved by another American, the journalist Robert Underwood Johnson who, in Coronation year, 1911, enjoyed the Athenaeum's hospitality for a month. In *Remembered Yesterdays* he looked back on it:

The secretary was exceedingly courteous to me and made me acquainted with the haunts and corners of the club associated with Thackeray, Dickens, Gladstone . . . I deeply appreciated its hospitality and enjoyed its tranquillity and seclusion. In America we go to clubs for conversation; in England, at least as far as the Athenaeum is concerned, men go for privacy. Even if I were inclined to violate the sanctity of a club by revealing anything that might be embarrassing, I should not be able to do so in this case, since in the month of my membership, I did not exchange a word with anyone in the club, Mr Tedder the secretary, and the servants excepted. No one spoke to me, and I did not feel at liberty to speak to anyone else, except one occasion, when, at a buffet luncheon to members who were awaiting the Coronation parade, I accidentally trod upon the foot of a gentleman, and in this way struck up a conversation. But I revelled in the quiet alcoves, the well-furnished library and reading room and the charming atmosphere.

The charming atmosphere did not suit all temperaments. In fiction, Bertie Wooster narrates:

Once a year the committee of the Drones decide that the old club could do with a wash and brush-up, so they shoo us out, and dump us down for a few weeks at some other institution. This time we were roosting at the Senior Liberal, and, personally I had found the strain pretty fearful. I mean, when you've got used to a club where everything's nice and cheery, and where, if you want to attract a fellow's attention, you heave a bit of bread at him, it kind of damps you to come to a place where the youngest member is about eighty-seven, and it isn't considered good form to talk to anyone unless you and he went through the Peninsular War together.

Elizabeth Longford tells an apposite story:

While the Guards Club was closed for seasonal cleaning, its members were enjoying the hospitality of the Oxford and Cambridge. A young visitor from the Guards threw himself into a chair next to an elderly gentleman hidden behind a newspaper.
'I say,' drawled the affable visitor, 'you fellows in the middle classes do yourselves well and no mistake.' The newspaper was lowered to disclose the face of the Duke of Wellington, wearing, one may surmise, the expression immortalized by the painter Haydon.

Clubs store up such stories like income. Michael Meyer in his lively memoirs tells a story set nearer Mayfair, in the Savile Club in 1938. The young V.S. Pritchett, already a travel and story writer, sits down at an empty table.

Almost immediately the place on his right was taken by W.B. Yeats and, a minute later, that on his left by H.G. Wells, who began to eat greedily with his mouth open. Yeats, who had only a few months to live, apparently hated any talk of death. Pritchett says the following dialogue then took place across him.

Wells.   'Isn't it Yeats?'
Yeats.   'Ah. Good morning, Wells.'
Wells.   'You're looking very old, Yeats.'
Yeats.   (*goes slightly grey*): 'None of us gets younger, Wells.'
Wells.   'Ah, the days when we were young. Do you remember how we used to walk on Hampstead Heath with X and Y?'
Yeats.   'Yes. I wonder what they're doing nowadays.'

Wells.	(*eating noisily*) 'Dead.'
Yeats.	(*greys further*) 'Both of them?'
Wells.	'Yes. And when we went together to the Bedford to see Dan Leno with young Z.'
Yeats.	'How is Z now?'
Wells.	'Dead.' (*pause*) 'And Yeats, do you remember the time we went boating at Richmond and took those girls with us? One of them wore a pink dress and had beautiful long gold hair?'
Yeats.	(*moved, puts down his knife and fork*) 'Yes, I remember her. She was very beautiful. What's happened to – surely she can't be dead? She was much younger than us?'
Wells.	'No, she isn't dead.'
Yeats.	'Thank heavens for that!'
Wells.	(*illustrating graphically*) 'Paralysed all down one side. (*to waiter*) I think I'll have the steak.'

London clubs abound in fiction, gathering pace after Trollope's Bear Garden with its spirited young gamblers and heiress-hunters. Part of a make-believe West End remains occupied by Saki's witty, insouciant, world-weary and exquisite Clovis and Reginald: by such clubmen as Miles Malpractise, John Beaver and Arthur Box-Bender at Bellamy's in Evelyn Waugh's steely comedies. Clubland can also introduce grimmer currents. In his *The Soul of London*, Ford Madox Ford was aware that London security was always at risk, not only on such high occasions as Chartist riots and Fenian bombings. Violence always lurked, like a fire smouldering beneath a nursery floor:

Go down Piccadilly to Hyde Park Corner on a pleasant summer day. On the right of you you have all those clubs with all those lounging and luxuriating men. On the left is a stretch of green park, hidden and rendered hideous by recumbent forms. They lie like corpses, or like soldiers in a stealthy attack, a great multitude of broken men and women, they too, eternally at leisure. They lie, soles of boots to crowns of heads, just out of arm's reach one from the other for fear of being rifled by their couch-mates. They lie motionless, dun-coloured, pitiful and horrible, bathing in leisure that will never end. There, indeed, is your London at leisure; the two ends of the scale offered violently for inspection, confronting and ignoring steadily the one the other. For in the mass, the men in the windows never look down; the men in the park never look up. In those two opposed sights you have your London, your great tree in its leisure, making for itself new sap and new fibre, holding aloft its vigorous leaves, shedding its decayed wood, strewing on the ground its rotten twigs and stuff for graveyards.

This hint of menace reappears in *The Three Hostages*, when John Buchan's General Sir Richard Hannay, of Fosse Manor, leaves the élitist Thursday Club after dining in its pomp as the guest of Dominic Medina, MP, subtle poet, popular in clubs, drawing-rooms and country houses but also kidnapper, hypnotist and terrorist. The club with its spirited talk and famous names now behind him, Hannay walks home alone, through a spring evening:

The West End of London at night always affected me with a sense of the immense solidity of our civilization. These great houses, lit and shuttered and secure seemed the extreme opposite of the world of half-lights and perils in which I had sometimes journeyed. I thought of them as I thought of Fosse Manor, as sanctuaries of peace. But to-night I felt differently towards them. I wondered what was going on at the back of those heavy doors. Might not terror and mystery lurk behind that barricade as well as in tent and slum? I suddenly had a picture of a plump face all screwed up with fright muffled beneath the bed-clothes.

Such misgivings would not have overtaken members of the Drones – Oofy Prosser, Gussie Fink-Nottle, Bertie Wooster, Bingo Little, Catsmeat Potter-Pirbright. In *Mulliner Nights* Wodehouse gives a typical dialogue:

'Hullo, Oofy, old man! How are you, Oofy, old man?
I say, Oofy, old man, I do like that tie you're wearing.
What I call something like a tie. Quite the snappiest
thing I've seen for years and years and years and years.
I wish I could get ties like that. But then, of course,
I haven't your exquisite taste. What I've always said
about you, Oofy, old man, is that you have the most
extraordinary *flair* – it amounts to genius – in the selec-
tion of ties. But, then, one must bear in mind that
anything would look well on you, because you have
such a clean-cut, virile profile. I met a man the other
day, who said to me: "I didn't know Ronald Colman
was in England." And I said: "He isn't." And he said:
"But I saw you talking to him outside the Blotto Kitten."
And I said "That wasn't Ronald Colman. That was my
old pal – the best pal any man ever had – Oofy Prosser."
And he said: "Well, I never saw such a remarkable resemblance." And I said: "Yes, there is a great resemblance,
only, of course, Oofy is much the better-looking." And
this fellow said: "Oofy Prosser? Is that '*the*' Oofy Prosser,
the man whose name you hear everywhere?" And I
said: "Yes, and I'm proud to call him my friend. I don't
suppose," I said, "there's another fellow in London in
such demand. Duchesses clamour for him, and if you ask
a princess to dinner, you have to add: 'To meet Oofy
Prosser,' or she won't come. This," I explained, "is
because, in addition to being the handsomest and best-
dressed man in Mayfair, he is famous for his sparkling
wit and keen – but always kindly – repartee. And yet,
in spite of it all, he remains simple, unspoilt, unaffected."
Will you lend me twenty quid, Oofy, old man?'

'No,' said Oofy Prosser.

TWO PALACES

With its dark stone, its turrets and its red sentry, St James's
Palace separates St James's Street from its park, a plaything
of a palace, where Thackeray's Becky, now married, attends
a royal function:

We are authorised to state that Mrs Rawdon Crawley's 'costume de cour' on the occasion was of the most elegant and brilliant description. Some ladies we may have seen – we who wear stars and cordons, and attend the St James's assemblies, or we who in muddy boots, dawdle up and down Pall Mall, and peep into the coaches as they drive up with the great folks in their feathers – some ladies of fashion, I say, we may have seen about two o'clock of the forenoon of a levee day, as the laced-jacketed band of the Life Guards are blowing triumphal marches seated on those prancing music-stools, their cream-coloured chargers – who are by no means lovely and enticing objects at that earlier period of noon. A stout countess of sixty, décolleté, painted, wrinkled with rouge up to her drooping eyelids, and diamonds twinkling in her wig, is a wholesome and edifying, but not a pleasant sight. She has the faded look of a St James's Street illumination, as it may be seen of an early morning, when half the lamps are out, and the others are blinking wanly, as if they were about to vanish before the dawn.

Behind the Palace, along the tree-lined Mall, under the column supporting the Brave Old Duke of York – perched there, people said, to evade his creditors – is St James's Park, where Charles II, like Swift after him, loved to walk, and had the lake laid out and filled with what Pepys called 'a great variety of fowl which I never saw before'.

Pepys was often there. In 1668:

So I to the Park, and there walk an hour or two; and in the King's garden, and saw the Queen and ladies walk, and there I did steal some apples off the trees; and there did see my Lady Richmond, who is of a noble person as ever I did see, but her face worse than it was considerably by the small-pox.

Here, too, he saw 'one man basted by the keeper for carrying some people over on his back through the water'. In its essentials, the Park has not greatly changed since Pepys' day. The waterfowl, first established by Charles II, continue to breed: civil servants and politicians still take their walks.

A living poet, Diana Witherby, opens her poem 'St James's Park':

> Pelican and willow droop
> In this garden like a print;
> Boys are throwing nails
> Into sky as dark as flint.
> Rain smokes through the feathers, foliage,
> Slants down the beak and branch
> Carved in this open-air cage.
> The pencil lines and light reflect
> In artificial lake, and grasses drown
> In fans of wind and vapour; while under trees
> The leaf-green chairs are spurting water down.

At the end of the Park, Buckingham Palace is inescapable, ponderous, formal, without grace. Inside, formalities at one time lapsed into the markedly informal. Sir Frederick Ponsonby, who served in the Royal Household under Victoria, Edward VII and George V, left an entertaining account of his experience:

> When I attended a 'Court', I was always struck by the incongruous music the band played, and determined to do what I could to have this remedied. The majority of the Household, being quite unmusical, clamoured for popular airs, and Sir Walter Parratt, the Master of the Music, who cared only for classical music and looked down on any other sort of music, complied with the demand. I argued that these popular airs robbed the ceremony of all dignity. A presentation at Court was often a great event in a lady's life, but if she went past the King and Queen to the tune of 'His Nose was Redder than it Was,' the whole impression was spoilt.

At the Palace Tennyson read aloud to Victoria and Dickens presented amateur theatricals. Robert Graves, on being presented, is said to have referred the Queen to their mutual

descent from the Prophet Mahomet. None would have envied
the predicament of the art historian and editor Benedict
Nicolson who, as Assistant Keeper of the Royal Paintings,
was, at a palace gathering, trapped into playing the Blind Man
in one of George VI's favourite pastimes, Blind Man's Buff.
Nicolson, shy, learned and awkward, fumbling for the identity
of some mute figure, mistook through misapplied fingers the
present Queen Mother for a footman.

The Palace, thanks to the later monarchs appointing capable
advisers, contains an opulent art collection, which includes surprises. Stanley Weintraub gives one instance:

> Male beauty had been an obsession with the young
> Victoria, and life with Albert, however satisfying physi-
> cally, had not changed that. Her eye still caught striking
> examples, in life and in art, and she would continue
> their cultivation. At a time when nudity in pictures
> was denounced from some pulpits, as morally corrupt,
> when the virile Thackeray thought that William Etty's
> nudes should be hidden by 'a great, large curtain of
> fig-leaves', and the prudish, pontifical Ruskin judged
> William Mulready's nude drawings 'degraded and bes-
> tial', Victoria bought nudes. A century later, when
> the novelist Compton Mackenzie trod the corridors of
> Buckingham Palace en route to being knighted, he passed
> an 'almost nude' canvas of Diana, and asked himself
> what Victoria would have thought of it. Then he read
> the inscription – that it was one of the young Queen's
> wedding presents to Albert. She even bought a black
> and red Mulready drawing for her husband in which a
> muscular young man is seen at full length wearing
> nothing but a beard and an anxious expression.

Crowds still stare at the Palace and fantasize on the
comings and goings, like that imagined by Virginia Woolf,
in *Mrs Dalloway*:

> A small crowd meanwhile had gathered at the gates
> of Buckingham Palace. Listlessly, yet confidently, poor
> people all of them, they waited; looked at the Palace

itself with the flag flying; at Victoria, billowing on her
mound, admired her shelves of running water, her gera-
niums; singled out from the motor cars in the Mall
first this one, then that; bestowed emotion, vainly, on
commoners out for a drive; recalled their tribute to keep
it unspent while this car passed and that; and all the
time let rumour accumulate in their being and thrill the
nerves in their thighs at the thought of royalty looking
at them; the Queen bowing; the Prince saluting; at
the thought of the heavenly life divinely bestowed upon
Kings; of the equerries and deep curtsies; of the Queen's
old doll's house; of Princess Mary married to an Englishman, and the Prince – ah! The Prince! who took wonder-
fully, they said, after old King Edward, but was ever so
much slimmer. The Prince lived at St James's; but he
might come along in the morning to visit his mother.

BOND STREET

As Piccadilly lunges towards Hyde Park Corner, its atmosphere
turns aside into Bond Street. Gibbon had a house there, hearing
the coaches rattle, but usually preferring to read in solitude.
Brummell had a tailor there, Mr Weston, and Lewis Melville
records him drawling: 'That fellow Weston is an inimitable
fellow – a little defective, perhaps, in his linings, but irre-
proachable for principal and buttonholes.' Cecil Beaton noted
that Guards' overcoats are still cut to Brummell's taste; that his
influence keeps London a world centre for masculine elegance.
  In *Lothair* Disraeli acknowledged elegance in the street's
elaborate window-displays and rich interiors:

> Business had not long commenced when Lothair entered
> the shop, somewhat to the surprise of its master. Those
> who knew Bond Street only in the blaze of fashionable
> hours can form but an imperfect conception of its
> matutinal charm, when it is still shady and fresh, when
> there are no carriages, rarely a cart, and passers-by gliding
> about on real business. One feels as in some continental
> city. Then there are time and opportunity to look at

the shops; and there is no street in the world that can furnish such a collection, filled with so many objects of beauty, curiosity, and interest. The jewellers and gold-smiths and dealers in rare furniture; porcelain, and cabinets and French pictures, have long fixed upon Bond Street as their favourite quarter, and are not chary of displaying their treasures; though it may be a question whether some of the magazines of fancy food, delicacies culled from all the climes and regions of the globe, par-ticularly at the Matin hour, may not, in their picturesque variety, be the most attractive. The palm, perhaps, would be given to the fishmongers, with their exuberant exhibi-tions, grouped with skill, startling often with strange forms, dazzling with prismatic tints, and breathing the invigorating redolence of the sea.

Virginia Woolf's Mrs Dalloway felt similarly, after the Great War:

Bond Street fascinated her; Bond Street early in the morning in the season; its flags flying; its shops; no splash; no glitter; one roll of tweed in the shop where her father had bought his suits for fifty years; a few pearls; salmon on an ice block.

A little further up, with eyes half-closed, snuffing in, after the street noises, the scent and coolness in Mulberry's, the florist, she suddenly contemplates the flowers:

How fresh, like frilled linen clean from a laundry laid in wicker trays, the roses looked; and dark and prim the red carnations, holding their heads up; and all the sweet peas spreading in their bowls, tinged violet, snow white, pale – as if it were the evening and girls in muslin frocks came out to pick sweet peas and roses after the superb summer's day, with its almost blue-black sky, its delphiniums, its carnations, its arum lilies, was over; and it was the moment between six and seven when every flower – roses, carnations, irises, lilac – glows; white, violet, red, deep orange; every flower seems to burn by itself, softly, purely in the misty beds; and how she loved the grey white moths spinning in and out, over the cherry pie, over the evening primroses!

MAYFAIR

Between Bond Street and the Park, the wide lawns, trees and statues of Grosvenor Square and Berkeley Square and the mansions of Curzon Street contribute to Mayfair, where the wealthy have long lived and played, though with decreasing style, and where, in all decades, life amongst the rich could be richly pursued by those who themselves lacked riches. Thackeray's Becky and Rawdon Crawley enjoyed a lavish existence in fashionable Curzon Street, employing a versatile repertoire of dishonesty. In *Vanity Fair*:

> it was wonderful to see the pertinacity with which the washerwoman from Tooting brought the cart every Saturday and her bills week after week. Mr Raggles (the landlord) himself had to supply the greengroceries. The bill for the servants' porter at the Fortune of War public house is a curiosity in the chronicles of beer. Every servant also was owed the greater part of his wages, and thus kept up perforce an interest in the house. Nobody in fact was paid. Not the blacksmith who opened the lock, not the glazier who mended the pane; nor the jobber who let the carriage; nor the groom who drove it; nor the butcher who provided the leg of mutton; nor the coals which roasted it; nor the cook who basted it; nor the servants who ate it; and this, I am given to understand, is not infrequently the way in which people live elegantly on nothing a year.

At the west end of Curzon Street, in Park Lane, facing Hyde Park, lived a very different fictional character. Shirley Robin Letwin characteristically asserts:

> The most perfect gentleman in Trollope's novels is Madame Max Goesler. She was the daughter of a humble

German Jewish attorney, and her only endowments by
birth were beauty and intelligence. But she inherited a
fortune from her husband and with these assets Marie
Goesler moved from Vienna to London, hoping to make
her way into the top social circles. She succeeded so well
that the highest duke of all offered her his coronet.

Refusing this, Marie Goesler was probably something of an
exception in a locality where Dukes were welcomed, less for
being themselves than for possessing a title. In later fiction, as
in Michael Arlen's novels, and in social history, a sense remains
of people with charm, intelligence, humour and occasional
wit, flawed by arrogance and complacency, and with insuffi-
cient employment so that the débâcle of 1914, far from being
deplored by many of its young, insouciant victims, could
be welcomed as a further chance for sensation, relief from
boredom, a change from the cricket and hunting fields.
Their mansions – Londonderry House, Dorchester House,
Grosvenor House – are gone or transformed into hotels, where
their receptions, balls and dinners are nightly travestied. Soon
few save readers will remember the nights now displaced.
Osbert Sitwell captures the fragile, perfumed atmosphere:

Night after night, during the summers of 1913 and 14,
the entertainments grew in numbers and magnificence.
One band in a house was no longer enough, there must
be two, three even. Electric fans whirled on the top of
enormous blocks of ice, buried in banks of hydrangeas like
the shores from which the barque departs for Cythera.
Never had there been such displays of flowers; not of
the dehydrated weeds, dry poppy-heads and old-man's
beard that characterised the interbellum years, when a
floral dessication that matched the current beige walls
and self-toned textiles and carpets was in evidence; but
a profusion of full-blooded blossoms, of lolling roses and
malmaisons, of gilded musical comedy baskets of carnations and sweet-peas, while huge bunches of orchids,
bowls of gardenias and flat trays of stephanotis lent to
some houses an air of exoticism. Never had Europe seen
such mounds of peaches, figs, nectarines and strawberries

all in season, brought from their steamy tents of glass. Champagne bottles stood stacked on the sideboards . . . and to the rich, this show was free.

As guests, only the poor of every race were barred. Even foreigners could enter, if they were rich. The English governing classes – though still struck dumb with horror if a foreigner entered the room, and albeit when obliged to talk to him, they still shouted at him in English baby-language, a result of the Public School system – had grown used to the idea that foreigners existed and were – well, foreigners.

The hothouse luxury of Park Lane and Grosvenor Square, the sensuality amongst the frock coats and bare shoulders within boudoir, salon and ballroom, contained a further element. Social life, H.G. Wells declared in *The Passionate Friends*, was honeycombed and rotten with the secret and the hidden: 'Thousands of people of our sort are hiding and shamming about their desires, their gratifications, their love relationships.'

HYDE PARK

Park Lane descends southwards to join Piccadilly at Hyde Park Corner. Here, London, without warning, presented one of those sudden sharp illuminations, often in unexpected juxtaposition, that can fix themselves more permanently in the imagination than coronations, jamborees or festivals. Aldous Huxley observed, in *Antic Hay*:

In the warm yellow light of the coffee-stall at Hyde Park Corner loitered a little group of people. Among the peak caps and the chauffeurs' dust-coats, among the weather-stained workmen's jackets and the knotted handkerchiefs, there emerged an alien elegance. A tall tubed hat and a silk-faced overcoat, a cloak of flame-coloured satin, and in bright coppery hair a great Spanish comb of carved tortoise shell.

Such a scene appeals to what an adopted Londoner, Sybille Bedford, has called 'that sense of lighter heart, of deep-grooved pleasures, daylight and proportion'.

Like all pleasure places, Hyde Park has several aspects. Pepys enjoyed a visit to the cake-house there with two attractive ladies, Mrs Pierce and the actress Mrs Knepp, but in his *Journal to Stella*, Swift wrote:

> This morning at eight, my man brought me word that the Duke of Hamilton had fought with Lord Mohun, and killed him, and was brought home wounded. I immediately sent him to the Duke's house, in St James's Square, but the porter could hardly answer him for tears, and a great rabble was about the house. In short, they fought at seven this morning. The dog Mohun was killed on the spot; and while the Duke was standing over him, Mohun shortening his sword, stabbed him at the shoulder to the heart. The Duke was helped toward the cake-house by the Ring in Hyde Park (where they fought) and died on the grass before he could reach the house; and was brought home in his coach by eight, while the poor Duchess was asleep.

Long after Swift, snobbery developed between areas north of the Park and south, baffling to sensible Londoners but of concern to the foolish. The contemporary author Jeremy Lewis grew up in the 1950s, and in his autobiography, *Playing for Time*, remembered this very clearly:

> The London I grew up in as a child was, of course, rigid with men in bowler hats, along with small boys in grey flannel shorts and fairisle sleeveless jerseys, ex-soldiers with pudding-basin hair-cuts and tight-waisted demob suits, policemen with snake-clasps to their belts, charwomen with turbans on their heads and flower-patterned pinnies with strings at the back, and all the much-loved familiars associated with Ealing comedies, every frame of which I scan for a fleeting glimpse of the London I dimly remember – innocent of tower blocks, the public buildings mercifully uncleaned, the taxis upright and

hooded, soot and peeling stucco all about.

It went without saying that my mother was – and still is – a firm believer in that great and famous divide that separates Londoners north of the Park from their fellow-citizens to the south of that mightiest of natural frontiers. From an early age I remember being told that 'no one' lived north of the Park. Were those endless houses stretching away on either side of the Edgware Road but empty façades, a vast Potemkin village erected to persuade gullible foreigners that London was indeed – as we were so often informed – the largest city in the world? Or were those people I spotted hurrying about their business, for all their apparent normality, close relations of 'Homo Sapiens', similar but not the same? Such were the speculations aroused by my mother's stern, exclusive words.

Hyde Park like St James's, provided a fine show for the curious onlooker. The rich paraded with their parasols and canes, their gloves, tall hats, flowered hats, expensive dogs. The riders in Rotten Row (*Route de roi*) usually maintained considerable studied grace, or at least poise. A valued immigrant, Joseph Conrad, in his novel *The Secret Agent*, was concerned with neither, but

Through the park railings he beheld men and women riding in the Row, couples cantering past harmoniously, others advancing sedately at a walk, loitering, groups of three or four, solitary horsemen looking unsociable, and solitary women followed at a long distance by a groom with a cockade to his hat, and a leather belt over his tight-fitting coat. Carriages went bowling by, mostly two-horsed broughams, with here and there a victoria with the skin of some wild beast inside and a woman's face and hat emerging above the folded hood. And a peculiarly London sun – against which nothing could be said except that it looked bloodshot – glorified all this by its stare. It hung at a moderate elevation above Hyde Park Corner with an air of punctual and benign vigilance. The very pavement under Mr Verloc's feet had an

old-gold tinge in that diffused light, in which neither
wall, nor tree, nor beast, nor man cast a shadow. Mr
Verloc was going westward through a town without
shadows in an atmosphere of powdered old gold. There
were red, coppery gleams on the roofs of houses, on the
corners of walls, on the panels of carriages, on the very
coats of the horses, and on the broad back of Mr Verloc's
overcoat where they produced a dull effect of rustiness.

KENSINGTON

Separated from Hyde Park by the Serpentine, are Kensington
Gardens. To the south, the Albert Hall covers the site of
Gore House, where Lady Blessington and Count d'Orsay once
entertained the famous and the fashionable; where Addison
died; and where Cromwell issued orders. Here, Hans Andersen
first met his hero, Dickens: 'He is just what I thought he
would be. We understood each other at once, clasped each
other's hands and talked English – I unfortunately not well.'
The Gardens themselves have more graciousness and variety,
more trees, than Hyde Park. About them, Thomas Tickell,
Under-Secretary of State under Addison himself, wrote in
1772:

> Where Kensington high o'er the neighbouring lands
> 'midst greens and sweets, a regal fabric stands,
> And sees each spring, luxuriant in her bowers,
> A snow of blossoms, and a wild of flowers,
> The dames of Britain oft in crowds repair
> To gravel walks and unpolluted air.
> Here, while the town in damps and darkness lies,
> They breath in sunshine, and see azure skies;
> Each walk, with robes of various dyes bespread,
> Seems from afar a moving tulip-bed,
> Where rich brocades and glossy damasks glow,
> And chintz, the rival of the showering bow.

Kensington had been green for centuries, its Gardens adjoining a sedate Palace, of which Matthew Arnold mused in 1852:

In this lone, open glade I lie,
Screen'd by deep boughs on either hand;
And at its end, to stay the eye,
Those black-crowned, red-boled pine-trees stand.

Humbert Wolfe knew the Gardens well:

Queen Victoria's
statue is
the work of her daughter Louise.
The shape's all wrong
and the crown doesn't fit,
but – bless her old heart!
She was proud of it.

In 1836, an anonymous writer considered that 'there are three classes – men, women and governesses'. Charlotte Brontë wrote, 'None but those who have been in the position of a governess could ever realise the dark side of respectable human nature.' These last, and their colleagues, fellow gossips and rivals, the nannies, were an institution in Kensington Gardens and have played an important though under-considered part in history. Dickens, who nightly heard from his nurse the saga of *Captain Murderer*, poisoner and cannibal, reckoned: 'If we all knew our own minds, I suspect that we should find our nurses responsible for most of the dark corners we are forced to go back to against our will.' In 1977 the historian Lawrence Stone noted that many early nineteenth-century governesses ended their days in an asylum.

Ezra Pound lived for thirteen years in London, mainly near Kensington Church Street. Imagism, he claimed, began in Church Walk, with Richard Aldington, H.D. (Hilda Dolittle) and himself, aiming to show 'an intellectual and emotional complex in an instant of time'. Pound thus compressed a Metro station into

The apparition of these faces in the crowd:
Petals on a wet, black bough.

In London, he acquired his distinctive tone: dapper, sardonic, ironic, with a quick-witted insolence threatened by vulgarity.

> Like a skein of loose silk blown against a wall,
>   She walks by the railings of a path in
>   Kensington Gardens,
> And she is dying piece-meal
>   Of a sort of emotional anaemia.
> And round about there is a rabble
>   Of the filthy, sturdy, unkillable infants
>   of the very poor.
> They shall inherit the earth.
>
> In her is the end of breeding.
>   Her boredom is exquisite and excessive.
> She would like someone to speak to her,
>   And is almost afraid that I
>   will commit that indiscretion.

However neat and green the Gardens, however grandiose the churches and museums, department stores and mansions, Kensington too has its seedier aspects. The drab saloon and the shabby lodging house remain in back streets and dull squares, where one can still expect to find characters from Patrick Hamilton's *Twenty Thousand Streets under the Sky*: the scheming and chilly barmaid, the bored servant girl and flashy suitor, experienced in journeys to Brighton.

Recreation grounds, like art galleries, literary conferences and public baths, always attract oddities. Kensington Gardens has an existence beyond the toy yachts on the Round Pond, the Orangery in Kensington Palace, the Peter Pan statue, the prams, the flowers, the trees. In *Journey Without Maps*, Graham Greene reflected:

> It isn't a gain to have turned the witch or the masked secret dancer, the sense of supernatural evil, into the small human viciousness of the thin, distinguished military grey head in Kensington Gardens with the soft lips and the eye which dwelt with dull lustre on girls and boys of a certain age.

He was an old Etonian. He had an estate in the Highlands. He said: 'Do they cane at your school?' looking out over the wide flat grass, the nursemaids and the children, with furtive alertness. He said: 'You must come up and stay with me in Scotland. Do you know any girls' school where they still – you know – ' He began to make confidences, and then, suddenly taking a grip of the poor sliding brain, he rose and moved away with stiff military back, the old Etonian tie, the iron-grey hair, a bachelor belonging to the right clubs, over the green plain among the nursemaids and the babies wetting their napkins.

And Jeremy Lewis remembers further:

On Sundays we often went for a walk in Kensington Gardens to watch the model boats on the Round Pond and climb about a large statue of a naked, muscle-bound figure on horseback waving a sword. A diversion of a gloomier kind was provided by an elderly man in a brown overcoat who came to feed the ducks with crusts from a brown paper bag. Every week an ambulance stood on duty; every week he had an epileptic fit by the side of the pond, and dropped his brown paper bag, which was whisked away by a gust of wind; every week he was promptly and punctually spirited away by the waiting ambulancemen; and every week he returned with a fresh supply of crusts, and the sad ritual was repeated once again. I found a terrible pathos in the sight of his brown paper bag and its scattering of crumbs – very similar to that excited, in later life, by a pair of worn and highly polished shoes set out in a lonely bedroom.

Outside the Gardens is Kensington itself, which, when a seventeenth-century village, possessed a health resort, the Gravel Pits, to cure the gravel, a bladder complaint. Swift wrote to Stella: ' 'Tis good for us to live in gravel pits but not for gravel pits to live in us.'
Later, as the Royal Borough, it gathered traits and associations ponderous and aloof, as the Gardens are aloof from the

more democratic Park. In *The Wings of a Dove*, Henry James shows the impact of a Lancaster Gate mansion on a youngish writer with means too small for his ambitions:

> Never, he flattered himself, had he seen anything so gregariously ugly – operatively, ominously so cruel. He was glad to have found this last name for the whole character; 'cruel' somehow played into the subject for an article – that his impression put straight into his mind. He would write about the heavy horrors that could still flourish, that lifted their undiminished heads, in an age so proud of its short way with false gods; and it would be funny if what he should have got from Mrs Lowder were to prove, after all, but a small amount of copy. Yet the great thing, really the dark thing, was that, even while he thought of the quick column he might add up, he felt it less easy to laugh at the heavy horrors than to quail before them. He couldn't describe and dismiss them collectively, call them either Mid-Victorian or Early; not being at all sure they were rangeable under one rubric. It was only manifest they were splendid and were furthermore conclusively British. They constituted an order and they abounded in rare material – precious woods, metals, stuffs, stones. He had never dreamed of anything so fringed and scalloped, so buttoned and corded, drawn everywhere so tight, and curled everywhere so thick. He had never dreamed of so much gilt and glass, so much satin and plush, so much rosewood and marble and malachite. But it was, above all, the solid forms, the wasted finish, the misguided cost, the general attestation of morality and money, a good conscience and a big balance.

Outside, on the wide opulent Exhibition Road, H.G. Wells, James's friend, had young George Ponderevo in *Tono-Bungay* contemplate the Kensington scene:

> It shone, pale amber, blue-gray, and tenderly spacious and fine under clear autumnal skies, a London of hugely handsome buildings and vistas and distances, a London

of gardens and labyrinthine tall museums, of old trees
and remote palaces and artificial waters.

The South Kensington Science Museum seems to have
helped instigate Wells's *The Work, Wealth and Happiness of
Mankind*, one of those volumes which made him, for thousands, a one-man university determined to change the world:

> We spent an hour or so over the development of the steam
> engine; we went on to the story of the ship. Then we
> went up to the evolution of optical science. My friend
> began to show signs of brain fag. We went to that central
> place on the top floor which gives a glimpse of all the
> floors and galleries. 'This is fascinating,' said my friend,
> 'but it isn't like reading a history or a novel. It doesn't
> take you on from a beginning to an end. It's a multitude
> of strands woven together. Each one is different, but
> they all go the same way. I would like you to tell
> me now what it is all about; to take me to this exhibit
> or that to illustrate this point or that, but I have no
> use for it all. I like to know it is here. I like to know
> what the main divisions are. But nobody sane would
> want to explore all these galleries, just as nobody sane
> would dream of reading through an encyclopaedia from
> beginning to end. This stuff is for reference. You tell
> me what it is all about – if you can.

In his book, Wells attempted to do so.
Other writers abounded between the High Street and Not-
ting Hill Gate. One of them, Patricia Hutchins, was living in
Kensington after the Great War:

> The gaiety of bands in the street was offset by the
> first sight of a mutilated man, hat held out for pennies.
> This one had known something of the same London as
> Ezra Pound – its smell of horses and cars, and curtained
> houses with cedarwood boxes, conservatories, knife-
> cleaner powder, maids in white uniform, those bobbled
> mantlepieces loaded with curiosities, and, after shopping,
> tea in the brown, steaming comfort of an ABC.

Kensington, like all areas, hides as much as it reveals: domestic tensions, racial and political conflicts, social grievances and ambitions. Angus Wilson trained a colder eye on a Kensington of nervy social relations and dislocations under the 1945 Labour government, in his story 'Saturnalia' set in Mendel Court Hotel:

> There was no doubt that the first hour of the staff dance had proved very sticky; servants and guests just wouldn't mix. Chef had started the evening in the customary way, by leading out Mrs Hyde-Green, and the Commander had shown the young chaps the way to do it in a foxtrot with Miss Tarrant, the receptionist. But these conventional exchanges had somehow only created greater inhibitions, a class barrier of ice seemed to be forming and though a few of the more determinedly matey both of masters and men ventured from time to time into this frozen no man's land they were soon driven back by the cold blasts of deadened conversation. A thousand comparisons were made between this year's streamers and last year's fairylights; every measurement possible and impossible was conjectured for the length of the lounge; it would have verged on irony to have deplored even once more the absence through illness of the head waitress who had been such a sport the year before – by nine o'clock the rift was almost complete.

In *Life at the Top* John Braine's affluent but disillusioned Joe Lampton visits London from the North, and pauses in Kensington for a moment of desolation.

> Kensington High Street seemed deserted; I wondered gloomily where everyone went at night. When I was younger there always seemed to be a lot of people about; now there were only cars. When you came close to them you saw there was always someone in the driving-seat; but it wouldn't always be so. One day they'd drive themselves without passengers, to whatever destination cars choose for themselves and we'd all hide indoors waiting

for them to pass. But they'd never stop passing; it was like watching Chinese march by.

This is another glimpse of that further London, just beyond reach, which all writers periodically experience. Cheerful is a recollection by Susan Hill who, in the early 1960s, was a student in South Kensington. Contributing to Alan Ross's *Living in London*, published in 1974, she revives youthful sensations:

In the space of a single October weekend, every idea I had received was knocked aside. I saw a new heaven and a new earth and my way of looking at the world has been different ever since. I am proud, too, that I discovered Victorian buildings entirely by and for myself. I had no idea that they had become quite fashionable. I had not then heard of Betjeman . . . The first, amazing moment of that revelatory weekend came as I walked past the Albert Memorial one Saturday afternoon. It was intensely cold, with a glazed blue sky and a very bright, still sun, rimmed with frost. The edges of all the buildings were razor-sharp. As I went by the Memorial, I saw how beautiful was the curve of Albert's back, against the light. It startled me. I turned, and saw the Albert Hall, round as a cake, and decorated like one, too, with its stiff, graceful friezes. Scales (about which I had also read) dropped from my eyes. I walked on, up to the Round Pond, to watch the boats sail about on the glassy black water. When I came back again, the Memorial and the Hall were the same, my eyes had not cheated me. Much later, I looked out of my window, high above the Cromwell Road. The last of the sun was right behind the rose-red brick of the Natural History Museum, and I saw that it, too, was beautiful. I opened the window and leaned out and looked down the long road, towards the dome of Brompton Oratory, and the V and A. They were all beautiful. It was the first, real, visual discovery of my life.

EARL'S COURT

Stately Kensington leads into Earl's Court, a gaudy mass
of boarding-houses, brothels, cafés, cosmopolitan loafers, amateur revolutionaries, strident disc jockeys, pushers, hookers,
polyglot tongues and regional accents, far-ranging students
and smartish beggars. Also in *Living in London* is the late
Shiva Naipaul, Trinidadian novelist and traveller, who once
sojourned there: 'It is uncompromisingly urban, a conglomeration of solitary individuals. Relinquishing responsibility, it
offers frenzy. Therein lies its attraction. Nothing is permanent
in Earl's Court.'

With experience of London not at its best – 'Room to Let
Kolored Pipple need not apply' – in Notting Hill, Stockwell,
Fulham and Ladbroke Grove, Naipaul retained forbearing
humour, observing the offers in shop windows:

> Grounded Air Hostess Seeks New Position.
>   Chocolate Baby Teaches French. Very strict.
> Handsome Young Man Willing to Walk Dog.

Travelling through Salzburg, Hilaire Belloc refused to leave
his train to see the city where Mozart had worked, explaining
that it reminded him of Earl's Court.

KNIGHTSBRIDGE AND CHELSEA

Between Piccadilly and Kensington is Knightsbridge, its broad
road covering a medieval plague pit. From here, reaching
south towards the river, Sloane Square and Chelsea, Cadogan
Gardens passes the Cadogan Hotel, with its tall, rounded turret
and stone curlicues, where Oscar Wilde's arrest is mordantly
imagined by Betjeman:

> Mr Wilde, we 'ave come for tew take yew
>   Where felons and criminals dwell;
> We must ask yew to leave with us quoietly
>   For this *is* the Cadogan Hotel.

He rose, and he put down THE YELLOW BOOK.
  He staggered – and, terrible-eyed,
He brushed past the palms on the staircase
And was helped to a hansom outside.

The Gardens end at Sloane Square, Chelsea. Here, at the Court Theatre between 1904 and 1907, Granville-Barker and Shaw, in alliance with J.E. Vedrenne, first attempted to align British drama with the most advanced in Europe. Years later, they had not totally succeeded. In 1924, Arnold Bennett's Journal shows he attended the first night at the Court of Shaw's *Back to Methuselah*:

Walls of box dead black and of stone. We could see the empty orchestra, and the nakedness of Adam and Eve. Curtain going up announced by a sort of clash of a cymbal. I was very bored by the play, I could see nothing in it; neither action nor character nor a sermon nor wit. The game of finding new words played by the characters seemed silly. It was too far round to go to smoke in the interval, so we stayed in our tomb. In the second act I went to sleep and had to be wakened for fear a snore might be heard on the stage. A most depressing night.

Bennett might have been more entertained by a private performance in 1886 by the Shelley Society of their poet's banned play, *The Cenci*, though, according to Shaw, writing in the *Star*: 'The critic William Archer slept very soundly, then fell forward flat on his face with a tremendous noise, leaving a dent in the floor which may still be seen by curious visitors.'

West from Sloane Square, on either side of the King's Road, parallel to the river, is Chelsea Village. Thomas More's statue stands near the river, Smollett lived here, there are memories of Carlyle and Swinburne, Rossetti, Turner, Whistler, George Eliot and G.H. Lewes, of Wilde and Henry James.

Readers of Boswell's *London Journal* might be perplexed, without editorial assistance. On 9 June 1763:

At night I went to Chelsea and saw Johnson ride, standing upon one and then two horses at full gallop, with all his feats of agility. I was highly diverted. It was a true English entertainment. The horses moved about to the tune of 'Shilinagarie', for music, such as it is, makes always a part of John Bull's amusement.

The Chelsea Johnson was, of course, a celebrated professional equestrian.

The Cremorne Pleasure Gardens in Chelsea were very popular until they closed in 1877. Gathering material for his book on prostitution, the Victorian sociologist William Acton discovered little:

A jolly burst of laughter now and then came bounding through the crowd that fringed the dancing-floor and roved about the adjacent sheds in search of company; but that gone by, you heard very plainly the sigh of the poplar, the surging gossip of the tulip-tree, and the plash of the little embowered fountain that served two plaster children for an endless shower-bath. The RATUS PUELLA RISUS was put in a corner with a vengeance, under a colder shade than that of chastity itself, and the function of the very band appeared to be to drown not noise, but stillness.

Nearby, at 16, Tite Street, lived Oscar and Constance Wilde, as their son Vyvyan Holland recalled:

To the right of the front door . . . was my father's study, in which most of his work was done, and a table that had once belonged to Carlyle. The motif of this room was red and yellow, the walls being painted pale yellow and the woodwork enamelled red; on a red column in one corner stood a cast of the Hermes of Praxiteles. A few small pictures hung upon the walls; a Simeon Solomon, a Monticelli, and Beardsley's exquisite drawing of Mrs Patrick Campbell. But most of the wall-space was occupied by the bookshelves, filled with copies of the Greek and Latin Classics, French literature, and presentation copies of the works of contemporary authors. It was a place of awe, and it was sacrosanct; a place in the vicinity of which no noise was to be made, and which must only be passed on tiptoe. When my father was there we were not allowed into it except by special invitation; and even when he was not in the house it had a sort of 'A' certificate attached to it, in that we were forbidden to enter it unless accompanied by an adult. Whenever my brother and I did manage to penetrate into this Holy of Holies, we always made straight for the waste-paper basket in search of treasure trove. The basket was often half full of discarded manuscript for which collectors would probably fight one another to-day; and there were gaily-coloured boxes that once held cigarettes and had a lovely grown-up smell. Waste-paper baskets seem to have a fascination for all children . . .

It was from my father's study that the hooligans stole everything that they could lay their hands upon when he lay in prison and we were in exile.

Hilaire Belloc's quatrain 'On Chelsea' still squares with the bright-garbed, talkative groups in the King's Road:

> I am assured by Dauber's wife
> That Dauber's always true to life.
> I think his wife would far prefer
> That Dauber should be true to her.

This road was not seen at its brightest in an episode involving Edith Wharton and Henry James. Devoted to the Master, Mrs Wharton must have had her full share of the untoward and exasperating. In *A Backward Glance* she recounted how she strove to direct an inexperienced chauffeur:

While I was hesitating and peering out into the darkness James spied an ancient doddering man who had stopped in the rain to gaze at us.

'Wait a moment, my dear – I'll ask him where we are'; and leaning out he signalled to the spectator.

'My good man, if you'll be good enough to come here, please; a little nearer – so,' and as the old man came up: 'My friend, to put it to you in two words, this lady and I have just arrived here from *Slough*; that is to say, to be more strictly accurate, we have recently *passed through* Slough on our way here, having actually motored to Windsor from Rye, which was our point of departure; and the darkness having overtaken us, we should be much obliged if you would tell us where we are now in relation, say, to the High Street, which, as you of course know, leads to the Castle, after leaving on the left hand turn down to the railway station.'

I was not surprised to have this extraordinary appeal met by silence, and a dazed expression on the old wrinkled face at the window; nor to have James go on: 'In short' (his invariable prelude to a fresh series of explanatory ramifications), 'in short, my good man, what I want to put to you in a word is this: supposing we have already (as I have reason to think we have) driven past the turn down to the railway station (which in that case, by the way, would probably not have been on our left hand, but on our right) where are we now in relation to – '

'Oh, please,' I interrupted, feeling myself unable to sit through another parenthesis, 'do ask him where the King's Road is.'

'Ah – ? The King's Road? Quite right! Can you, as a matter of fact, my good man, tell us where, in relation to our present position, the King's Road exactly is?'

'Ye're in it,' said the aged face at the window.

In 1930, Vera Brittain and Winifred Holtby were living in Glebe Place, Chelsea, described in Vera Brittain's *Testament of Friendship*:

Whenever we were not working, or entertaining, or visiting friends, or consoling relatives, Winifred and I went for walks in Battersea Park or along Chelsea Embankment. For the first year or two we also struggled with the garden, conscientiously sowing seeds, tugging the heavy roller, or planting cuttings . . . But try as we would the flowers refused to grow, and thanks to cats, slugs, small active feet and the marks of toy wheel-barrows and perambulators, the oblong of tussocky grass resisted all our efforts to turn it into a lawn. In the end we gave it up and, like other Chelsea and Battersea residents, adopted the Old English Garden in Battersea Park as our private Elysium. Whenever we were tired or sought peace from interrupters we ran to it across the suspension bridge, and it always consoled us. Each time we saw it we felt inclined to cry: 'But this is the best yet!'

In May, the flame and crimson of giant tulips blazed from the scented shadow of lavender-blue lilac and snow-white hawthorn. In October, enormous dahlias in sulphur, crimson, magenta and scarlet made a wild clamour of audacious colour against shoulder-high Michaelmas daisies in every shade of mauve from royal purple to the faintest off-white. Even in winter the garden possessed its gusty exhilaration of wind, sea-birds, flying petals and scuttling leaves. On summer Sundays the fountain played, the bronze goldfish slid like flaming quicksilver beneath the pink-petalled, golden-hearted water-lilies, and poor but exuberant Chelsea lovers shared the spectacle with overworked Battersea mothers as proudly as if they were exhibiting their own garden. Watching them crowd down the narrow gravelled path to the crazy paving between the flower-beds, and observing on every face the same shock of surprised delight in the glory of this communal treasure, we would whisper triumphantly to each other: 'The Revolution has come!'

Stephen Gardiner, architect and critic, has known Chelsea since boyhood. In a *London Magazine* essay he comments:

How lucky one was, brought up in the leafy lanes of Chelsea and Kensington. How lucky one is, for that matter, to be around there still. As the past with its squares and avenues dissolves into the present it is sur-prising to find so few changes – The structure of the neighbourhood remains intact; what differences there are seem to have more to do with personal experiences . . . than any redevelopments of the last twenty years.

The factors that bring Chelsea, in particular, into sharp human focus are still there, despite a good deal of commercialisation. It's the mix that is so important, and this is also a characteristic of London as a whole. It is full of surprises; walk through darkest Fulham and you suddenly hit the river and a view of country: take a tube through the slums and desolate point blocks of Stratford and Leyton and five minutes later you are within a stone's throw of the unspoilt paradise of Epping Forest. Chelsea's like a microcosm of this; cross the Fulham Road and Edwardian heaviness vanishes up the sleeve of the Regency cottage architecture of Old Church Street: walk on to Chelsea Bridge with the howls of the Battersea Dog Home in your ears and there is the Royal Hospital by Wren, one of the most magnificent pieces of building in England; turn a corner off the embankment with some marvellous eighteenth-century terraces in your mind and the street narrows to a cul-de-sac of cottages, a run-down church and a state-school. Late nineteenth-century Victorian red-brick overlooks the best in Upper Cheyne Row, and the best in Upper Cheyne Row overlooks a school playground. This is the mixture on which Chelsea thrives rather than survives . . .

A few large elements hold the bits of the fragile picture in position. There is the river, the decisive finish to the long walk downhill from Hampstead Heath. The maze of little streets and small squares suddenly open up into the enormous space of slow moving water, the great curve round Wandsworth on the right and Battersea Park straight ahead.

8

PICCADILLY CIRCUS TO NOTTING HILL

We have taken the details of classical pediment and
swag, the bric-a-brac pillaged from the ruins of
the past, and made New Regent Streets of them.

Alasdair Clayre

REGENT STREET

Though with fine streets and squares on both sides, Regent
Street's past is virtually obliterated, and its present is a mass
of depersonalized commerce. George Augustus Sala, a colleague of Dickens, remembered, in *Twice Round the Clock*
(1859), the colonnades and strict proportions of Nash's Old
Regent Street, its classical columns and porticoes, its serene
curve towards Oxford Circus, its secluded courtyards:

There was a delightful bird-stuffer's shop at the corner of
a court, with birds of paradise, parrots, and humming-
birds of gorgeous plumage, and strange creatures with
white bodies and long yellow beaks and legs that terrified
while they pleasured us. Then there was the funeral
monument shop, with the mural tablets, the obelisks,
the broken columns, the extinguished torches, and the
draped urns in the window, and some with the inscriptions into the bargain, all ready engraved in black and
white. There was Swan and Edgar's, (with a real Mr Swan
and a real Mr Edgar) . . . How many times have I listened
to the enthusiastic cheers of Swan and Edgar's young

men on the occasion of the proprietors giving their annual banquet to their employees?

Old Regent Street had an atmosphere different from that of the genteel, polyglot shoppers thronging it today. Nearly a century later, Mrs Robert Henrey added:

Those were the days when Regent Street abounded in gambling houses with their regiments of rogues, called 'Greeks', who decoyed strangers into their abominable dens. The judases, the smoke-blackened ceilings, the dark-panelled walls, the guttering tallow candles shedding their light on the green tables – those grasping hands, those bloodshot eyes staring at the dice with incipient madness; these nightmares require an effort of the imagination . . .

At the time Sala wrote about, there were bakers' shops, stationers, and opticians who had models of steam-engines in their windows. The little grocers sold marmalade, brown sugar, and Durham mustard. You could buy a penny cake of chocolate. There were music shops, shawl shops, jewellers, French glove shops, perfumery, and point lace shops, confectioners, and milliners.

Soon the little shawl shop became a vast, palatial building with marble pillars supporting the roof, mirrors lining the walls, turkey carpets covering the floor, and eastern vases adorning the windows.

Mrs Henrey evokes a later era, Christmas 1947. In Regent Street:

Across the road the lights of Dickins and Jones glittered on the damp pavement of this warm drizzly evening, and beckoned one inside to admire the riches of this magnificent store with its high walls, half cedar wood, half cream, its huge Christmas Tree with the fairy waving her wand on the topmost branch, and its masses of daffodils, which even decorated the smart little desks of the chief saleswomen. There was a delicious smell of fir-tree, spring flowers, and Lanvin's Arpège, which for some reason seemed to dominate all the other perfumes from the great French fashion houses. But most tempting and disturbing of all were the moirés with silver threads running through their rich texture, the satin brocades, the velvets, the pure silks, and the cotton zephyrs from Lyons which gleamed and shimmered and spread their enticing folds all round one, inviting one to turn them into dresses for every occasion.

E.M. Forster was less enchanted with this avenue of stone and glass. In an essay, 'London is a Muddle' (1951), he sighs:

> If you want a muddle, look around you as you walk from Piccadilly Circus to Oxford Circus. Here are ornaments that do not adorn, features that feature nothing, flatness, meanness, uniformity without harmony, bigness without size. Even when the shops are built at the same moment, they manage to contradict one another.

Oxford Circus itself cuts across Regent Street, separating it from its upper reaches and Broadcasting House, alongside which, until its destruction by German bombs, was the Queen's Hall, famous for its music, particularly the Promenade Concerts, though it also housed literary events. Frank Swinnerton, born in 1884, heard debates there from the age of about sixteen:

> Sometimes Shaw would debate with Chesterton, sometimes with Belloc; once, I recall, he debated with Chesterton while Belloc took the chair and rang an infuriating bell; on another occasion he met Belloc in the large Queen's Hall, when an audience of three thousand heard these two discuss the question of whether a Democrat who was not also a Socialist could possibly be a Gentleman, and came away with the problem unsolved after two hours of resolute hard hitting.

OXFORD STREET AND MARBLE ARCH

Of Oxford Street De Quincey lamented in 1821: 'stony-hearted stepmother: thou that listenest to the sighs of orphans and drinkest the tears of children'.

Peter Ackroyd's fictional Oscar Wilde remarks that it is all Street and no Oxford. Like Regent Street it is another avenue of shops, with nothing to linger over, admire and absorb, though it has escape passages, into the squares of Mayfair and Marylebone. A memory flickers of Byron being born in Holles Street in 1788, where the John Lewis Company built an emporium, wrecked by wartime bombs; of Gibbon living awhile in Bentinck Street, Cavendish Square, 'in a small house between a street and a stableyard'. Thomas Hardy's verse, from his early poem, 'Coming up Oxford Street: Evening', envisaged:

A city clerk, with eyesight not of the best,
Who sees no escape to the very verge of his days.
From the rut of Oxford Street into open ways;
And he goes along with head and eyes flagging forlorn,
Empty of interest in things, and wondering why he was
                                                                                    born.

These lines contain youth's muffled rebelliousness, packed into a grey shadow, into a few lines. Claustrophobia, from traffic, from department stores, is finally relieved when the sky broadens over Marble Arch and Hyde Park North, where Speakers' Corner has attracted audiences for well over a century, replacing Primrose Hill.

Marble Arch, of course, covers the old Tyburn gallows. In his anthology, *London is London*, D.M. Low recalls the writer John Thomas Smith and his *Nollekens and his Times* (1829):

I remember well, when I was in my eighth year, Mr Nollekens calling at my father's house in Great Portland Street, and taking me to Oxford-road to see the notorious Jack Rann, common called 'Sixteen-string Jack', go to Tyburn to be hanged for robbing Dr William Bell, in Gunnersbury Lane, of his watch and eighteen-pence in money; for which he received sentence of death on Tuesday the 26th of October 1774. The criminal was dressed in a pea-green coat, with an immense nosegay in the button-holes, which had been presented to him at St Sepulchre's Steps; and his nankin small-clothes, we are told, were tied at each knee with sixteen strings. After he had passed, and Mr Nollekens was leading me home by the hand, I recalled his stooping down to me, and observing, in a low tone of voice, 'Tom, now, my little man, if my father-in-law, Mr Justice Welch, had been High-Constable, we could have walked by the side of the cart all the way to Tyburn.'

Until 1783, Tyburn Tree overshadowed much of London's sensational literature and private thoughts. Though an assiduous attender of public executions, 'the attractions of repulsion', Dickens was foremost in striving for their abolition, partly through his belief that they pandered to the exhibitionist tendencies of criminals.

With the removal of the gallows the area became more gentrified, with prosperous houses and hotels replacing rookeries and low taverns. Norman Collins, in *London Belongs to Me*, enthuses:

The crowds at Marble Arch actually stop where they are – whereas at Piccadilly Circus everyone is always on the way to somewhere else. Choose any fine summer evening and at the Marble Arch you'll find a crowd of several hundred people standing about greedily savouring the simple but tremendous pleasure of merely being there. It's a good spot. As dusk falls, the Park in the background becomes vast and mysterious, and the gas lamps that light your way along the main paths dwindle into the distance like lanterns in Illyria. But somehow or other it remains London, with the buses that cruise up Park Lane twinkling through the railings, and the air filled with the roar and rustle of innumerable wheels. Yes, it's London all right. But it's also somewhere right outside it. Sufficiently far out for you to be able to look up into the sky as the dusk deepens and see the gigantic

upturned bowl of brightness that the West End has
erected above itself. You can, in fact, stand at the Marble
Arch and be just wherever you want to be, in London
or in the country. That's the magic of the place. Or
rather, that's how it was in 1939.

BAYSWATER

Along the north side of the Park, leading directly from Marble
Arch, Bayswater Road extends to Notting Hill. A few yards
north of it, covered by tennis courts and houses and probably
unknown to Galsworthy's Forsytes, assembling at Uncle
Timothy's in this road, is an ancient burial-ground. Here lay
Laurence Sterne, of whom V.S. Pritchett has written that
he constantly reckoned up how much he was going to feel
before he felt it.

Yellowy stuccoed hotels dominate Bayswater, and thick
blocks of flats. The Forsytes have departed, yet in any age
one can never be certain of what, or who, may wait behind a
dim window or tight door. In 1923, Harold Acton visited lofty
Pembridge Villas, Moscow Road, a few steps off Bayswater
Road. In his *Memoirs of an Aesthete*, Sir Harold describes his
ascent:

> One climbed forever, pitying anyone forced to live in
> such an eyrie. Remembering the magnificence of her
> father's mansion at Montegufoni, rising above an ocean
> of olive groves and vineyards, I wondered at the contrast.
> The view of chimney-pots and slate roofs from the
> window of her small sitting-room had been standardized
> by the London Group of Painters.

His hostess was Edith Sitwell. In his book on the Sitwells,
John Lehmann comments:

> Harold Acton's heart sank at what seemed the utter
> joylessness of these surroundings, particularly on a raw
> December morning. The atmosphere changed, however,
> when Edith Sitwell glided into the room in a dress of

emerald brocade. 'A rare jewel, a hieratic figure in Limoges enamel,' I thought, 'clamped in some biscuit box, but rarer, more hieratic against this background.' The pale oval face with its almond eyes and long thin nose had often been carved in ivory by true believers. Her entire figure possessed a distinction seldom to be seen outside the glass cases of certain museums.

WEST LONDON HOSTESSES

By Holland Park Avenue, between Notting Hill Gate and Addison Road, one wing of Holland House, begun in 1607, survives from the Second World War air-raids: not so the Long Gallery, where Addison himself is said, during periods of composition, to have placed a bottle of wine at each end to fortify his imagination. The park of Holland House remains, with its arched loggias and trees, its herbaceous flowers glowing within box-hedge symmetries, and its peacocks. In *The Crying Game*, John Braine's narrator maintains: 'Of all London parks it was the most private in atmosphere, the one furthest away from the twentieth century.'

If ladies were not foremost in clubs, foremost ladies could be dominant in their own mansions – Holland House and Gore House, then Londonderry House and Grosvenor House – out of their own interest, often too in their husbands' interests, making something of an art of entertaining, encouraging conversation and wit, and patronizing the arts. They were not always suitably rewarded. One hostess, while dispensing Dr Johnson twenty-five cups of tea, received in return less than that number of words.

Rivals of Lady Blessington and Count d'Orsay at Gore House, Lord, and particularly Lady Holland, devotee of Napoleon, reigned at Holland House. In his biography of Byron, Peter Quennell compares her tyranny to that of Proust's Madame Verdurin. Here could be met, amongst many gaggles of celebrities, literary and political, Samuel Rogers, poet, conjurer, snob, giver of breakfast parties, and who, Quennell adds, 'if one borrowed five hundred pounds from him, would control his natural spitefulness until one came to pay it back'.

Lady Holland, 'the Witch' in Carlyle's letters, did not cringe before big names. Dickens could have seen her halting Rogers in full torrent: 'Your poetry is bad enough so pray be sparing of your prose', or, 'Never bring any more of your guests to Holland House who are not blessed with bridges to their noses' – discharged at a friend who had ventured to introduce a popular author lacking that amenity.

Una Pope-Hennessy describes an evening under the more casual Blessington–d'Orsay regime, at Gore House, nearer Kensington:

Mr Disraeli, who when worked up talked 'like a racehorse approaching a winning post,' one evening described Beckford's *Italy* and went on to tell of its author's fantastical life at Bath where he was said to own two houses joined by a covered bridge, his servants living on one side and he and his companion, a Spanish dwarf, 'who believes himself a duke and is treated as such on the other.' Then he told of a high tower lined with books and of a grave below the pavement in which he was arranging a double sepulchre for himself and the dwarf. Victor Hugo and his newest books also came in for discussion, champagne flowed, and all the while d'Orsay kept up the conversation by a running fire of witty parantheses in French and English. Usually silent and often aloof, in a corner of the saloon sat Prince Louis Napoleon, the future Emperor of the French.

From a debt-laden London exile, through two imprisonments and an imperial extravaganza, the Prince achieved not only a final exile but also a transformation into literature: in at least some of Disraeli's 'King Florestan' in *Endymion* and in all of Browning's *Prince Hohenstiel-Schwangau*, a poetic monologue in which he defends his career with dignity and intelligence to a courtesan in Leicester Square:

The world knows something of my ups and downs . . .
King, all the better he was cobbler once,
He should know sitting on the throne, how tastes
Life to who sweeps the doorway.

Browning has him confess:

> But life's hard,
> Occasion rare; you cut probation short,
> And being half-instructed, on the stage
> You shuffle through your part as best you can,
> And bless your stars as I do.

Louis Napoleon wrote considerably: on poverty, artillery, canals, Bonapartism, Julius Caesar; he contemplated a novel, and he began a History of England which like so many of his intentions and indeed utterances remained uncompleted. Surviving fragments suggest that in that corner at Gore House he may have been thinking more than his sleepy demeanour suggested. For that projected history he wrote: 'The history of England says very clearly to kings: March at the head of the ideas of your century, and these ideas follow and support you. March behind them, and they drag you after them. March against them, and they will overthrow you.'

Glamour can derive from distance. In his *Encounter* memoirs, 'One of my Londons', Cyril Connolly remembered Logan Pearsall Smith saying that

> Holland House must have been terribly dull. He had met in his youth one of the survivors of that world where the conversation used to consist of long monologues which displayed your general knowledge and reading (in the case of the survivor, Aberdare, his topic was the route of Alexander's Indian expedition) while all the other old gentlemen sat around like croquet-players, waiting to cut in at the first cough.

The salons did not vanish with Lady Blessington and Lady Holland, both dead by 1850. In 1917 Virginia Woolf wrote of the London encountered by the young American Henry James, nearly fifty years before:

> The main facts about that London, as all witnesses agree in testifying, were its smallness compared with our city, the limited number of distractions and amusements

available, and the consequent tendency of all people worth knowing to know each other and to form a very accessible and, at the same time, highly enviable society. Whatever the quality that gained you admittance, whether it was that you had done something or showed yourself capable of doing something worthy of respect, the compliment was not an empty one. A young man coming up to London might in a few months claim to have met Tennyson, Browning, Matthew Arnold, Carlyle, Froude, George Eliot, Herbert Spencer, Huxley and Mill. He had met them; he had even offered something of his own. The conditions of those days allowed a kind of conversation which, so the survivors always maintain, is an art unknown in what they are pleased to call our chaos. What with recurring dinner parties and Sunday calls, the country visits lasting far beyond the week-ends of our generation, the fabric of friendship was solidly built up and carefully preserved. The tendency perhaps was rather to a good fellowship in which the talk was wide-sweeping, extremely well-informed, and impersonal than to the less formal, perhaps more intense and indiscriminate intimacies of to-day. We read of little societies of the sixties, the Cosmopolitan and the Century, meeting on Wednesday and on Sunday evenings to discuss the serious questions of the times, and we have the feeling that they could claim a more representative character than anything of the sort we can show now. We are left with the impression that whatever went forward in those days, either among the statesmen or among the men of letters – and there was a closer connection than there now is – was prompted or inspired by members of this group. Undoubtedly the resources of the day – and how magnificent they were! – were better organised; and it must recur to every reader of their memoirs that a reason is to be found in the simplicity which accepted the greatness of certain names and imposed something like order on their immediate neighbourhood. Having crowned their king they worshipped him with most wholehearted loyalty. Groups of people would come together at Freshwater, in that old garden where the

houses of Melbury Road now stand, or in various London
centres, and live as it seems to us for months at a time,
some indeed for the duration of their lives, in the mood
of the presiding genius. Watts and Burne-Jones in one
quarter of the town, Carlyle in another, George Eliot in
a third, almost as much as Tennyson in his island,
imposed their laws upon a circle which had spirit and
beauty to recommend it as well as an uncritical devotion.

Of the next literary generation, J.B. Priestley continues the
theme, in *Delight*:

When I first settled in London, in the early nineteen-
twenties, it was still the fashion for literary hostesses
to give very large evening parties, to which all manner
of writers, old or young, famous or unknown were
invited . . . It is quite possible that the disappearance
of these parties, and the consequent lack of any spacious
meeting ground for old and young writers, the established
and the newly arrived, has helped to disintegrate, almost
to atomise our literary life. And certainly their absence
has robbed newcomers to London, the lads who are
now in the position I was in 1922, of one peculiar bit
of delight. This came from suddenly finding oneself in
the same room as the celebrities of one's profession. There
you were – the fellow-guest of giants, of figures that
were almost mythological. There they were – eating and
drinking and chattering, solid beings existing in the
same world. If it came to a push – though you would
be well advised not to try – you could actually offer a
whisky-and-soda and a ham sandwich to Bernard Shaw.
Just when the voice of H.G. Wells was rising to a
coloratura height of derision, you could crash in and
contradict him. You could steal up to Arnold Bennett
and whisper balefully that he was old-fashioned. There
was nothing, except your reverence for that commanding
personage, to prevent your asking W.B. Yeats to use
his imagination. Belloc and Chesterton, in full stride
over the Pyrenees and blowing the horn of Roland, could
be halted with a demand for them to define their terms.

None of these would have been wise moves, but they could have been made, as you realised to your delight, just because there, not two plates of sandwiches away, were the genuine monsters themselves. I will admit that circumstances were different then. Our literary values were more stable. As a youngster, before 1914, I had read and revered these writers, who occupied far more space, just because there was more space to spare in those easy old days, than any writers do now. It was much easier then to create the legends. Their figures had not to be seen against to-day's towering background, lit with hell-fire or world drama. The stage on which they played was domestic and easy.

Such assemblies were usually genial, stimulating and also free. However, there were other West London hostesses on hand: in his poem, 'The Harlot's House', Oscar Wilde shows a scene familiar enough in Bayswater and Notting Hill, Kensington and Chelsea, and indeed in almost all London's 'villages':

> Like strange mechanical grotesques,
> Making fantastic arabesques
> The shadows raced across the blind.
>
> We watched the ghostly dancers spin
> To sound of horn and violin,
> Like black leaves wheeling in the wind,
>
> Like wire-pulled automatons,
> Slim silhouetted skeletons
> Went sidling through the slow quadrille.
>
> They took each other by the hand,
> And danced a stately saraband;
> Their laughter echoed thin and shrill.
>
> Sometimes a clockwork puppet pressed
> A phantom lover to her breast;
> Sometimes they seemed to try to sing.

> Sometimes a horrible marionette
> Came out and smoked a cigarette
> Upon the steps like a live thing.

NOTTING HILL

Macaulay lived at Notting Hill in Holly Lodge during his last years. Laurence Hutton saw the house:

> Holly Lodge, now [1976] called Airlie Lodge, occupies the most secluded corner of the little labyrinth of by-roads, which, bounded to the east by Palace Gardens and to the west by Holland House, constitutes the district known as Campden Hill. The villa – for villa it is – stands in a long and winding land, with its high back paling, concealing from the passer-by everything except the mass of dense and varied foliage, [and] presents an appearance as rural as Streatham presented twenty years ago.

Early in this century, around Notting Hill, gathered young literary trouble-makers, scenting new attitudes, then creating them – 'the first organised youth racket', Wyndham Lewis asserted. One resident, Ford Madox Ford, remarked in 1913: 'I would rather read a picture in verse of the emotions of a Goodge Street anarchist than recapture the song the sirens sang.'

His mistress, Violet Hunt, was a novelist and friend of Ruskin, Browning and Dante Gabriel Rossetti. The young journalist and biographer Douglas Goldring would visit her house, South Lodge, on Campden Hill, between Holland Avenue and Kensington High Street:

> Up to 1914 young men who paid formal calls or went to Sunday tea parties had to wear top hats and 'London clothes' and to carry gloves and canes. At South Lodge – before the incursion of Ford Madox Ford and Ezra Pound – these proprieties were rigidly enforced . . .
> The transformation of South Lodge from a rather stuffy and conventional Campden Hill villa, into a stamping ground for *les jeunes* was brought about far more by

Ezra Pound than by Ford. Ezra's irreverence towards
Eminent Literary Figures was a much needed corrective
to Ford's excessive veneration for those of them he elected
to admire . . .

Of Ezra, in those days, Ford remarks: 'His Philadel-
phian accent was comprehensible if disconcerting; his
beard and flowing locks were auburn and luxuriant; he
was astonishingly meagre and agile. He threw himself
alarmingly into frail chairs, devoured enormous quantities
of your pastry, fixed his pince-nez firmly on his nose,
drew out a manuscript from his pocket, threw his head
back, closed his eyes to point of invisibility and, looking
down his nose, would chuckle like Mephistopheles and
read you a translation from Arnaut Daniel.

Bridget Patmore witnessed Pound's first meeting with his
fellow-Imagist, Richard Aldington, at South Lodge.

Ezra was gentle and fatherly until the name of Milton was
brought up to support an aggressive claim of Richard's.

'That confounded rhetorical old blank, blank son of
a so-and-so,' Ezra ground out through set teeth. 'No, my
dear fellow, you're far away on the wrong track. Give
them all up. Throw them away! Don't you realise that
an Englishman's brain clamps down when he's twenty-
one and never opens to admit an idea after that? Those
people are poison, you must keep alive and find what's
in yourself.'

Pound's habitual nonchalance reminded her of the pianist,
Paderewski, with his 'extremely slow, calm advance on a
platform to receive the wave of applause'.

At one of Ford's parties, Douglas Goldring saw

a little quiet grey old man wearing a red tie, who turned
out to be Thomas Hardy. I was standing next to Hugh
Walpole at the back of the room, when he was pointed
out to me. The conversation among the lion cubs in our
neighbourhood was no doubt very brilliant and very
'literary' but suddenly there came the usual inexplicable

hush. It was broken by Hardy who, turning to an elderly lady by his side, remarked with shattering effect
    'And how is Johnny's whooping cough?'

Wyndham Lewis, at Notting Hill, was Pound's friend, colleague and sparring partner. Founder of Vorticism, with its fierce upthrusting strokes, he painted the American, in the portrait now in the Tate. Like Pound, he was prepared to bait all comers, particularly famous middle-brows, and frequently did so, notably in his short-lived review *Blast* (1914):

Blast Sir Thomas Beecham. Blast the years 1837 to 1900. Blast Croce, Marie Corelli, John Galsworthy, Sidney Webb, the Stracheys, the Meynells, A.C. Benson. Bless George Robey and Harry Weldon, Chaliapin and Gertie Miller, Pope Benedict and castor oil.

His verbal portraits included one of Ford reported by Douglas Goldring:

A flabby lemon and pink giant who hung his mouth open as though he were an animal at the zoo inviting buns – especially when ladies were present. Over the gaping mouth damply depended the ragged ends of a pale lemon moustache.

Literary life has continued here to the present day, in small theatres, which began to disappear after 1950; in literary clubs and bars; in coteries and societies, though it possesses no South Lodge, no hefty quarrels or combative journals.

9

PICCADILLY CIRCUS TO BLOOMSBURY AND ST JOHN'S WOOD

'My dear fellow,' said Sherlock Holmes, as we sat on either side of the fire in his lodgings at Baker Street, 'Life is infinitely stranger than anything which the mind of man could invent. We would not dare to conceive the things which are mere commonplaces of existence. If we could fly out of that window hand in hand, hover over this great city, gently remove the roofs, and peep in at the queer things which are going on, the strange co-incidences, the plannings, the cross-purposes, the wonderful chains of events, working through generations, and leading to the most outré results, it would make all fiction with its convention-alities and foreseen conclusions most stale and unprofitable.

Sir Arthur Conan Doyle, 'A Case of Identity'

SHAFTESBURY AVENUE

Eros in Piccadilly Circus aims down Shaftesbury Avenue, the glittering double line of theatres, shops and restaurants that crosses Cambridge Circus on its way towards Bloomsbury and the north-west. Near Cambridge Circus, bounded by Charing Cross Road and Tottenham Court Road, the streets that invade Soho and Fitzrovia retain a personality more compressed and vivid than those of Shaftesbury Avenue and Leicester Square, flakes of history still giving clues to a lost city.

T.R. Fyvel, editor, journalist, meticulous observer, friend of
Orwell and long-settled immigrant, born in the glum after-
math of the First World War, noted in his *Tribune* column in
1948:

> Most of the Shaftesbury Avenue-Leicester Square triangle
> dates from Victorian days; the region reached a peak of
> night-life during the hey-day of Victorian Music Hall.
> 'Goodbye Piccadilly, farewell Leicester Square' was a
> refrain of the troops in 1914–18; but already by 1939 that
> West End nostalgia sounded age-old. And today,
> bombed, chipped, Shaftesbury Avenue looks third-rate.

The Avenue was repaired, refaced and smartened, but largely
remains a veneer for expensive showbiz, the transitory and the
tawdry. Fyvel added a reminder, still topical, that behind
garish lights and specious invitations is that other, shadowy
London of half-held secrets, alcoves easily overlooked, barely
discovered mementoes, tiny hushed spaces and privacies amid
traffic, pleasure-seekers, drinkers and hooligans:

> Shaftesbury Avenue has its nobler ruins too, such as the
> bombed hulk of the 17th century church of St Anne's,
> Soho. Only the brick belfrey stands, and the two walls.
> But there is a patch of green grass in the small churchyard,
> some struggling trees, and a few benches. One wall, still
> standing, bears an old stone tablet, stating that here, on
> 3 October 1786, 'the completion of the centenary of
> St Anne's was celebrated by a very numerous and respec-
> table meeting of the inhabitants of Soho.' And on the
> other side, there is a memorial tablet of the 1914–18
> War – 'Lest We Forget' – with a list of the names of
> those who died to make it 'possible for others to live in
> freedom.' A bomb in the Second World War knocked off
> the top of the wall, but the tablet was preserved.
>   I went across to the other side. There, among the old,
> worn graves, a few people were sitting on the benches
> under the trees; women were knitting, some children
> playing, while pigeons were pecking among the litter
> where the rubble lies. Most of the older inscriptions on

the weather-worn stones have been washed away. But one
memorial tablet, mid-18th century, is for King Theodore
of Corsica, who 'died immediately after leaving the King's
Bench [Debtor's] Prison on 11 December 1756, in consequence of which he registered his Kingdom of
Corsica for the use of his creditors.' Next to it, a modern
tablet points to the grave of William Hazlitt – died 18
September 1830.

There are yellow tulips round Hazlitt's grave, which
is well tended. As I turned away into the street, I
encountered two young girls in khaki – both military
police, one a girl sergeant, the other a corporal – head
straight, shoulders back, walking in slow, straight step,
as it might be Cumberland's redcoats advancing at
Fontenoy. Their faces under the red caps were girlish;
they wore lipstick; they were laughing away, completely
absorbed in themselves, as only the very young can be,
as they walked with their artificial stride through the
sunshine towards Leicester Square.

SOHO

'Soho' seems to have been a hare-coursing cry. Near here,
north of Soho Square, the Duke of Monmouth had his mansion, and chose 'Soho' for his battle-cry at Sedgemoor, at which
Defoe may have fought, though he covered his tracks well.
Monmouth's ill-timed adventure ended not in courage on a
western plain, nor with a nervous executioner on Tower Hill,
but in a clutch of historical romances, mostly lush; probably
the best are R.D. Blackmore's *Lorna Doone*, Conan Doyle's
Micah Clarke and John Masefield's *Martin Hyde, The Duke's
Messenger*. Monmouth's Soho acreage survives outside today's
Soho in unromantic Monmouth Street.

In Soho itself, streets and restaurants are more obviously
cosmopolitan, their inhabitants Greek, Polish, Chinese, Italian
or French. A mid-Victorian Italian exile, living in Charlotte
Street, Gabriele Rossetti, father of Christina and Dante
Gabriel, became professor of Greek at King's College, London.
The surrounding pubs and cheap restaurants were long a

standby for writers, painters, musicians and their retinues. Grub Street had outposts in Soho, the bars crammed with Prince Charlies wearily or defiantly seeking a moor at Culloden or claiming an odds-against triumph, some plagued by what Ben Jonson called the leprosy of wit. And a Mrs Theresa Berkely once kept a late Victorian brothel at 28, Charlotte Street, with a cat-o'-nine-tails, leather straps and birch canes kept flexible in water.

Soho can be romanticized by ageing writers, though J.B. Priestley described it caustically. In his novel, *Angel Pavement*, a young man, anxious to entertain a girl on the cheap, is recommended to a Soho restaurant by his friend, Mr Warwick:

He beamed at her through his rimless eyeglasses. 'Nothing I enjoy better than studying these queer types,' he whispered. 'A place like this is a treat to me, if only for that reason. Old Warwick told me I'd enjoy that part of it. He's had some very funny experiences in his time. I must try to remember some of the yarns he's told me, once or twice when I've been sitting up with him over a pipe at the Chestervern.'

While Miss Matlock was asking idly what sort of man Mr Warwick was and Norman was telling her, the waitress had brought them the two halves of a grapefruit, the juice of which had apparently been used some time before. They had not finished with old Warwick, who seemed to Miss Matlock a silly old man, when the waitress returned to give them some mysterious thick soup, which looked like gum but had a rather less pronounced flavour.

Miss Matlock tried three spoonfuls and then looked with horror at her plate. Something was there, something small, dark, squashed. There were legs. She pushed the plate away.

'What's the matter, Lilian. Don't you like the soup?'

She pointed with her spoon at the alien body. Mr Birtley leaned across and peered at it through his glasses.

'No, by George, it isn't, is it? Is it really? Oh, I say, that's not good enough, is it? That's the worst of these foreigners. Do you think I ought to tell them about it?'

Soho has always had its productive regions – in Frith Street, T.E. Hulme held his regular Friday-night discussions – but its reputation is of different standing. In the 1940s, Julian Maclaren-Ross encountered the Ceylonese J. Meary Tambimuttu, editor of *Poetry London*, who declared: 'A poet is a citizen of the world. All mankind is a country. My principality is everywhere. The Principality of the Mind.' Maclaren-Ross, however, first met him in Soho, where for some years he mostly confined himself, a familiar bright-eyed, tangle-haired figure talking rapidly about his friends the famous poets, T.S. Eliot and Edith Sitwell, before demanding whether his listener carried any money. Reassured, he might continue: 'That is good. I am a Prince in my own country and princes don't carry money you know.' This method of finance long served him well enough. Through him Maclaren-Ross, aspiring writer, was introduced to 'Fitzrovia':

> 'Well, I thought to finish some work tonight,' I said. Tambimuttu said: 'Yes, work is good but you are a writer, you must meet people and it is better you meet them under my aegis. That is so, isn't it?' and the supporters raised a sullen murmur of agreement like a lynching mob getting ready to string someone up at the behest of a rabble rouser.
>
> 'Only beware of Fitzrovia,' Tambi said, quelling the mob with a flicker of his amazing fingers. 'It's a danger-ous place, you must be careful.'
>
> 'Fights with knives?'
>
> 'No, a worse danger. You might get Sohoitis you know.'
>
> 'No, I don't. What is it?'
>
> 'If you get Sohoitis,' Tambi said very seriously, 'you will stay there always day and night and get no work done ever. You have been warned.'

Alan Ross, poet and cricketer, long-time editor of the *London Magazine*, also knew Soho:

> Among other regulars in the Wheatsheaf was Nina Hamnett, painter, author of a lively autobiography,

Laughing Torso, and one-time model and bed-companion of Modigliani and Gaudier-Brzeska, to name only two. Nina was by now in her late fifties, her unconventional features mottled by drink, her country voice fruity. 'Modi said I had the best breasts in Europe,' she was wont to remark, apropos of nothing, hauling up her striped jersey to demonstrate. 'You feel them, they're as good as new.' They certainly were good, needing no support, but the rest of Nina was disastrous. She carried what little money she had in a tin box, rattling it from time to time for contributions. 'Got any mun, dear?', a leper-like noise that soon got on one's nerves. Nevertheless, with her endless stories of Parisian low life and studio anecdotes – dancing naked for Van Dongen, working for Aleister Crowley, drinking with Picasso – she was a true whiff of Bohemia.

Another impressive Soho Bohemian was the poet Paul Potts, friend of Orwell, admired by George Barker, tall, beaky, a lively, somewhat inflamed contributor to literary journals of marked excellence and small circulation. He sometimes seemed to be in several pubs simultaneously, arguing about poetry, Israel, underdogs, socialist politics, parliamentary mountebanks, with old friends and enemies – these could interchange rather abruptly – and with strangers. With the last he did not long disdain a nudge towards his glass, always more half-empty than half-full, and a request, perhaps peremptory, for a loan. Unpredictable, impoverished, generous, a child-lover, passionate about Jewish liberties, though himself a Canadian gentile, he wrote in his autobiography, described by Cecil Day-Lewis as the best bad book ever written: 'I had kept my hat on because this is an act of reverence in the Jewish world. I was lucky to have one, as I seldom wear a hat. But I had bought it a few months before, so that I could take it off, to a person who at that time was being sneered at.'

Fitzroy Square has witnessed many sights under its elms and lilacs, its stone terraces designed by the Adam brothers giving a dignified setting to some anecdotes probably embroidered through the years.

For a while, Bernard Shaw lived there with his mother –

'I did not throw myself into the struggle for life, I threw my mother into it.' Shaw well understood that, though writers may pledge themselves to Truth at all costs, the cost may involve minor truths. In an article in *The Star* (1890), he tells how, walking home late after a Vincenti ballet, he found Fitzroy Square deserted:

And such a magnificent hippodrome that I could not resist trying to go round it just once in Vincenti's fashion. It proved frightfully difficult. After my fourteenth fall I was pulled up by a policeman. 'What are you doing here?' he said, keeping fast hold of me. 'I 'bin watching you for the last five minutes.' I explained eloquently and enthusiastically. He hesitated a moment, and then said, 'Would you mind holding my helmet while I have a try? It dont look so hard.' Next moment his head was buried in the macadam and his right knee was out through its torn garment. 'I never was beaten yet,' he said, 'and I wont be beaten now. It was my coat that tripped me.' We both hung our coats on the railings and went at it again. If each round of the square had been a round in a prize-fight we should have been less damaged and disfigured; but we persevered in getting round twice without a rest or a fall, when an inspector arrived and asked him bitterly whether that was his notion of fixed point duty. 'I allow it aint fixed point,' said the constable, emboldened by his new accomplishment, 'but I'll lay half a sovereign you cant do it.' The inspector could not resist the temptation to try (I was whirling round before his eyes in a most fascinating manner); and he made rapid progress after half an hour or so. We were subsequently joined by an early postman and by a milkman, who unfortunately broke his leg and had to be carried to hospital by the other three.

Self-styled Joey the Clown, G.B.S., bringer of the inspired untruths of comedy without malignity, once demanded whether, were the world only one of God's jokes, we should work any the less hard to make it a good joke instead of a bad one.

A degree more probable is T.E. Hulme settling an argument

with Wyndham Lewis by hanging him upside down over the railings in Fitzroy Square, Lewis having asserted that touch vitally assisted communication. 'He must', Patricia Hutchins considers, as she relates the tale, 'have found this well illustrated'.

Living in the Square as a boy was Ford Madox Ford, of whose novel of Tudor politics, *The Fifth Queen*, Graham Greene wrote admiringly that one can believe anything by torchlight. In her book, *Ezra Pound's Kensington*, Patricia Hutchins refers to the child Ford, with long fair hair, dressed in a velvet suit:

> He would greet visitors after dinner. On other evenings he used to sit on the other side of the rustling fire, listening to his grandfather and William Rossetti revive the splendid ghosts of the Pre-Raphaelites, and talk of Shelley, Browning, Mazzini and Napoleon III.

He might have heard talk of another Italian, whose lurid story has been chronicled by Michael St John Packe:

> As Orsini wandered off into Soho, grey muffled shapes slid purgatorially past him in the fog. Cabs clopped along, spattering him with mud. Dray horses in blinkers whinnied steam. At a street corner he slipped on an oozy patch of pavement, and stumbled into a covey of young mudlarks. Pointing at his foreign beard, they began to shriek in chorus. He brushed past them, but they pursued him, chanting. When he turned on them angrily, they ran away, and pelted him with half-frozen balls of horse-dung.

The children's instincts were sound. Orsini was an Italian terrorist, soon to be methodically manufacturing bombs to be transported from Soho to Paris, disguised as gas-fittings, and thrown at Napoleon III, on behalf of United Italy. This was indeed done, at the cost of some scores of imperial outriders, policemen, horses, and damage to the Emperor's nose and his wife's left eye – 'The hazards of our trade', Louis Napoleon remarked to the blood-spattered Eugénie.

Less spectacular is the Irish poet Austin Clarke's recollection of a party in Fitzroy Square, with W.B. Yeats telling stories of fairies:

> Suddenly he peered down at the threadbare rug before the fender and, in a chanting tone, murmured: 'I see an abyss and far down in it is a hawk with poised wings.'
> 'I can see nothing,' complained his sceptical companion, noticing a large hole in the rug.

BLOOMSBURY

The commonplace Tottenham Court Road separates Soho from Bloomsbury, traditionally more high-minded, influenced by its two hubs, London University and the British Museum. Bloomsbury is tinged with an aura of learning, civilized order and discussion. It possesses, too, an air of tranquillity and repose, derived from the plane trees, roses and lawns of Bloomsbury Square which, like Russell Square, was designed by a landscape gardener, Humphry Repton.

Victorian London was an intellectual power-house in which native Londoners mingled with Continental refugees. They could meet at the British Museum Library; Karl and Eleanor Marx, Bernard Shaw and Rebecca West, William Morris and Prince Kropotkin. Virginia Woolf, in *Jacob's Room*, summed up the Museum:

> Stone lies solid over the British Museum, as bone lies cool over the visions and heat of the brain. Only here the brain is Plato's brain and Shakespeare's; the brain has made pots and statues, great bulls and little jewels, and crossed the river of death this way and that incessantly, seeking some landing, now wrapping the body well for its long sleep; now laying penny pieces on the eyes; now turning the toes scrupulously to the East. Meanwhile, Plato continues his dialogue; in spite of the cat whistles, in spite of the woman in the mews behind Great Ormond Street who has come home drunk and cries all night long, 'Let me in! Let me in!'

A shy young romantic, John Masefield, later Poet Laureate, was using the Reading Room simultaneously with a man who was neither, researching for *Materialism and Empirico-Criticism*, unlikely to excite the author of *Dauber* and *The Tragedy of Nan*, though the latter wrote to Florence Lamont in 1964:

I often saw Lenin in the British Museum reading room and always said to myself 'I wonder who that extra-ordinary man is,' for anyone must have seen that he was an extraordinary man certain to make a mark on the wall. Once, as I was leaving the room, I saw that he was just behind me, so that I held the door open for him till he had passed. He smiled at me and muttered some words of thanks, and that was the nearest I ever got to him.

The Ionic design of the Museum, with its pediment and columns, together with Wilkins' ten Corinthian pillars, and dome, of University College, give Bloomsbury a patrician serenity, suggesting dignified people of superior ways.

Bloomsbury indeed has a significance not only as a noun, a place of green squares, gardens, statues, libraries and studies, but also as an adjective, an attitude, a sensibility agnostic, sceptical, teasing, wary of dogma, manifestoes, majority votes, utopias, of 'telegrams and anger', E.M. Forster's phrase, though the sensibility once veered towards silliness when he hesitated to plant oaks on his property because of their patriotic associations.

The most well-remembered Bloomsbury figures were approachable, not always amiable, never rollicking. For Lord David Cecil:

Though most of Bloomsbury was cultivated and sensitive, I don't think it was exactly poetical. It was a very solid group and, when I first went to a party there, I was very much aware of this. I don't think it is at all true to call them affected. It was like any other close group – it had its mannerisms of voice and phrasings. They had a rather breathless way of talking, and a very solemn face. This was a little alarming. When they shook hands they didn't smile, they just handed the hand. And if you didn't know them, this grave look and this limp handshake were not welcoming.

The most celebrated of 'Bloomsbury' reputations is that of Virginia Woolf, of whom Raymond Mortimer considered that her words were all alive, like a shoal of fish jumping in a net – 'never a cliché, nothing heavy'. Of her and her friends, in Tavistock Square, John Lehmann would see

> Roger Fry eagerly spinning his latest art theories; or Aldous Huxley, leaning in willowy length against the chimney-piece as he discoursed on recondite problems of anthropology or philosophy; or William Plomer, mocking and teasing and turning everything to absurdity; or Lytton Strachey's beautiful niece Julia, with her husband, the gifted and melancholy sculptor-poet Stephen Tomlin; and many others, luminaries and disciples of the Bloomsbury world. Virginia sat in her chair smoking in a long holder the strong cigarettes she always rolled for herself, sometimes leading the talk, sometimes contenting herself with brief interjections, or asking questions to draw her guests out to further confessions or declarations. I found it difficult to take my eyes off her countenance, in which intellect, imagination and finesse of feature were so rarely mixed. I think of Edith Sitwell's description:
> 'Virginia Woolf had a moonlit transparent beauty. She was exquisitely carved, with huge, thoughtful eyes that held no foreshadowing of that tragic end which was a grief to everyone who had ever known her.'

Her teasing mood is captured by Christopher Isherwood in his 1941 obituary. He was having tea with her, accompanied by the best-selling novelist Hugh Walpole, himself of Piccadilly, Cumberland and Cornwall, far from 'Bloomsbury', but devoted to her despite her disdain for his books. Isherwood here calls Walpole 'Jeremy', the boy hero of many Walpole stories:

> 'You know, Jeremy,' she tells him, smiling, almost tenderly, 'you remind me of a very beautiful prize-winning cow. . .'

'A cow, Virginia . . .?' the novelist gulps but grins bravely at me, determined to show he can take it.

'Yes . . . a very, very fine cow. You go out into the world and win all sorts of prizes, but gradually your coat gets covered with burrs, and so you have to come back again into your field. And in the middle of the field is a rough old stone post, and you rub yourself against it to get the burrs off. Don't you think, Leonard . . .' she looks across at her husband, 'that that's our real mission in life? We're Jeremy's old stone scratching-post.'

Married to a Fabian and internationalist, friend of Maynard Keynes, co-publisher of Freud, she was scarcely the Ivory Tower aristocrat sometimes imagined. Gillian Beer suggests:

The real world of Virginia Woolf was not solely the liberal-humanist world of personal and social relation-ships: it was the hauntingly difficult world of Einsteinian physics and Wittgenstein's private language.

What did Mrs Woolf think of herself and Bloomsbury? Rose Macaulay remembered:

that throaty, deepish, wholly attractive voice, throwing out some irrelevant and negligent inquiry, starting some hare – 'Is this a great age?' or, 'Can there be Grand Old Women of Literature, or only Grand Old Men? I think I shall prepare to be the Grand Old Woman of English letters. Or would you like to be?' Or 'All this rubbish about Bloomsbury . . . I don't feel Bloomsbury; do you feel Marylebone (or Chelsea, Kensington or Hampstead?)'

Bloomsbury, of course, had many, rather different, literary occupants. One of its projects was aborted, sadly for Dickens's mother, less so for local children. As Una Pope-Hennessy relates:

At Michaelmas, 1823, Mrs Dickens, who had the rather scrambling notion of making money by running a small school for the children of parents living in the Indies, rented No. 4 Gower Street North, in her own name with money said to have been guaranteed by Christopher Huffam. Partly furnishing the house and fixing a brass plate upon the door with the words 'Mrs Dickens' Establishment', she caused handbills to be printed for distribution in the neighbourhood. Charles and the other children were called upon to push them into letter-boxes. None of them drew custom and no pupil appeared. Her son was to crystallise the venture in 'Mrs Micawber's Boarding Establishment for Young Ladies.'

Christopher Huffam, of Limehouse Hole, where some of *Our Mutual Friend* was enacted, was Charles's godfather, and had some characteristics of Captain Cuttle in *Dombey and Son*. Dickens himself was to live in Doughty Street, now a Dickens Museum. Jane Welsh Carlyle, in a letter of 1843, shows him at a Christmas party, conjuring, for an hour, 'the best conjurer I ever saw', ending

with a plum pudding made out of raw flour, eggs – all the raw usual ingredients – boiled in a gentleman's hat and tumbled out reeking – all in one minute before the eyes of the astonished children, and astonished grown people – that trick, and his other of changing ladies' pocket-handkerchiefs into comfits – and a box full of bran into a box full of a live guinea-pig! would enable him to make a handsome subsistence let the bookseller trade go as it please.

Dickens also lived awhile in nearby Torrington Square, where Hans Andersen visited him:

On the first floor was a rich library with a fireplace and a writing table, looking out on the garden; and here it was that in winter Dickens and his friends acted plays to the satisfaction of all parties. The kitchen was underground, and at the top of the house were the bedrooms. I had a snug room looking out on the gardens; and over the tree-tops I saw the London towers and spires appear and disappear as the weather cleared or threatened.

Some other Bloomsbury writers were probably more inclined towards Dickens, Morris, Ruskin, Shaw and Wells than to Virginia Woolf and Lytton Strachey. Eleanor Marx and Edward Aveling organized a local Marxist cell, though 'Bloomsbury' may have giggled at Marx's mother's remark: 'If only Karl had made Capital instead of writing about it!' Also in Bloomsbury, Mrs Humphry Ward, earnestly concerned with ethics, education and morals, stigmatized Strachey's *Eminent Victorians* as 'unpatriotic'.

Max Beerbohm, for whom London was still sufficiently small to be considered a cathedral city, disliked Bloomsbury and regretted the university, as a place for filling minds and starving souls. He felt Bloomsbury residents to be lustreless, too much indoors, lacking self-confidence and juvenile swagger, though praised by elderly reviewers. He excepted one, a foreigner, a

tall, thin, keen-faced man with short side-whiskers; and he wore a kind of tam-o'-shanter, a brick-coloured cloak, a long robe to match, and a pair of sandals; and his brown hair fell to the back of his waist, and in windy weather streamed out behind him with immense vivacity. He attracted great attention always, and comment too, of course. The best comment on him that I overheard was made by one of two costermongers whom he had just passed by. 'Well, Bill,' said the one to the other, who was grinning widely, 'at any rate 'e's got more courage than wot *we've* got.' These words, so typical of cockney wisdom and tolerance, impressed me deeply.

In this broadcast, made in 1940, Beerbohm went on to say that he felt Bloomsbury needed a strong, purging river, whereas Chelsea he enjoyed, 'so fresh and tonic was the air of it; so gay were the artists of that village (for village it still seemed to be) by the riverside'.

MARYLEBONE

North of Soho, and flanked by Regent's Park, lies Marylebone with its neat, professional streets: Wimpole Street, Harley Street, Welbeck Street. Marylebone Road aims at Baker Street, and Paddington beyond, with periodic glimpses of the Park. It penetrates a further area of art galleries, churches, squares, straight thoroughfares to the West End and Marble Arch, to Hampstead and Golders Green. The tall columns of the Ionic portico of Sir John Soane's Holy Trinity Church on Marylebone Road are praised by the exacting authority on British architecture, Pevsner, but Marylebone Road owes its popularity not to Soane, nor to the church's musical tradition, but to a young French refugee who had witnessed the French Terror in 1792–4, Madame Tussaud. Her permanent exhibition of waxworks attracts not only Londoners. The Czech playwright, Karel Capek, wrote in a letter:

> At Madame Tussaud's I had a rather unpleasant discovery; my incapacity to read human faces, or the deceptions within the faces themselves. Thus, I was at once charmed by a gentleman in a chair with a goatee. No. 12. The catalogue revealed him as Thomas Neill Cream hanged in 1892. 'Poisoned Matilda Glover with strychnine.' He was also convicted of murdering three other women. Really, his face is very suspect. Well! No. 20, a clean-shaven gentleman of honest enough appearance – Arthur Devereux, hanged 1905, known as 'the trunk killer', for concealing his victims in trunks. Very nasty. No. 21 – no, this excellent person cannot be 'Mrs Dyer, the Reading baby-killer!' Now I see that I have muddled the catalogue and have to revise my impressions. The gentleman in the chair, No. 12, is merely Bernard Shaw; No. 13 is Louis Blériot, and No. 20 only Gugliemo Marconi.

Baker Street is of course famed not for itself but, like Wimpole Street, for its literary fictions. Very typical is Dr Watson's entry in 'The Sign of Four':

> Holmes gave a shrill whistle, on which a street arab led across a four-wheeler and opened the door. The man who

had addressed us mounted to the box, while we took our places inside. We had hardly done so before the driver whipped up his horse, and we plunged away at a furious pace through the foggy streets.

The situation was a curious one. We were driving to an unknown place, on an unknown errand.

REGENT'S PARK

Bordered under Primrose Hill by the Regent's Canal, Regent's Park, spread to the north between the Hill and Camden Town, is fringed with Nash's terraces of classical columns, friezes and porticoes, and adorned with lake, rose garden and theatre. The dreamy, pre-1914 atmosphere which Edith Sitwell describes in her 1937 novel, *I Live under a Black Sun*, still lingers:

Mrs Vanelden's house was situated in one of the moon-coloured Crescents, or Circuses, bordering on the edge of Regent's Park. Two Crescents, one on either side, overlooked large gardens full of huge purring leaves and great bright flowers, pale yellow begonias that made you think of South America because of their Creole complexions; and here, shrouded by the great leaves of trees and bushes, the young people played tennis; from the windows of the houses, or if you sat beneath the awnings that sheltered the balconies, you could hear their voices calling to each other, although you could not see them, you could only, at moments, see a white dress, a glint of gold or bird-dark, bird-glossy hair as they passed among the trees. No old people ever walked in the gardens, but sometimes a dark foreign-looking woman would pass by, like a sudden patch of shade, and with her a child, looking like a tired August moon in her white dress.

The Crescents and gardens alike had a faint Regency character, partly, perhaps, because they faced remote light blue distances, such as one sees in water-colours of the period. Mrs Vanelden's house looked light and temporary, as if it were a house in which one lived for the summer only; as if when at last the summer was over and the voices and the white dresses flashing among the leaves in the gardens were gone, the house itself might crumble into a little moon-coloured dust, or be packed away with the muslin dresses. The feeling that it must always be summer in the Crescents was increased, too, by the fact that nearly always a barrel-organ seemed to be playing in one or other of the Crescents, light tunes, dropping like water, that one could imagine being played on xylophones and queer wooden instruments and guitars and flutes in Mexico and Peru, under a huge tropical parrot-feathered sun, or waltzes that were fashionable fifty years ago and that were bright-coloured and waxen as the begonias in the garden.

ST JOHN'S WOOD

A deep-fielder's throw from the Regent's Canal, tree-surrounded in St John's Wood, is Lord's Cricket Ground, beloved by many, though not by Pevsner. Its more recent embellishments would probably not have modified his contempt: 'Lord's settled down on this site in 1814. The buildings are a jumble without aesthetic aspirations, quite unthinkable in a country like Sweden or Holland.'

With three centuries of records, anecdotes, diaries and tall stories behind it, cricket itself has built an imaginative prism flashing with nostalgic incidents, outsize performers, momentous occasions, at times sentimental, but with the trivial apt to produce a tint worth remembering. The length and procedures of each game encourage the growth of the singular performance and the eccentric personality. Neville Cardus, musical and sporting critic, provides an instance of the trivial from a traditional schoolboy match at Lord's in 1910, a fixture in which, a century before, Byron had played.

The scene at Lord's that evening stays always in the mind. Two batsmen at bay – one of them Fowler, against conquering bowlers. Over the ground came the cries of 'Play up, Harrrow!' On the edge of the field a sequence of top hats was to be observed standing upside-down; Etonian brows required to be cooled.

The next morning Eton collapsed; they were all out for 65. Only Fowler with 21 reached double figures for Eton, who had to follow on 165 behind. Again did Eton collapse, five wickets going for 65. Etonians of great age were unable to watch the issue now. During the lunch interval I saw, in one of the boxes near the Nursery end, a well-preserved peer attending to his colours with a hammer in his hand.

Around the boundary were aristocratic coaches and carriages flaunting partisan emblems. Cardus continues:

> I imagined he was battling with emotion. To this day I have wondered in what manner the hammer and nails came into the possession of one whose life so obviously was removed from the paths of labour. Did he bring the implement to Lord's himself? – in the depths of his coat-tails. Or did he, with great foresight, remind Perkins the night before, as he was going to bed: 'There's the chicken and tongue, Perkins; there's the trifle and champagne – and, oh, Perkins, don't forget the hammer and nails. The same hammer we had last year will do; no doubt you'll be able to find it somewhere.' Strange that memory of Fowler's Match should cling to the sight of an aristocrat performing with a hammer!

With Eton needing 100 to save an innings defeat, Fowler knocked up 64, mostly in boundaries. Ten thousand watched Harrow bat again, needing but 55 for victory. Fowler took 8 wickets for 23 and Eton won by 9 runs.

The memorialist of this area is William Sansom, who discerned the bizarre and dramatic in this solid, in parts hushed, area of wide streets, tall churches, parks, conservatories, thick bushes, covered drives and reticent windows: its clerical fêtes, half-memories of faded celebrities, and its old people, very rich, sometimes very drunk, moving shakily behind dogs that often resemble live porcelain:

The Wood is full of history. One is considerably conscious of it. Apart from all the famous who lived there – from George Eliot to Alma-Tadema, Lily Langtry and Gaby Deslys – the Grove of the Evangelist was wellknown in the eighteen sixties and seventies for the expensive Cyprian maintained in a commodious villa by a gentleman from the Park Lane area (incidentally, a Gentleman in those days wore *brown* boots and white trousers with his dark morning coat, thus exploding today's nonsensical snobbism that a Gentleman only wears Black shoes). The Wood then, among the decorative lilacs and laburnams, was discreetly orgiastic. Relics of this time are still to be seen – a number of the high front garden doors, stoutly placed between pillars surmounted by eagle or pineapple, still have peepholes. When the Paying Lord rolled up in his darkened berlin and had his tiger ring the garden-gate bell, there was time enough for the maid to run out, peep and send a message back to get the handsome non-paying ostler out of the boudoir double-quick. Kate Hamilton, who ran the biggest brothel in the West End, lived in The Wood and contributed munificently to a neighbouring Church Fund. My own favourite character was a Mr Cooper, who reversed the usual situation, set himself up in a villa and invited a flow of West End ladies of difficult virtue to visit him. His personal curriculum involved one of the earliest recorded jam sessions. Once a week a baker's cart arrived in the afternoon with a large load of melt-in-the-mouth jam tarts. Then, after dark, carriage after carriage rolled up, each containing an equally juicy lady-tart. What then happened was finally reported by a keyholing housekeeper. Mr Cooper would sit himself in the centre of some capacious room with the jam tarts piled up beside him. The ladies, either naked or diaphanously veiled, would then troop round the room, just within tartthrow. Then old Cooper would get going with his ammo, shying tarts at the tarts as they pranced around him. This went on regularly for some years. I would dearly like to know more of it. Was there a scoreboard?

10

EUSTON TO
HAMPSTEAD AND
HIGHGATE

Half the leaves have fallen, so that one can see the
fading glory of those that remain; yellow and
brown and pale and hectic red, shining like golden
guineas and bright copper coins against the rich,
dark, business-like green of the trees that mean to
flourish all the winter through, like the tall slanting
pines near the Spaniards, and the old cedar trees,
and the hedges of yew and holly, for which
Hampstead gardens are famous.

George du Maurier, *Peter Ibbetson*

EUSTON AND CAMDEN TOWN

North of Bloomsbury, dulled by the great railway termini –
Euston, King's Cross, St Pancras – ranges a wide crescent of
railway lines and canals, massed lodging houses, shabby parks,
furtive side-streets, small shops for collectors of stolen watches,
parrots, condoms, camping equipment, frayed clothes, racing-
pigeon journals, with window cards advertising clairvoyance,
dubious cars, lost cats, mediums and the benefits of 'Enid',
measurements and telephone number added.

Disraeli's Lothair journeyed from Marylebone to Euston,
through

endless boulevards, some bustling, some dingy, some
tawdry and flaring, some melancholy and mean; rows of

garden gods, planted on the walls of yards full of vases and
divinities of concrete, huge railway halls, monster hotels,
dissenting chapels in the form of Gothic churches, quaint
ancient almshouses that were once built in the fields, and
tea-gardens and stingo [beer] houses and knackers' yards.
They were in a district far from the experience of Lothair,
which indeed had been exhausted when he had passed
Eustonia, and from that he had long been separated. The
way was broad but ill-lit, with houses of irregular size
but generally of low elevation, and sometimes detached
in smoke-dried gardens. The road was becoming a bridge
which crossed a canal, with barges and wharves and
timber yards, when their progress was arrested by a
crowd. It seemed a sort of procession; there was a banner,
and the lamp-light fell upon a religious emblem.

Stevie Smith, in *Over the Frontier*, revives the spirit of lost
railways and North London evenings:

In the London and North-Eastern Railway Carriages,
those delightful museum pieces that take you right back
into the middle of the factory laws and the chimney-
sweeping babies of the 'thirties and 'forties, to link up
maybe with colds in the head, antimacassars, muffins for
tea and evensong, Freddy and I have often had a very
close and comforting rapprochement.

It is the sickly green gaslight that does it. I am partial,
in my Mrs Humphry Wardish way, to sickly green
gaslight. I like to have the smuts thick on the windows,
the glass broken in front of some Gothic hotel, photo-
graphed in sepia and overscrawled with obscenity. I like
to have the horsehair stuffing coming out of the cushions
and over all and everything I will have a patina of railway
dust. In such a setting, half suffocated by the fumes of
sulphur from the tunnel in which we always stop, I have
no rightmindedness about social intercourse, I am wholly
Freddy's.

The purlieus of King's Cross and the Pentonville Road,
and that ominous dark lane that runs to the side of the
suburban platform, have seen us too, late at night-times,

under the gas lamps to meet. And then, under the green gaslight he is looking suddenly so lost and betrayed, so somehow sweet, I think, I must hug him a little he is looking so sweet.

On such a train, in wartime, Paul Bloomfield, Hampstead biographer, teacher and critic, of European sensibility, always tireless in addressing strangers, was reading *Walden*:

There were two American G.I.s in my compartment, and in the course of conversation I told them that the book in my hands was an American classic.
They had never heard of Thoreau. His opting for solitude amazed them; they couldn't quite believe it.
'Was there a girl in it?' one of them asked. I said there was not.
'I guess he must 'a been crazy.'

In a grey North London dusk, Bloomfield saw a sudden sunset, 'the lemon-yellow and boot-polish brown of the open sky, with indigo clouds above: no red or pink, an astringent, dry-sherry effect, very beautiful'. His companion replied: 'Ah, it's the humidity of the atmosphere acting like a prism, breaking up the light.'
Something of the atmosphere, lingering still, around Camden Road, from Eustonia to Camden Town, can be recognized in H.G. Wells's *Tono-Bungay*:

Their 'ménage' was one of a very common type in London. They occupied what is called the dining-room floor of a small house, and they had the use of a little inconvenient kitchen in the basement that had once been a scullery . . . There was, of course, no bathroom or anything of that sort available, and there was no water supply except to the kitchen below. My aunt did all the domestic work, though she could have afforded to pay for help if the build of the place had not rendered that inconvenient to the pitch of impossibility. There was no sort of help available except that of indoor servants, for whom she had no accommodation. The furniture was

their own; it was partly second-hand, but on the whole
it seemed cheerful to my eye, and my aunt's bias for cheap,
gay-figured muslin had found ample scope. In many ways
I should think it must have been an extremely inconvenient and cramped sort of home, but at the time I took
it, as I was taking everything, as being there and in the
nature of things. I did not see the oddness of decent,
solvent people living in a habitation so clearly neither
designed nor adapted for their needs, so wasteful of
labour and so devoid of beauty as this was . . . It strikes
me now as the next thing to wearing second-hand clothes.

Beneath the nob hills of Hampstead and Highgate, leafy and
spacious with the airy Heath and trim Primrose Hill, itself once
rowdy and rebellious, and touching Regent's Park, the green
air slumps into the several greys of Camden Town, Gospel Oak
and Kentish Town.

Camden Town has a residue of wide streets and solid houses.
On its edge, at the end of Parkway, with its cafés and odds-and-
ends, is Regent's Park Terrace, facing Primrose Hill, near the
Zoo, and which prompted Bernard Spencer's poem of that
name.

The noises round my house. On cobbles bounding
Victorian fashioned drays laden with railway goods
and their hollow sound like stones in rolling barrels:
the stony hoofing of dray horses.

Further, the trains themselves; among them the violent
screaming like frightened animals, clashing metal;
different the pompous, the heavy breathers, the aldermen,
or those again which speed with the declining
sadness of crying along the distant routes
knitting together weathers and dialects.

Between these noises the little teeth of a London
silence.

Finally the lions grumbling over the park,
angry in the night hours,

cavernous as though their throats were openings up
   from the earth;
hooves, luggage, engines, tumbrils, lions,
hollow noises, noises of travel, hourly these unpick
the bricks of a London terrace, make the ear
their road, and have their audience in whatever
hearing the heart or the deep of the belly owns.

The nineteenth-century Regent's Canal, then the railway,
extinguished or distorted local villages, transformed fields
to parks or embankments, and ejected such cultural establish-
ments as Mr Jones' Classical and Commercial Academy, where
Dickens once, very briefly, studied. He lived for a while in
Bayham Street in boyhood, exploring it as he did adjacent
Kentish Town and Somers Town, before the Canal and the
Railway. He recalled Bayham Street as 'shabby, dingy, damp
and mean a neighbourhood as one would desire not to see. It
shut the street doors, pulled down the blinds, screened the
parlour windows with the wretchedest plants in pots, and
made a desperate stand to keep up appearances. The genteeler
part of the inhabitants, in answering knocks, got behind the
door, . . . and endeavoured to diffuse the fiction that a servant
of some sort was the ghostly warder.' Una Pope-Hennessy
observed:

> The whole neighbourhood appears and reappears in
> his books. Bob Cratchit lived in Camden Town, so
> did Jemima Evans: Traddles lived there with Micawber:
> the Toodles family lived in Stagg's Garden, 'Camberling'
> Town: Heyling in *Pickwick* ran down his victim in
> Little College Street, Camden Town, 'a desolate place
> surrounded by fields and ditches'.

Much of the area's past is one of poverty, violence and racial
tension incited by Gaelic-speaking navvies building the canal,
railway tracks and tunnels, men who were reckless and casually
pagan, for whom marriage was solemnized by the couple
jumping over a broomstick.
For ten years George Bernard Shaw was a local Camden
councillor in the St Pancras Vestry. He told Stephen Winsten:

'the prophet of the race will be the political economist. There is nothing like prosaic work. I had a grand time in the Vestry, worrying about drains, dust destructors, and instituting women's lavatories.'

For him, a curious mixture of personal geniality and academic cruelty, such matters were more urgent than 'the silly visionary fashion-ridden theatres' of Shaftesbury Avenue, St Martin's Lane and Drury Lane which he resolved to replace. In the British Museum Library he had studied not only Wagner but also Marx. Marx himself had lived in Soho, Hampstead and Kentish Town, writing to Engels in Regent's Park Road in 1866:

I am forced to borrow small sums here and there in London, just as in my worst days as a refugee – and this among a very restricted and indigent circle – merely to make the most necessary payments. On the other hand the tradesmen are menacing; some of them have cut off our credit and are threatening to sue.

Alongside Camden Town, barely a mile from St Pancras Station, is Kentish Town, where Goldsmith, in his essay 'Travellers' Tales', saw the road lying

through a fine champaign country, well-watered with beautiful drains, and enamelled with flowers of all kinds, which might contribute to charm every sense, were it not that the odoriferous gales are often more impregnated with dust than perfume.

ISLINGTON

From Camden Town, a walk along the Regent's Canal will reach Islington. The walk gives views which change by the minute, like those of the companion North London Railway: sloping back gardens, derelict Victorian warehouses, wharves, foundries, domestic boat-sheds, dripping tunnels, painted pleasure-launches and long houseboats, grimy barges, secret playgrounds and intricate wrought-iron balconies.

E.M. Forster, having castigated Regent Street, advised:

Go, for a change, up the Caledonian Road, and lean over
the bridge which crosses the Canal. A much pleasanter
muddle awaits you. A queer smell hangs about, sweetish
and not disagreeable, and seems to rise from the water.
The surroundings are grubby and cheerful, the colouring
quiet, as is usual with London colouring, the district
poor.

Civic roots are deep. Goldsmith saw Islington as 'a pretty
neat town, mostly built of brick, with a church and bells; it
has a small lake, or rather pond in the midst, though at present
much neglected'. Blake mentioned 'the fields from Islington to
Marylebone, to Primrose Hill and St John's Wood': in 1823,
Charles Lamb was living within them. To Robert Southey he
gave the address: 'Colebrook Cottage, Colebrook, Islington,
close to the New River end of Colebrook Terrace, left hand
from Sadlers Wells.'
Writing to Bernard Barton, he described more:

I have a cottage . . . a cottage, for it is detached; a white
house with six good rooms; the New River (rather
elderly by this time) runs (if a moderate walking-pace can
be so termed) close to the foot of the house; and behind
is a spacious garden with vines (I assure you), pears,
strawberries, parsnips, leek, carrots, cabbages, to delight
the heart of old Alcinous. You enter, without passage,
into a cheerful dining-room, all studded over and rough,
with old books; and above is a lightsome drawing-
room, three windows full of choice prints. I feel like a
great lord, never having had a house before.

Around him were orchards, pleasure gardens, stables and
riding-masters and, in neighbouring Sadler's Wells, a small spa
with waters recommended to cure 'dropsy, jaundice, scurvy,
greensickness and other distempers not to be mentioned'. Also
an entertainment emporium, for spectacles, farces and concerts.
Smollett's Winifred Jenkins, in *Humphry Clinker*, writes to
Mary Jones:

I was afterwards at a party at Sadler's Wells, where I saw
such tumbling and dancing upon ropes and wires, that I
was frightened, and ready to go into a fit – I tho't it was
all inchantment; and, believing myself bewitched, began
for to cry – You know as how the witches in Wales fly
upon broom-sticks; but here was flying without any
broom-stick, or thing in the varsal world, and firing of
pistols in the air, and blowing of trumpets, and swinging,
and rolling of wheel-barrows upon a wire (God bless us!)
no thicker than a sewing-thread; that, to be sure, they
must deal with the devil! – A fine gentleman, with a pig's
tail, and a golden sword by his side, came to comfit me,
and offered for to treat me with a pint of wind; but I
would not stay; and so, going through the dark passage,
he began to show his cloven futt, and went for to be rude.

At Sadler's Wells, in 1783, *The Deserter* was acted by dogs,
trained by who knows what cruelties, but which Edmund
Kean endured; and clowns, acrobats and castrated singers suffered. Another featured artiste was a 'learned pig'.

HAMPSTEAD

From Camden Town and the High Street, the road passes on
to Chalk Farm, from where Haverstock Hill, then Rosslyn
Hill, climb to Hampstead. Surmounting the dense plains
below, 'the Village' is fresher, and considers itself more
individual than most London districts. Here, amongst trees and
birds, perched high above Kentish Town, Camden Town,
Cricklewood and Golders Green, one can sometimes escape
what Somerset Maugham called 'the vague low song of
London, like the distant hum of a mighty engine'. Local
place-names give echoes: Keats Grove, Leigh Hunt Cottage,
Constable Close, the Sir Richard Steele.
   Robert Louis Stevenson praised Hampstead Heights: 'Coming up out of London is like going to the top of Kir Yetton.'
A character in E.M. Forster's *A Passage to India* calls it 'an
artistic and thoughtful little suburb of London'. Beerbohm, in
youth, knew it as 'a little old remote village'. Ezra Pound

seldom thought it of sufficient value for the bus fare, calling it, in 1913, 'a more hideous form of Boston, with its particles of information and gossip', though he expunged some unenthusiastic lines about Hampstead in T.S. Eliot's *The Waste Land*.

Defoe noted that the steepness of the hill 'did check the Humour of the Town'. Mineral waters, remembered in Flask Walk and Well Road, briefly gave Hampstead a spa, though Defoe remained discouraging, observing at the Wells 'more gallantry than modesty'. A seventeenth-century witness, John MacKay, confirmed this: 'Its nearness to London brings so many loose women in vampt-up clothes to catch the City apprentices, that modest company are ashamed to appear there.'

The rowdiness in the Pump Room and Assembly Room, together with the gambling, offended Steele in *The Tatler*, though three years later, Swift reported that Steele himself had been arrested 'for making a lottery'. Pope and Gay took the waters together, Pope rescuing his friend from 'writer's block' by kindness and encouragement, thus ensuring the successful *The Beggars' Opera*, its satirical plot suggested by Swift. Fanny Burney describes the Assembly Room dances in *Evelina*. An eighteenth-century Hampstead writer, Anna Barbauld, living in Church Row, said of Burney that she was 'the greatest object of interest this season, that is, after the balloon which goes up at the Pantheon'.

Like St Pancras and Kilburn, Hampstead in the eighteenth century possessed pleasure gardens, the Bellsise (*sic*) Gardens, with music, gambling and dancing, the quality protected by 'twelve stout fellows, completely armed'. For a time, these competed with Ranelagh and Vauxhall, though unable to rival the latter's Rotunda, decorated by Canaletto and compared to Rome's Pantheon, where in 1764 the child Mozart performed.

Johnson asserted that one man could learn more in a journey by the Hampstead coach than another could in making the Grand Tour. Certainly, most of the famous London writers, painters and actresses of the period made the journey, sometimes for meetings of the Kit Kat Club at the Upper Flask Inn, with Addison, Steele, Pope, Congreve, Vanbrugh and Arbuthnot assembling in the summer under a mulberry tree.

The inn appeared in Richardson's novel, *Clarissa*, the designing Lovelace taking the heroine there. Under its roof, visiting the Shakespearian scholar, George Steevens, Dr Johnson began *The Vanity of Human Wishes*.

'Lovely-browed Hampstead,' Leigh Hunt wrote, 'from my little packing case dignified with the name of a house . . . Yet it has held Shelley and Keats and half a dozen friends in it at once; and they have made worlds of their own within the rooms.'

These visitors were celebrated by Cornelius Webb:

> Our talk shall be (a theme we never tire on)
> Of Chaucer, Shakespeare, Milton, Byron,
> (Our England's Dante) – Wordsworth – Hunt, and
> Keats,
> The Muses' son of promise; and what feats
> He yet may do.

One day in 1817, Keats himself casually mentioned to the painter Benjamin Robert Haydon that he had met Wordsworth that morning on the Heath. Both poets knew Leigh Hunt, who had already written a sonnet, with its sight of

> A steeple issuing from a leafy rise,
> With forms, fields in front and sloping green,
> Dear Hampstead, is thy southern face serene.

The forms have vanished, but Christchurch steeple still hovers gracefully above the grass, between the trees.

Here Keats walked with Coleridge in 1819, recalling the other's talk, 'far above singing . . . about Nightingales, Poetry – on Poetical sensation – Metaphysics – Different genera and species of Dreams – a dream accompanied by a sense of touch – a single and double touch – a dream related.'

A few steps from the Heath, Keats heard his own nightingale during a luxuriant spring and, years later, Thomas Hardy wrote a poem on Keats's house in Hampstead, beginning:

> O poet, came you haunting here
> where streets have stolen up all around
> and never a nightingale pours one
>   Full-throated sound?

William Blake was less rhapsodical: 'A journey to Hampstead without due consideration would be a mental rebellion against the Holy Spirit, and only fit for a soldier of Satan.' Yet he gave sufficient consideration for journeys to the Linnell family in North End, though the night air did not suit him. Samuel Palmer's son remembered, in his reminiscences:

> Fortunately for my father, Broad Street lay in Blake's way to Hampstead, and they often walked up the village together; the aged composer of the *Songs of Innocence* was a great favourite with the children, who revelled in those poems, and in his stories of the lovely spiritual things and beings which seemed to him so real and so near. Therefore, as the two friends neared the farm, a merry troup hurried out to meet them. Here Blake might often be found, standing at the door to enjoy the summer air, playing with the children, or listening to the simple Scotch songs sung by the hostess.

Palmer mentions 'cold winter nights, when Blake was wrapped up in a shawl by Mrs Linnell and sent on his homeward way, with the servant, lantern in hand, lighting him across the Heath'.

In Hampstead occurred a correspondence between Burke's friend, Lord Chancellor Thomas Erskine, of Erskine House, near the Spaniards Inn, and William Cowper, who succeeded in preventing him felling nine gracious elms. On the Heath, Erskine proved less amenable. A pioneer of animal rights, he rebuked a man for savaging his dog. 'Can't I', the bully demanded, 'do what I like with my own?'

'Well,' Erskine retorted, 'So also can I. This stick is *my* own!' And thrashed the fellow.

Dickens, ever restless, oppressed by domesticity and inner turbulence, sought refuge in exhausting walks. 'You don't feel disposed, do you,' he invited his future biographer John

Forster, 'to muffle yourself up and start off with me for a good brisk walk over Hampstead Heath? I know of a good house [Jack Straw's Castle] where we can have a red-hot chop for dinner and a glass of good wine.'

Much of Bill Sikes's trail, after Nancy's murder, survives:

> He went through Islington, strode up the hill at Highgate on which stands the stone in honour of Whittington; turned down to Highgate Hill unsteady of purpose, and uncertain where to go; struck off to the right again, almost as soon as he began to descend it; and taking the foot-path across the fields, skirted Caen Wood, and so came out on Hampstead Heath. Traversing the hollow by the Vale of Health, he mounted the opposite bank, and crossing the road which joins the villages of Hampstead and Highgate, made along the remaining portion of the Heath to the fields at North End, in one of which he laid himself down under a hedge and slept.

Dickens's friend, Wilkie Collins, lived awhile in Church Row. The first narrator in *The Woman in White* sets out after midnight to walk from the Heath to Regent's Park. He reaches the crossing of four roads: 'There in the middle of the broad, bright high road – there as if it had that moment sprung out of the earth, or dropped from the heaven – stood the figure of a solitary woman, dressed from head to foot in white.' This seemingly derived from an actual incident.

On the lower slopes, George Orwell once lived in Parliament Hill. His biographers, Stansky and Abrahams, emphasize its specifically Hampstead nature:

> What made it remarkable was that one stepped from the front door and almost immediately was on the Heath, had only to ascend a knoll and there before one were great grassy stretches of field; clumps of woodland; birds and insects and plants to observe, the life of nature that Orwell would always value; and far in the hazy distance the panorama of London, unfolding as far as the eye could see.

The social essence of Hampstead was long concentrated on the hill-top, parallel to the Heath's summit: Church Row, Heath Street, Downshire Hill, Well Road, Holly Mount and Perrins Lane, with their many mews, closes, cobbled courtyards, passages and alleys.

John Braine's Tim Harnforth, in *These Golden Days*, delights in Hampstead, a hill village of casual strollers, friendly café and pub encounters and sudden vistas of Heath, trees, sky:

What I'm here for is to take you with me now, twice left, once right and then into Perrins Lane and under the verandah outside the Coffee Cup in Hampstead High Street. There are two young men and two young women sitting there. I take my seat and the waitress finishes serving the four young people, smiles at me, and goes into the café. She appears a moment later with a mug of cappuccino and hands it to me. She knows what I want. This is one of the minor pleasures of living here; one never feels anonymous, merely a consumer unit.

I'm absolutely content sitting there in the sunshine . . . I wouldn't be anywhere else, sitting here with my coffee. The High Street is a live street, the main street of a village and yet metropolitan, a place where all the action is. The trees are now so luxuriant in foliage that they meet to form a sort of green tunnel, to give a little shade. The foliage is even more luxuriant on Rosslyn Hill. Trees make the dullest of streets interesting, and the High Street, with its mixture of styles, is never dull. And even now buildings like the Laura Ashley shop fit in; jerry-built glass-and-concrete monstrosities aren't allowed.

Paul Bloomfield, from his home off the High Street, could also observe the London panorama, thick wedges of roof and stack, chimney and tree, sloping down towards Golders Green and Hendon, Bloomsbury, Baker Street and Maida Vale, to St Paul's dome and distant, misty hills:

My cynosure is now the beetroot-coloured tube-station which has this minute disgorged a load of passengers from underground. They are all sorts and kinds: two Indian

girls in charming saris, a twisted old woman, a jaunty
young man with a beard who may be a painter, a boy
munching an apple; and there goes a BBC man in a
Whitehall hat, an actress I know a little whose pretty grey
eyes I can't of course see from up here, and close behind
her a well-known immigrant physicist.

Bloomfield once had an encounter perhaps common enough
in Hampstead and Chelsea. He was hurrying for the No. 24 bus
to the British Museum when, passing the Bricklayers' Arms,
an unknown woman grabbed him from a bench outside.
    'Tell me, why are you looking so grumpy?'
    'Madam, I had not realised I was looking so grumpy.'
    She grabbed him more firmly. 'Well, come in and tell me all
about it.'
    After several drinks and the stranger's monologue of vivid
non sequiturs, Bloomfield escaped, fleeing for the bus in South
End Road, opposite the bookshop managed by George Orwell.
The bus was empty, save for a friend whom Bloomfield had
not seen for some years – Aldous Huxley.
    Each street of this small acreage is clustered with stories.
Church Row has its Georgian parish church amongst cedars
and yews, its bust of Keats and memorial to Constable, and
is used in many films that wish to show a London of patrician
calm and moderate-sized, well-proportioned architecture. Here
lived H.G. Wells, named by David Hughes 'the Man who
Invented To-morrow'. On the death of Mrs Wells, one of
his mistresses is said to have exclaimed, 'I suppose this means
we all move up one.'
    The famous man surprised the young novelist David
Garnett:

I only went once or twice to tea with the Wellses and
remember being rather flabbergasted at the energy and
noise H.G. put into some of the games he made us play.
There was rampageous bumping round a table and knock-
ing over of chairs when I had expected to sit around, on
my good behaviour, listening to highbrow conversation.
And then I was dragged into a nursery where a little war
was in progress and saw H.G. in a whirlwind of tactical

enthusiasm, ousting his small sons Frank and Gyp from the peaceful enjoyment of their toy soldiers.

Ivy Low, born in Maida Vale in 1889, later lived in Hampstead where, in 1914, she met a Russian dissident and associate of Lenin, Maxim Litvinov, whose friends gaped when she demanded whether Tolstoy or Marx did most for socialism. Neville Braybrooke, a Hampstead author and historian of London's parks, introduces a 1988 edition of her stories, 'She Knew She was Right':

> In her early days in Hampstead when she and Maxim used to have tea at the Express Dairy in Heath Street, she would provide him with reading lists. Years later, when he was appointed the People's Commissar for Foreign Affairs, he told her that despite all the Bernard Shaw and Fabian tracts on Marxism and English socialism that he had waded through, he had learnt far more about English society and politics by following up her advice and reading Trollope.

Henry James had neither the build nor the inclinations of an athlete but would nevertheless walk from Piccadilly to Hampstead to meet George du Maurier who, in Leon Edel's words,

> had for years lived his private Hampstead life with his wife and children and dog, his drawing-board and his notations of London comedy and London society. Then he had written *Trilby* as a piece of natural and intimate story-telling, and it had taken the public by storm. The amateur, writing his tale as if it were on the edge of his drawing-board, had achieved what James with his consummate art of story-telling could never do. He was not jealous of his friend, but he was amazed by the paradox of 'success.' In the end, *Trilby* seemed to have murdered her creator. The old witty du Maurier disappeared; in his place there remained a melancholy successful man.

Strolling in Bayswater, du Maurier had originally offered the gist of the tale to James himself, who refused it, from his ignorance of music, feeling it should be left to du Maurier.

Stephen Spender had a Hampstead boyhood, his father a famous political journalist, J.A. Spender. His autobiography has a poignant memory:

> We lived in a state of austere comfort against a background of calamity. Little of our money seemed spent on enjoyment, but most on doctors and servants, on maintaining a standard of life. My mother, who died when I was twelve, was a semi-invalid, and her ill-health provided the background to our childhood. We walked by her bedroom on tiptoe, knowing that to talk too loud was to give her a headache. Once, when we had been playing trains in the nursery, which was above her bedroom, the door suddenly opened and she appeared on the threshold, with a white face of Greek tragedy, and exclaimed like Medea: 'I now know the sorrow of having borne children.'

HIGHGATE

From Heath Street, the road crosses the Heath, forking leftwards to Golders Green, right to Highgate. Both Hampstead and Highgate, with their trees and grass, owls and foxes, testify the strength of Gerard Manley Hopkins' lines:

> What would the world be, one bereft
> Of wet and of wilderness? Let them be left,
> O let them be left, wildness and wet.
> Long live the weeds and the wilderness yet.

Balancing Hampstead, the green dome of St Aloysius gleaming across the Heath, Highgate on its wooded hill now gives an atmosphere more obviously individual. Since John Braine, Hampstead Village has wilted into boutiques and restaurants but, amongst video emporia and supermarkets, Highgate retains art galleries, odds-and-ends shops, an antiquarian bookshop, 'The Village Tuckshop', a merchant chandler, a

communal square, a notable park, a hillside ghost and tradi-
tions not only of Marvell and Cromwell, but also of Francis
Bacon in 'Bacon's Lane', Coleridge, Rossetti, Priestley and
Betjeman.

Of the High Street, with the adjoining Pond Square, South
and North Grove, and the former Green, Pevsner allows that
it is 'one of the most delightful in London to recover the
character of a favourite residential village near London'.

A vast Victorian cemetery droops down the hillside, with
mournful figurines, winged and draped, busts, lichened pillars,
overgrown monuments, Karl Marx's massive head, a city of
the dead, its gardens tended only by ghosts and in consequence
wild. There, in 1869, in tribute to his wife and model, the
beautiful and talented Elizabeth Siddal, dead from an overdose
of laudanum, Rossetti buried between her cheek and hair his
unpublished poems. Seven years later, as if in a queer old
tale, he exhumed them, for publication. William Gaunt tells
the story: 'When the book was lifted there came away with
it a strand of red-gold hair. It had to be saturated with
disinfectants.'

In Highgate Cemetery, Galsworthy's ageing Soames Forsyte
broods:

> dreaming his career, faithful to the scut of his possessive
> instinct, warming himself even with its failures.
> 'To Let' – the Forsyte age and way of life, when a man
> owned his soul, his investments and his woman, without
> check or question. And now the State had, or would have,
> his investments, his woman had herself, and God knew
> who had his soul. 'To Let' – that sane and simple creed.
> The waters of change were foaming in, carrying the
> promise of new forms only when their destructive flood
> should have passed its full. He sat there, subconscious of
> them, but with his thoughts resolutely set on the past – as
> a man might ride into a wild night with his face to the
> tail of his galloping horse. Athwart the Victorian dykes
> the waters were falling on property, manners and morals,
> on melody and the old forms of art – waters bringing to
> his mouth a salt taste as of blood lapping to the foot of
> this Highgate Hill where Victorianism lay buried.

Highgate's laureate is John Betjeman. The narrator in his 'False Security' climbs West Hill to a children's party in The Grove, Highgate, as the keeper rings the closing bell in Waterlow Park, the lights starting to fizzle and burst into mauve. Then:

I ran to the ironwork gate of number seven
Secure at last on the lamplit fringe of Heaven.
Oh who can say how subtle and safe one feels
Shod in one's children's sandals from Daniel Neal's,
Clad in one's party clothes made of stuff from Heal's?
And who can still one's thrill at the candle shine
On cakes and ices and jelly and blackcurrant wine?
And the warm little feel of my hostess's hand in mine?
Can I forget my delight at the conjuring show?
And wasn't I proud that I was the last to go?
Too over-excited and pleased with myself to know
That the words I heard my hostess's mother employ
To a guest departing, would ever diminish my joy,
I WONDER WHERE JULIA FOUND THAT
STRANGE, RATHER COMMON LITTLE BOY?

On the further side of Highgate, straddling Muswell Hill Road, are Highgate Woods – Gravel Wood and Queen's Wood, only five miles from the City, yet with coots and moorhens, water-rats and dragon-flies, as Norman Collins discovered, in his novel *Bond Street Story* (1965):

There may be other places that are more central. And more fashionable. Like the Round Pond in Kensington Gardens, for instance. But fashion never had any connection with serious yachting. And centralness is exactly what isn't wanted. There is no feeling of escape, of being away from it all, with just the wind in your face and the splash and ripple of water coming up at you, if you can hear the sound of motor horns from all quarters and see the red sides of buses as they go trundling along Knightsbridge.
    Up at Highgate, there is nothing but green Nature. Great park-land trees. And rolling meadows. And the

placid, duck-bearing surface of the lake. Standing on the little wooden jetty there is not a house to be seen. Not one. Not even in the misty distance. Just reed-beds and osiers. And willow-herb. And the massive forest skyline from Ken Wood where the whole dangling necklace of ponds begins in a dark, ferny grotto.

From these slopes, H.G. Wells's Stephen Stratton, in *The Passionate Friends*, desolate in frustrated love, was overtaken by one of those vistas that London so unexpectedly discloses:

My sense of the enormity of London increased with the twilight, and began to prevail a little against my intense personal wretchedness. I remember wastes of building enterprise, interminable vistas of wide dark streets, with passing trams, and here and there at strategic corners coruscating groups of shops. And somewhere I came along a narrow street suddenly upon the distant prospect of a great monstrous absurd place on a steep hill against the last brightness of the evening sky, a burlesque block of building with huge truncated pyramids at either corner, that I have since learnt was the Alexandra Palace. It was so queer and bulky that it arrested and held my attention, struck on my memory with an almost dreamlike quality, so that years afterwards I went to Muswell Hill to see if indeed there really was such a place on earth, or whether I had had a waking nightmare during my wanderings.

From Waterlow Park, or beneath Highgate Church, looking down on the golden cross of St Paul's floating far below through a late autumn afternoon, one can watch all London dissolve into vague outlines, then fill up, and become a unity – Highgate, Clerkenwell, Bermondsey, Shadwell – merging in further stratas of time. From here Londoners watched a comet, the anti-aircraft guns fire and the balloons rise, the Crystal Palace burn; the fairs, the rioters, the militia bands. From here, under the sky, above the City, Lawrence Norfolk's evocation of a hot, eighteenth-century London summer in *Lemprière's Dictionary* can seem contemporary.

The heat seemed to cage itself and concentrate, building up to burn holes in the City's fabric with an eerie specificacity. Children: they drowned, two of them while bathing in the Thames; were burned when a draper's house was consumed in Union Street; crushed by a coach overturning on the Lambeth turnpike; took their own lives after viewing a hanging in Pulteney Street; had their skulls caved in, a flower pot, a servant's carelessness on a third floor in Berwick Street. Collapses: a summer storm would sap the foundations of the Coal Meter's Office, cracks would appear in the paving over the Fleet River, in the cobbles of Leadenhall Street, four houses in Wapping would disappear overnight heralded by neither agitation in the air, disturbance of the earth nor subterranean rumblings of any sort. A small earthquake would be reported in Norwood, swallowing two, and a whirlwind at Deptford would raze a cottage and four sheds, firing their contents aloft so as to cause a monstrous hazard of the air. A man would be killed by a descending fruit barrow. Finally, limbs: Lord Chatham's foot would be taken with gangrene from a gash of his shoe-buckle; a leg and a thigh, female by the shoe, would be washed up at White Friar's Dock; arms jutting from the port-holes of a brig at Blackwall would discover stowage of slaves, above three hundred dead, above sixty dismembered for concealment; a single finger would be delivered to Sir John Fielding at the Examiner's Office, only that, quite clean and without explanation.

11

SUBURBIA

I heard the hundred pin-makers
Slow down their racking din,
Till in the stillness men could hear
The dropping of the pin:
And somewhere men without the wall, beneath the
    wood, without the wall,
Had found the place where London ends and
    England can begin.

G.K. Chesterton, *Collected Poems*

London has been expanding since Chaucer's day, breaking out over the city walls and threatening the outlying villages. Smollett announced in 1711 that 'Pimlico and Knightsbridge are now almost joined to Chelsea and Middlesex.' In *Humphry Clinker*, provincial youngsters swarm to the capital, to become thieves and sharpers in 'the immense wilderness in which there is neither watch, nor ward of any signification, nor any order of police . . . This misshapen and monstrous capital, without head or tail, members or proportion.'

The process of expansion was incessant, quickening with the railway. In Robert Browning's boyhood Camberwell was becoming suburban. He recalled, in a letter of 1841, how he would once run from the village to Bond Street, but added that he had now moved further out, though to another suburban house 'with a garden, and trees, and little green hills of a sort to go out on'.

Wild woods, riverbanks, blue-remembered hills surrendered. Ford Madox Ford noted where the soot began, darkening rural trees. Once, in 1911, E.M. Forster at sunset helped E. Nesbit and her family set fire to models of suburban villas and industries. In *The Earthly Paradise*, William Morris was nostalgic:

> Forget six counties overhung with smoke,
> Forget the snorting steam and piston stroke,
> Forget the spreading of the hideous town;
> Think rather of the packhorse on the down,
> And dream of London, small and white and clean.

And in 1944, Cyril Connolly reflected in *The Unquiet Grave*:

> In the past the clods were the peasants, now the brute mass of ignorance is urban. The village idiot walks in Leicester Square. To love according to nature we should pass a considerable time in cities, for they are the glory of human nature, but they should never contain more than two hundred thousand inhabitants: it is our artificial enslavement to the large city, too sprawling to leave, too enormous for human dignity, which is responsible for half our sickness and misery. Slums may be breeding-grounds of crime, but middle-class suburbs are incubators of apathy and delirium. No city should be too large for a man to walk out of in a morning.

Graphic memories emerge from all districts. On the plain north of Hampstead, Golders Green grew from village to suburb, alongside the tube trains. Jean MacGibbon knew it in childhood, writing about it years later in *I Meant to Marry Him*.

> My Golders Green, where I lived till I was twelve, was all green, dusted with buttercup pollen, a little furred at the edges. I hated that featureless name: 'Hampstead Garden Suburb'. My Golders Green was a safe, sunny, open place bounded to the east by the Wild Wood and Big Wood where in spring revels were held called 'Sanfairyann.' Near our houses was Wild Hatch where the nursery garden grew, smelling of sweet damp earth and young growth. Southwards rose up the forests of Hampstead, forbidden ground haunted by bad men, a Highwayman and a Headless Coachman. To the West,

trim houses, each bound by pale-green hedges square-clipped to a given height opened on to the Finchley Road where trams vented their tropical-birdlike screeches and the North London Underground, then at its terminus, continually swallowed and voided passengers.

'Suburban', like 'provincial', has become perjorative, for snobs, fake sophisticates, generalizers and those who, like H.G. Wells in Bromley, contained genius demanding to break the bonds. The suburb of rose-light and nookery is exposed by Dannie Abse, in verses from his poem, 'Odd'.

In front of our house in Golders Green
the lawn like a cliché, mutters 'Rose bushes'.
The whole suburb is very respectable.
Ugly men drive past in funeral suits,
from their necks you can tell they're overweight.

Sodium lamp-posts, at night, hose empty roads
With gold which treacles over pavement trees,
polishes brittle hedges, clings on closed, parked cars.
If a light should fly on in an upstairs room
odds on two someones are going to sleep.

It's unusual to meet a beggar,
You hardly ever see a someone drunk.
It's a nice, clean, quiet, religious place.
For my part, now and then, I want to scream:
thus, by the neighbours, am considered odd.

In 'Suburb' (1914), Harold Monro mused:

The stout contractor will design
The lazy labourers will prepare
Another villa on the line;
In the little garden-square
Pampas grass will rustle there.

Charles Pooter, in *The Diary of a Nobody*, supplies the accepted quintessence of suburbia.

My dear wife Carrie and I have just been a week in our
new house 'The Laurels', Brickfield Terrace, Holloway –
a nice six-roomed residence, not counting basement, with
a front breakfast-parlour. We have a little front garden;
and there is a flight of ten steps up to the front door,
which, by-the-by, we keep locked with the chain up.
Cummings, Gowing, and our other intimate friends
always come to the little side entrance, which saves the
servant the trouble of going up to the front door, thereby
taking her from her work. We have a nice little back
garden which runs down to the railway.

In our own century this remains familiar. T.R. Fyvel rated
his own suburb less favourably:

How Wembley sprawls, seen from the topmost platform
of the Stadium. I distinctly remember that when I was
a schoolboy in North-West London, there were still
batches of fields around Wembley. It grew between the
wars, the creation of the speculative builder; street upon
street of box-like, semi-detached houses sprung into full
existence, indistinguishable from those of other London
suburbs. There they all are; 'Chatsworth' beside 'Knole',
'Blenheim' next to 'Balmoral'; the tiny front gates, the
back gardens with patches of lawn and scarlet runners
and pink Alexandra roses; brick and mortar of English
suburb-life – a life where the youthful hero of the local
tennis club or amateur dramatic group seems far too
early changed to the captured young family man showing
snapshots of his offspring in the 8.42 to London, and,
almost before he knows, to 'Dad', middle-aged, working
in the garden and worrying over insurance installments
and school bills.
   A good life, a mild civilised life, whose superficiality
still masks native English strength (remember the Blitz!)
but not a life likely to produce English poets, adventurers,
empire builders – or Olympic champions.

P.G. Wodehouse's 'Wood Hills', in his *The Clicking of
Cuthbert*, seems very akin to the Dulwich of his youth, and

shares much of the ethos of Fyvel's Wembley. It is pastoral, idyllic, amiable. On its links, Mitchell Holmes would miss short putts 'because of the uproar of the butterflies in the adjoining meadows'.

Not wholly rural or urban, the social issues in 'Wood Hills' are not, perhaps, quite extinct.

Its inhabitants live in commodious houses, standing in their own grounds, and enjoy many luxuries – such as gravel soil, main drainage, electric light, telephone, baths (h and c) and company's own water, that you might be pardoned for imagining that life to be so ideal for them that no possible improvement could be added to their lot. Mrs Willoughby Smethurst was under no such illusion. What Wood Hills needed to make it perfect, she realized, was Culture. Material comforts are all very well but if the *summum bonum* is to be achieved, the Soul also demands a look in, and it was Mrs Smethurst's resolve that never while she had her strength should the Soul be handed the loser's end. It was her intention to make Wood Hills a centre of all that was most cultivated and refined, and, golly! how she had succeeded. Under her presidency the Wood Hills Literary and Debating Society had tripled its membership. But there is always a fly in the ointment, a caterpillar in the salad. The local golf club, an institution to which Mrs Smethurst strongly objected, had also tripled its membership.

Suburbia can foster the wistful, minor key lyricism. Vestigial countrysides are glimpsed from a cricket field, railway cutting or park. Memories linger, of distant green landscapes, started by a dim spire above trees, a slice of a long-lost village green outside the 'Goat and Compasses' ('God Encompasseth') and now strewn with garbage. John Betjeman provides a typical nostalgic nuance:

Parish of enormous hayfields
  Perivale stood all alone,
And from Greenford scent of mayfields
  Most enticingly were blown

Over market gardens tidy,
Taverns for the *bona-fide*,
Cockney anglers, cockney shooters,
Murray Poshes, Lupin Pooters
Long in Kensal Green and Highgate silent under soot and
                                                                            stone.

Yet the garden dwarf, trim gravel drive and comfortable
murmurs can be deceptive, as in Priestley's play, *Laburnum
Grove*. Laurel and privet, copper beech and monkey tree, have
had their place in pathos, in crime. Behind lace curtains the
familiar can turn terrible, children be terrorized, poisoned tea
be poured for his wife by an attentive smiler.

Conan Doyle had an eye for this. Harrow, Tooting, Hendon
and Wandsworth could harbour the criminal and the atrocious
as readily as Whitechapel, Barking Level and Plumstead
Marshes. In *The Lost Childhood*, Graham Greene praised his
poetic vision:

> Think of the sense of horror which hangs over the
> laurelled drive of Upper Norwood and behind the curtains
> of Lower Camberwell: the dead body of Bartholomew
> Sholto swinging to and fro in Pondicherri Lodge, the
> 'bristle of red hair,' the 'ghastly inscrutable smile,' and in
> contrast Watson and Miss Mortson hand in hand like
> children among the strange rubbish heaps.

A further illustration of suburban deceptiveness is supplied
in 'The Norwood Builder':

> 'Not clear? Well, if that isn't clear, what COULD be
> clearer? Here is a young man who learns suddenly that if
> a certain older man dies he will succeed to a fortune. What
> does he do? He says nothing to anyone but he arranges
> that he shall go out on a pretext to see his client that
> night; he waits until the only other person in the house
> is in bed, and then in the solitude of the man's room he
> murders him, burns his body in the wood-pile, and
> departs to a neighbouring hotel. The blood-stains in the
> room and also on the stick are very slight. It is probable

that he imagined his crime to be a bloodless one, and
hoped that if the body were consumed it would hide all
traces of the method of his death – traces which for some
reason must have pointed to him. Is all this not obvious?'

'It strikes me, my good Lestrade, as being just a trifle
too obvious,' said Holmes. 'You do not add imagination
to your other great qualities.'

Professor John Holloway's *A London Diary* recalls his
Norwood childhood during the 1920s – the piano upright in
the parlour, though never played, the zinc bath in the kitchen,
the panoramic streets with posters of Mary Pickford and
Rudolph Valentino, the dray horses and open-decked buses,
Tiger Tim and *The Modern Boy* at the corner shop, the grocer
who sold sugar a farthing a pound cheaper than elsewhere, and
those overhead shop railways. When you bought something,
the assistant wrote the bill, curled it round your coins and
placed it in a small metal car:

She let it go, that released the spring, a bell tinged loudly,
and capsule and wheel were shot off and rolled swiftly
along the wire making a noise like a tram, only quiet, not
loud. And it swayed from left to right like a tram, too.
There all day long, sat an extraordinary privileged
woman. She waited for the little chariots to arrive,
unwrapped the screws of paper in them, loaded them up
again with change, and fired them back along the wires
in all directions.

On Norwood Armistice Days, utter silence descended save
for distant booms of the Woolwich Maroons: 'The whole
thing was a real contact, for one day in the year, with grandeur,
solemnity and tragedy.'

The small Holloway envisaged territories beyond Norwood,
beyond brick and creeper. He would hear about 'the Cuckoo',
as if, like 'the Phoenix', there were only one. Woken at
night, he saw a nightingale, singing, mauve in the moonlight.
Impressions lingered forever; a furnace fire 'raking gently
backward, very smooth and flat and a fierce yellow'; the effect
of darkness on time, on touch; surprise at the greyness of light

upon snow; a sweep's brush suddenly poking from a chimney; a neighbouring family, each with deformed hands; fear of the brilliant flashing of electric trains on iced rails. Class distinctions were powerful, sometimes too powerful. Young Holloway feared darkness, out of which, arrogant and pitiless, 'a lord might emerge'.

Imagination must often have been needed to penetrate the apparent respectability that grew like demure tulips over the southern regions of London, in the secluded mansions of the professional classes – the Cedars, the Laurels, Cranbourne Lodge, Mountjoy Villa. On Tooting Common, Balham, in 1879 stood the Priory, around which, in *Doctor Gully*, Elizabeth Jenkins reconstructed a memorable drama:

> It was in the toy-castle mode, with one narrow wing, three storeys high, rising behind a square block of only two storeys. The first-floor windows projected under little battlements, and under them were the french windows of the ground floor. At each corner of the various roofs, was a turret with a battlemented top; they gave the whole building an effect of soaring into the wintry air. As the carriage came over the common, the house, to the right of the road, presented its garden front; the drive and entrance were round to the left opening on Bedford Hill. This long, sloping road ran down between commons, sprinkled with trees and thickets till it reached level ground. Here, at its foot, was the Balham railway station and a large imposing public house, the Bedford Hotel, which comprised bars, a billiard saloon and livery stables.

Suburban stuffiness? Yes. Victorian heaviness? Certainly. Yet behind the windows, under the turrets, three people watched each other and the servants whispered; a fourth would approach, look up at a window and pass on, until, for a few days, all Britain would, through every newspaper in the land, be staring at a beery room in the Bedford Hotel.

In the Priory a young, rising barrister, Charles Bravo, lived in apparent comfort. His story has an atmosphere peculiarly Victorian: a bride previously married unhappily and with an inclination towards the bottle, a disapproving mother-in-law, an enigmatic doctor intimate, perhaps too intimate, with the bride, and a powerful, rather sinister, white housekeeper from Jamaica. There followed quarrels, jealousy, Bravo's death by poison, an inquest, an exhumation, a second inquest in the hotel billiard room and a verdict which is still disputed.

A.S. MacNalty, connoisseur of bad behaviour, considered:

The Bravo mystery remains obscure, a theme for criminological speculation, and those who could have told us the solution have departed from among us with the secret unspoken. The story illustrates how slight a human action may set in train the march of dire events. Ordinarily, there is nothing significant in a holiday in Brighton or a chance meeting with an acquaintance on the sea-front. Yet here, with later knowledge, we see behind these trivial incidents the grim foreshadowing of bitter sorrow, ruined reputation and unnatural death.

In *People Who Say Goodbye*, P.Y. Betts conveys childhood memories of nearby Wandsworth, over seventy years ago:

Our suburb was a favoured one on account of its wide roads and many open spaces. Not only was there the Common, there was a nursery garden full of flowers, threaded with footpaths; there were enchanting glimpses through wrought-iron gates of the secret gardens of the big houses in the road between two commons where my grandparents lived. No wonder our estate, with its comfortable modern housing, pulled in youngish couples who were, they expected, going to get on in the world. There were so many trees. There was such an abundance of fresh air. It was incidental that much of the fresh air blew in from the domains of madness, crime, wounds and death, each of which required a large acreage of living space, if living is the word.

Wandsworth Prison resembled a fortress with a medieval gate, and possessed an execution shed. Periodically a crowd collected early, a warder posted up a notice, a black flag was run up and the crowd sighed. 'I thought of this enormous sigh as the last breath of the hanged murderer, all the breath that had ever been in his lungs going out into the world without him.'

Near the Common was also the lunatic asylum:

My mother of course had something to say about lunatic asylums because as a girl she had visited one. Her father had taken her when he went there on business. He was a Commissioner for Lunacy . . . While he went off to attend to what may have been gruesome business she remained behind, engaged in conversation with a pleasant gentleman to whom she had been introduced. They were on an upper floor with a view of the hall below, and when in due course her father came in sight, talking to an official, my mother's companion walked with her to the head of the stairs, where he bowed and took his leave, explaining regretfully that he was unable to accompany her down the stairs as his legs were made of glass and might break.

North London suburbs fit in here as easily as South. All possess a distinct flavour, sometimes one more memorable in print than during a casual day. Palmers Green is more famous for Stevie Smith and her 'Lion Aunt' than for Palmer. Her strange novel, *Over the Frontier*, with its winding trail of surprises, is not deeply concerned with the suburb, yet seems rooted there:

My aunt is cutting up bacon rind for our birds. She is doing this with rather a shaky hand, in half an hour the taxi will be here and I must say good-bye. The shadow of farewells is upon the bacon rind and to-day the birds will not have such a finely-chopped feast as yesterday. We take the rind and the breakfast crumbs and the crusts broken into pieces and put them on the lawn; now we stand back behind the window curtains and watch for cats. My aunt will have no cat in our garden. Also my aunt will see fair play between the birds, who sitting now and swinging gently upon the tree branches are about to have this lovely meal-o of bacon rind and crusty bread. It

is a sunny day and early in the morning, the grass is heavy
with dew and the sun low upon our neighbours'
roofs.

Yesterday the gardener was here, and now the garden,
newly prinked and tidied, the paths as neat and formal as
a parade, shines beneath this early morning sun that has
broken through to break the rain and storm clouds of past
months. How very spry the garden looks, like a good
child that has a washed face and a clean pinafore.

Holloway is another village that became what, in introducing *The Diary of a Nobody*, J.C. Squire called a typical suburb
of the impecuniously respectable kind. John Betjeman, in
'Thoughts on the *Diary of a Nobody*', imagined the Pooters in
their home, where a long-lost footpath led round elm and oak
to Muswell Hill:

> The Watney Lodge I seem to see
>   Is gabled gothic hard and red,
> With here a monkey puzzle tree
>   And there a round geranium bed.
>
> Each mansion, each new planted pine,
>   Each short and ostentatious drive
> Meant Morning Prayer and beef and wine
>   And Queen Victoria alive.
>
> Dear Charles and Carrie, I am sure,
>   Despite that awkward Sunday dinner,
> Your lives were good and more secure
>   Than ours at cocktail time in Pinner.

The Pooters' awkward Sunday dinner was with Mr Paul
Finsworth, hitherto unknown to them, at Muswell Hill:

There was also a large picture in a very handsome frame,
done in coloured crayons. It looked like a religious subject. I was very much struck with the lace collar, it looked
so real, but I unfortunately made the remark that there
was something about the expression of the face that was
not quite pleasing. It looked pinched. Mr Finsworth

sorrowfully replied: 'Yes, the face was done after death –
my wife's sister.'

I felt terribly awkward and bowed apologetically, and
in a whisper said I hoped I had not hurt his feelings. We
both stood looking at the picture for a few minutes in
silence, when Mr Finsworth took out a handkerchief, and
said: 'She was sitting in our garden last summer,' and
blew his nose violently, so I turned to look at something
else and stood in front of a portrait of a jolly-looking
middle-aged gentleman, with a red face and straw hat. I
said to Mr Finsworth: 'Who is this jovial-looking gentleman? Life doesn't seem to trouble him much.' Mr
Finsworth said: 'No, it doesn't. *He is dead too* – my
brother.'

Another typical episode occurred at Holloway itself:

As it was getting on for five, we four held a consultation,
and Gowing suggested that we should make for the
'Cow and Hedge' and get some tea. Stillbrook said: 'A
brandy-and-soda was good enough for him.' I reminded
him that all public-houses were closed till six o'clock.
Stillbrook said, 'That's all right – *bona-fide* travellers.'

We arrived; and as I was trying to pass, the man
in charge of the gate said; 'Where from?' I replied:
'Holloway.' He immediately put up his arm and declined
to let me pass. I turned back for a moment, when I saw
Stillbrook, closely followed by Cummings and Gowing,
make for the entrance. I watched them, and thought I
would have a good laugh at their expense. I heard the
porter say: 'Where from?' when, to my surprise, in fact
disgust, Stillbrook replied: 'Blackheath', and the three
were immediately admitted.

Gowing called to me across the gate, and said: 'We
shan't be a minute.' I waited for them the best part of an
hour. When they appeared they were all in most excellent
spirits.

Holloway, though, has another dimension, that averted
face of suburbia. North of Parkhurst Road is the women's

prison, a mock castle with its central tower said to imitate 'Caesar's Tower' in Warwick Castle. Here, in 1922, Mrs Edith Thompson waited in the condemned cell, having seen her lover, Freddie Bywaters, attack and kill her husband, in Endsleigh Gardens, Kensington. Older than Bywaters and uneasily conscious of it, she had been an Emma Bovary, thrilled by romantic fiction. She ended dreadfully, probably through a faulty presentation of her case, in a prudish era. She wrote to her friend, Bessie Aitken, on Christmas Eve, a few days from the straps and rope:

Dear Bessie,

I wanted to write to you yesterday and yet I couldn't. I could do nothing but sit and think. Who was it said, 'Some days we sits and thinks, and some we simply sits?' Well, yesterday was a 'sitting and thinking day.'

I got your little letter on Saturday. Yes, the result of the appeal was a great shock – I had such hopes of it – not only hopes for mercy, but hopes for justice; but I realise how very difficult it is to fight prejudice.

You talk about not having to suffer the extreme penalty. Do you know that I don't dread that at all. I feel that would be far easier than banishment – wrongful banishment for life. I feel no apprehension of what might lie ahead after this life.

Yesterday I was twenty nine; it's not really very old, I suppose, and yet it seems so to me.

I suppose when you're happy age doesn't count; it doesn't seem to matter; it's when you're not that the years seem so frightening.

Yesterday I was thinking about everything that has ever happened, it seems so to help in all sorts of ways when I do this. I realise what a mysterious thing life is. We all imagine we can mould our own lives – we seldom can, they are moulded for us – just by the laws and rules and conventions of this world, and if we break any of these, we only have to look forward to a formidable and unattractive wilderness.

I've often thought how good it would be to talk, to pour out everything; it might have pained as well, but it would be pain that comes with sudden relief of intolerable hurt.

However, I'm going to forget all that now. I'm going to hope – because everybody tells me so, I'm going to live in those enormous moments when the whole of life seems bound up in the absolute necessity to win.

Thank you so much for writing to me, and helping to keep me cheerful.

Edith

There is no need to overelaborate horror, distress, discreet perversions. Everywhere, people loved, yearned, laughed, wrote. Further to the indeterminate edge of London is Enfield where, in 1803, Keats was attending the village school. Cowden Clarke, Shakespearian critic and publisher, when an usher of, at the most, fifteen, recalled in 1861 the boys' gardens around the playground, and a pond surrounded by strawberry beds. By this pond,

beneath the iron railings which divided our premises from the meadow beyond, whence the song of the nightingales in May would reach us in the stillness of the night, there stood a rustic arbour, where John Keats and I used to sit and read Spenser's *Faery Queene* together, when he had left school, and used to come over from Edmonton, where he was apprenticed to Thomas Hammond the surgeon.

Enfield has a further claim to literary distinction. W.H. Auden, in his anthology *A Certain World*, discloses:

I read in a newspaper that a certain Mrs Winifred Venton, with the help of the Enfield College of Technology computer, has at last cracked the cipher of the 'sonnets'.

The message: Shakespeare was really King Edward VI who did not die, as the history books say, when he was sixteen, but at the age of 125. In addition to writing 'Shakespeare', he wrote not only all of Ben Jonson and Bacon, but 'Don Quixote' as well.

POSTSCRIPT

Throughout, London has been a city of movement, often dramatic, sometimes dangerous. Throughout, it has been cosmopolitan, often quarrelsome, at times petty and vindictive. It has never lost a personal character, a powerful presence. Much, however, of the London remembered here is virtually dead, like the significance of so many pub signs dangling above its streets – the Brazen Head, the Green Man, the Headless Woman, the Salisbury, the Sun in Splendour, the Magpie and Stump, the Tarpaulin Jacket – which contain legends, events, emblems, sayings, once shared in the civic memory. Time transforms the commonplace to the esoteric.

All ages are in transition. The leper and his pig's trotters have gone, like the walking lavatory, and the dockside cranes that dipped majestically at Churchill's funeral. Standardization may threaten the individual and secretive but, as the century nears its end, the angry and the ludicrous, the pathetic and the comic still remain, though less obvious, less outrageous, than they appeared to Smollett and Dickens.

As long ago as 1970, Jan Morris assessed London in a *Guardian* essay, which I was not to forget and still find pertinent:

Today she seems the most tentative of all the great capitals, the least confident of purpose or function, the least true to herself; but it is hard to believe that a city of such tremendous character can really have lost its spirit in two short decades. There is something about her decline that rings false – perhaps its very abruptness, for cities are like people, and do not easily rot. London feels as she does, I think, because she is a city that moves in cycles. She is an island capital, an off-shore meeting-place or conduit, through which ideas and influence pour in successive waves. She is a city of merchant venturers, whose fortunes depend on the enterprises of England – now in America, now in India, now in Africa, now in Europe itself.

She is also a city of actors, governed by a profound sense of timing – and just at the moment, restrained by caution, exhaustion, and a sort of historical aestheticism. London's malaise is not, I think, senility. She is biding her time. She has lost one kind of authority, and is waiting to assume another, has emerged from one cycle, and will presently enter the next. If she seems neurotic today, bitter, catty, light-headed, it is because her horizons have momentarily contracted, and she is left all alone at home. *Wait and see!*

SOURCES AND ACKNOWLEDGEMENTS

The author and publishers would like to thank all those responsible for giving permission to reprint copyright material. Unless otherwise stated, all sources were published in London.

William Abrahams and Peter Stansky, *Orwell: The Transformation*, 1979.

Dannie Abse, *Poems Golders Green*, 1962, © Dannie Abse. Reprinted by permission of Sheil Land Associates Ltd.

Peter Ackroyd, *The Last Testament of Oscar Wilde*, 1983. Reprinted by permission of Hamish Hamilton Ltd.

Harold Acton, *Memoirs of an Aesthete*, 1948. Reprinted by permission of David Higham Associates Ltd.

Dr William Acton, *Prostitution Considered in its Moral, Social and Sanitary Aspects in London and Other Large Cities and Garrison Towns*, 1857.

Joseph Addison, *Collected Spectator 1711-14*.

Harrison Ainsworth, *The Tower of London*, 1840.

Martin Amis, *Money*, Jonathan Cape Ltd, 1984.

Hans Andersen, *Memories of Dickens*, 1847.

Matthew Arnold, 'Kensington Gardens' in *Collected Poems*, 1950.

Cynthia Asquith, *Diaries*, 1917.

W.H. Auden, *A Certain World*, Faber & Faber Ltd, 1971.

Dudley Barker, *G.K. Chesterton*, 1973. © the estate of Dudley Barker. Reprinted by permission of Curtis Brown Ltd.

Nina Bawden, *Familiar Passions*, 1979. Reprinted by permission of the author.

Cecil Beaton, *Diaries 1955-63*. Reprinted by permission of the literary trustees of the late Sir Cecil Beaton.

Francis Beaumont, 'Ode on the Abbey Tombs' (undated), see G.C. Macaulay, *Francis Beaumont*, 1883; 'Letter to Ben Johnson', 1640.

Sybille Bedford, *As It Was*, Sinclair Stevenson, 1990. Reprinted by permission of the author.

Gillian Beer, *London Review of Books*, April 1977.

Max Beerbohm, BBC recordings, 1942; see also *Mainly on the Air*, 1957. Reprinted by permission of Mrs Eva Reichmann.

Hilaire Belloc, *The River of London*, 1912; *Charles the First*, 1933.

Arnold Bennett, *The Pretty Lady*, 1918; *Journals*, 1971; *Imperial Palace*, 1930.

John Betjeman, *Collected Poems*, 1958. Reprinted by permission of John Murray (Publishers) Ltd.

P.Y. Betts, *People Who Say Goodbye*, Souvenir Press, 1989.

William Blake, *Prophetic Books*, 1789–1804; *Songs of Innocence and Experience*, 1794.

Louis Blanc, see E.J. Dingwall, *Some Human Oddities*, 1947.

Eric Bligh, *Tooting Corner*, Martin Secker & Warburg Ltd, 1946.

Paul Bloomfield, *Journal 1939–49*, Gollancz Ltd, 1950.

Wilfrid Blunt, *The Haileybury Buildings*, 1936. Reprinted by permission of the author.

James Boswell, *London Journal*, Heinemann, 1950.

Elizabeth Bowen, 'Mysterious Kor' in *Collected Stories*, Jonathan Cape Ltd, 1980.

H.M. Brailsford, *Voltaire*, 1935.

John Braine, *Life at the Top*, Methuen London, 1962; *The Crying Game*, Methuen London, 1968; *These Golden Days*, Methuen London, 1985. Reprinted by permission of David Higham Associates Ltd.

Neville Braybrooke, Introduction to Ivy Low, *She Knew She Was Right*, 1988.

S.M. Brewer, *Design for a Gentleman*, Chapman & Hall Ltd, 1963.

Julia Briggs, *A Woman of Passion*, Hutchinson, 1987.

Vera Brittain, *Testament of Friendship*, Macmillan, 1940. Reprinted by permission of Paul Berry and Virago Press Ltd.

Charlotte Brontë, *Villette*, 1853.

Anita Brookner, *Look At Me*, Jonathan Cape Ltd, 1983. Reprinted by permission of A.M. Heath Ltd.

Tom Brown, *Amusements Serious and Comical*, 1700.

Robert Browning, 'Prince Hohenstiel-Schwangau', 1871.

Beau Brummell, see T.H. White, 'The Butterfly', *Windmill Magazine*, 1946.

Sir Arthur Bryant, *The Age of Elegance*, Collins Ltd, 1950. Reprinted by permission of HarperCollins Ltd.

John Buchan, *The Three Hostages*, 1924.

Rosina Bulwer, *Cheverley* (undated).

Thomas Burke, *The Streets of London*, Batsford Press Ltd, 1940.

Dorothy Burnham, *Through Dooms of Love*, Chatto & Windus Ltd, 1968. Reprinted by permission of Random Century Ltd and the estate of Dorothy Burnham.

A.S. Byatt, *Still Life*, Chatto & Windus Ltd, 1985.

Lord Byron, *Don Juan*, 1819–24.

Karel Capek, *Letters from London*, 1924.

Neville Cardus, *Cricket*, Longman Ltd, 1931.

Jane Welsh Carlyle, *Selected Letters*, 1883.

Thomas Carlyle, *Letters from Chelsea*, 1841.

C.E. Carrington and J. Hampden Jackson, *History of England*, Cambridge University Press, 1932.

Lord David Cecil, essay in *Recollections of Virginia Woolf*, ed. Joan Russell Noble, New York, 1972.

Geoffrey Chaucer, *Canterbury Tales*.

G.K. Chesterton, *Collected Poems*, 1936.

Marchette Chute, *Shakespeare's London*, Martin Secker & Warburg Ltd, 1941. Copyright 1949, renewed © 1977 by Marchette Chute. Reprinted courtesy of the publisher, Dutton, an imprint of New American Library, a division of Penguin Books USA Inc.

Austin Clarke, *A Penny in the Clouds*, Routledge Ltd, 1968.

Cowden Clarke, *Recollections of Keats*, 1861.

Alasdair Clayre, essay in the *London Magazine*, ed. Alan Ross, 1974. Reprinted by permission of Alan Ross.

0203456789012345

John Cleland, *Fanny Hill, c.* 1749.

Anne Cliff, 'All the Dandy O' in *The Windmill*, Vol. 1, ed. Reginald Moore and Edward Lane, Heinemann, 1946.

Harold P. Clunn, *The Face of London*, Spring Books, 1948.

Norman Collins, *London Belongs to Me*, Fontana, 1945; *Bond Street Story*, Fontana, 1959. Reprinted by permission of HarperCollins Publishers Ltd.

Cyril Connolly, *The Unquiet Grave*, Hamish Hamilton Ltd, 1944; 'One of My Londons' in *Encounter* magazine, 1955. Reprinted by permission of Rogers, Coleridge & White Ltd.

Joseph Conrad, *The Secret Agent*, 1907.

Diana Cooper, *The Rainbow Comes and Goes*, Hart-Davis, 1958. Reprinted by permission of the Viscount Norwich.

Henry Craik, *Jonathan Swift* (undated).

Roy Curtis, *East End Passport*, Macdonald, 1969.

Daniel Defoe, *Moll Flanders*, 1722.

Thomas Dekker, *The Shoemaker's Holiday*, 1609; *The Infection of the Suburbs, c.* 1608.

Charles Dickens, *Our Mutual Friend*, 1864–5; *Bleak House*, 1852–3; *Sketches by Boz*, 1836–7; *Great Expectations*, 1860–1; *Pickwick Papers*, 1837; *Little Dorrit*, 1855–7; *Oliver Twist*, 1837.

Benjamin Disraeli, *Lothair*, 1870.

Austin Dobson, *Collected Essays*, 1923–6.

Fyodor Dostoevsky, *Winter Notes on Summer Impressions*, Paris, 1962.

Arthur Conan Doyle, *The Complete Sherlock Holmes Stories*, John Murray, 1928.

Lawrence Durrell, 'A Ballad of the Good Lord Nelson', from *A Private Country*, Faber & Faber Ltd, 1943.

John Earle, *Micro-cosmographie*, 1628.

Leon Edel, *Henry James*, Collins Ltd, 1987. Reprinted by permission of HarperCollins Publishers Ltd.

Blake Ehrlich, *London on the Thames*, Cassell Ltd, 1968. Reprinted by permission of Macmillan Publishing Company.

T.S. Eliot, *The Waste Land*, Faber & Faber Ltd, 1922.

Alphonse Esquires, *The English at Home*, 1861.

John Evelyn, *Diary*, 1652.

Patricia Finney, *Firedrake's Eye*, Sinclair Stevenson, 1992.

Ronald Firbank, *Caprice*, 1917.

Ford Madox Ford, *The Soul of London*, 1905.

E.M. Forster, *Two Cheers for Democracy*, Edward Arnold, 1951.

John Forster, *Charles Dickens*, 1872–4.

T.R. Fyvel, *Tribune*, 1948; *And There My Trouble Began*, George Weidenfeld & Nicolson Ltd, 1989. Reprinted by permission of Mrs Mary Fyvel.

Richard le Gallienne, *New Poems*, 1909.

John Galsworthy, *The Forsyte Saga*, 1922.

Stephen Gardiner, essay in the *London Magazine*, ed. Alan Ross, 1974. Reprinted by permission of Alan Ross.

David Garnett, *The Golden Echo*, 1933.

William Gaunt, *The Pre-Raphaelite Dream*, Jonathan Cape Ltd, 1943.

S. Gelburg, 'Jewish London' in *Living London*, ed. George Sims, 1902.

Winifred Gérin, *Charlotte Brontë*, 1967.

Edward Gibbon, *Memoirs*, 1796.

Alexander Gilchrist, *William Blake*, 1863.

George Gissing, *Thyrza*, 1887.

Willy Goldman, 'The Way We Live Now' in *Penguin New Writing*, ed. John Lehmann, 1941.

Douglas Goldring, *South Lodge*, Constable Ltd, 1943.

Oliver Goldsmith, *Essays*, 1765.

Robert Graves and Alan Hodge, *The Long Weekend*, Faber & Faber Ltd, 1950. Reprinted by permission of A.P. Watt Ltd on behalf of the trustees of the Robert Graves Copyright Trust and Jane Aiken Hodge.

Thomas Gray, *The Bard*, 1757.

Henry Green, *Caught*, Chatto & Windus Ltd, 1943.

Roger Lancelyn Green, *A.E.W. Mason*, 1952.

Graham Greene, *Journey Without Maps*, © 1936 Verdant S.A.; *The Lost Childhood*, © 1947 Verdant S.A. Reprinted by permission of David Higham Associates Ltd.

George and Wheedon Grossmith, *The Diary of a Nobody*, 1892.

Thomas Hardy, 'Coming Up Oxford Street; Evening' in *Selected Poems*, 1978; 'On Keats' House' in *Collected Poems*, 1930.

J.F.C. Harrison, *The Common People*, Croom Helm Ltd, 1984.

John Harvey, 'The Mason's Skill' in *The Flowering of the Middle Ages*, ed. John Evans, 1966.

Mrs Robert Henrey, *London*, J.M. Dent, 1948.

Paul Hentzner, *Travels in England*, 1598.

Christopher Hibbert and Ben Weinreb, *The London Encyclopaedia*, 1987.

Susan Hill, essay in *Living in London*, ed. Alan Ross, 1974. © *London Magazine*. Reprinted by permission of Alan Ross.

Thomas Hinde, *Hinde's Courtiers*, 1986. Reprinted by permission of the author.

Vyvyan Holland, *Son of Oscar Wilde*, Penguin Ltd, 1957. Reprinted by permission of Merlin Holland.

John Holloway, *A London Diary*, Routledge Ltd, 1969.

Gerard Manley Hopkins, *Poems*, 1918.

Victor Hugo, *L'Homme qui rit*, Paris, 1869.

Leigh Hunt, *Sonnet to Hampstead*, 1815.

Patricia Hutchins, *Ezra Pound's Kensington*, Faber & Faber Ltd, 1965.

R.C. Hutchinson, *The Elephant and Castle*, Cassell and Co., 1949. Reprinted by permission of Macmillan Publishing Company.

Laurence Hutton, *Literary Landmarks of London*, 1892.

Aldous Huxley, *Antic Hay*, 1923.

Washington Irving, *Oliver Goldsmith*, 1846.

Christopher Isherwood, *Exhumations*, Methuen London, 1966.

W.W. Jacobs, *Dialstone Lane*, 1904.

Henry James, *A Small Boy and Others*, 1913; *Journal*, 1888; *English Hours*, 1905; *Princess Casamassima*, New York, 1886; *The Wings of a Dove*, 1902.

A.S. Jasper, *A Hoxton Childhood*, 1974.

Richard Jefferies, *After London*, 1885.

Elizabeth Jenkins, *Doctor Gully*, Michael Joseph Ltd, 1972. Reprinted by permission of Curtis Brown Ltd.

Jerome K. Jerome, *Three Men in a Boat*, 1889.

William Jesse, *Beau Brummell*, 1844.

Lionel Johnson, 'By the Statue of King Charles' in *Complete Poems*, 1953.

Robert Underwood Johnson, *Remembered Yesterdays*, 1923.

Dr Samuel Johnson, *Dictionary*, 1755.

Ben Jonson, *Bartholomew Fair*, 1614.

Philippe Jullian, *Oscar Wilde*, Constable Ltd, 1969. Reprinted by permission of Perrin, Paris.

Charles Lamb, *Letters*, 1834.

John Lehmann, *A Nest of Tigers*, 1968.

Shirley Robin Letwin, *The Gentleman in Trollope*, 1982.

Jeremy Lewis, *Playing for Time*, 1987. Reprinted by permission of the author.

Wyndham Lewis, *Blast*, 1914.

Jean Liddiard, *Isaac Rosenberg: The Half-Used Life*, Gollancz Ltd, 1975. Reprinted by permission of Sheil Land Associates Ltd.

Emanuel Litvinoff, *Journey Through a Small Planet*, 1973. Reprinted by permission of the author.

Elizabeth Longford, *Wellington: Pillar of State*, George Weidenfeld & Nicolson Ltd, 1972; *The Pebbled Shore*, George Weidenfeld & Nicolson Ltd, 1986.

D.M. Low (ed.), *London is London*, Chatto & Windus Ltd, 1949.

Donald Lupton, *London and the Country Carbonadoed*, 1632.

John Lydgate, *London Likepenny*, see John Lydgate, *Chaucer, c.* 1430.

Robert Lynd, *Dr Johnson and Company*, 1946.

Rose Macaulay, *The World My Wilderness*, Collins Ltd, 1947: essay in *Recollections of Virginia Woolf*, ed. Joan Russell Noble, New York, 1972. Reprinted by permission of the Peters, Fraser & Dunlop Group Ltd.

Thomas Babington Macaulay, *History of England*, 1849–55.

Kirsty McCleod, *The Last Summer*, Collins Ltd, 1983. Reprinted by permission of Toby Eady Associates Ltd.

Jean MacGibbon, *I Meant to Marry Him*, Gollancz Ltd, 1984. Reprinted by permission of the author.

Compton Mackenzie, *Poetry and the Modern World*, 1933.

Henry Mackenzie, *The Man of Feeling*, 1771.

Julian Maclaren-Ross, *Memoirs of the Forties*, London Magazine Editions, ed. Alan Ross, 1965. Reprinted by permission of Alan Ross.

John McManners, *Death and the Enlightenment*, Oxford University Press, 1981.

A.S. Macnalty, *A Book of Crimes*, 1929.

Louis Macneice, 'The Streets of Laredo' in *Collected Poems*, Faber & Faber Ltd, 1966.

Karl Marx, *Marx-Engels Letters*, George Weidenfeld & Nicolson Ltd, 1981.

John Masefield, *Letters to Reyna*, Buchan & Enright Ltd, 1983; *Collected Poems*, Heinemann, 1923.

A.E.W. Mason, *The Summons*, 1920.

W. Somerset Maugham, *A Writer's Notebook*, William Heinemann Ltd, 1949; *Cakes and Ale*, William Heinemann Ltd, 1930; *Of Human Bondage*, William Heinemann Ltd, 1915.

George du Maurier, *Peter Ibbetson*, 1891.

Henry Mayhew, *London Labour and the London Poor*, 1851.

Lewis Melville, *Beau Brummell*, 1924.

Michael Meyer, *Not Prince Hamlet*, Martin Secker & Warburg Ltd, 1989.

Naomi Mitchison, *You May Well Ask*, Gollancz Ltd, 1979. Reprinted by permission of David Higham Associates Ltd.

Timothy Mo, *Sour Sweet*, André Deutsch Ltd, 1983.

Harold Monro, 'Suburb' in *Collected Poems*, Duckworth Ltd, 1933.

Hannah More, *Thoughts on the Importance of the Manners of the Great to General Society*, 1788.

Thomas More, see Helen G. Nussey, *London Gardens of the Past*, The Bodley Head Ltd, 1939.

James Morris, essay in the *Guardian*, 1970. Reprinted by permission of A.P. Watt Ltd on behalf of Jan Morris.

William Morris, *Alfred Linnell Killed in Trafalgar Square, November 20, 1887*, 1887; *The Earthly Paradise*, 1868–70.

Arthur Morrison, *A Child of the Jago*, 1897.

H.V. Morton, *In Search of England*, Methuen London, 1927.

Iris Murdoch, *The Bell*, Chatto & Windus Ltd, 1958.

Shiva Naipaul, essay in *Living in London*, ed. Alan Ross, 1974. © *London Magazine*. Reprinted by permission of Alan Ross.

Bill Naughton, 'The Spiv' in *Pilot Papers*, see Anne Cliff, *The Windmill*, Vol. 1, ed. Reginald Moore and Edward Lane, Heinemann, 1946.

Edith Nesbit, *Wings and the Child*, 1913.

Lawrence Norfolk, *Lemprière's Dictionary*, Sinclair Stevenson, 1991.

Elizabeth d'Oyley, *Young Jemmy*, 1947.

Michael St John Packe, *The Bombs of Orsini*, Secker & Warburg, 1957.

Palmer (son of Samuel), see Anna Maxwell, *Hamsptead* (undated).

Ian Parsons, Introduction to Isaac Rosenberg, *Collected Works*, Chatto and Windus Ltd, 1979.

Bridget Patmore, *My Friends When Young*, Heinemann Ltd, 1968.

Samuel Pepys, *Diary*, ed. R. Latham & W. Matthews (11 vols., 1970–83).

Nikolaus Pevsner, *London*, 1952.

Sir Frederick Ponsonby, *Recollections of Three Reigns*, 1951.

Alexander Pope, 'Ombre at Hampton Court' in *Collected Works*, 1717; extract from *The Dunciad*, 1728.

Una Pope-Hennessy, *Charles Dickens*, Chatto & Windus Ltd, 1945.

Peter Porter, essay in *Living in London*, ed. Alan Ross. © *London Magazine*. Reprinted by permission of Alan Ross.

Paul Potts, *Dante Called You Beatrice*, 1963. Reprinted by permission of the author.

Ezra Pound, *Selected Poems*, Faber & Faber Ltd, 1928.

Nellie Priest, *The Island*, 1976. See J.F.C. Harrison, *The Common People*, Croom Helm Ltd, 1984.

J.B. Priestley, *Angel Pavement*, Heinemann Ltd, 1930; *Delight*, Heinemann Ltd, 1951. Reprinted by permission of the Peters, Fraser and Dunlop Group Ltd.

V.S. Pritchett, *London Perceived*, Chatto & Windus Ltd, 1962; *Collected Stories*, Chatto & Windus Ltd, Vol. 1, 1982; Vol. 2, 1983; *The Cab at the Door*, Chatto & Windus Ltd, 1968. Reprinted by permission of the author.

Peter Quennell, *Four Portraits*, 1947. © Peter Quennell, reprinted by permission of Curtis Brown Ltd; *Byron*, Collins Ltd. Reprinted by permission of Harper-Collins Ltd.

Thomas De Quincey, *Confessions of an English Opium Eater*, 1821.

Walter Ralegh, *History of the World*, 1614.

J. Hall Richardson, *From the City to Fleet Street*, 1927.

Wiliam Roper, *Life, c..* 1557.

Isaac Rosenberg, 'A Ballad of Whitechapel' in *Collected Works*, Chatto & Windus, 1979.

Alan Ross, *Blindfold Games*, 1988. Reprinted by permission of the author.

Dante Gabriel Rossetti, private letter to William Allingham, 1861.

Bertrand Russell, *Autobiography*, Allen & Unwin Ltd, 1967–9.

Michael Sadleir, *Fanny by Gaslight*, 1940.

Saki (Hector Hugh Munro), 'The Jesting of Arlington Stringham' in *The Chronicles of Clovis*, 1911.

George Augustus Sala, *Twice Round the Clock*, 1859.

William Sansom, *Lord Love Us*, 1945; *South*, 1948; 'Building Alive' in *Horizon* magazine, 1945; *Various Temptations*, 1947; essay in the *London Magazine*, 1947. Reprinted by permission of Elaine Green Ltd.

Siegfried Sassoon, *Collected Poems*, Faber & Faber Ltd, 1949. Reprinted by permission of George Sassoon.

César de Saussure, *A Foreign View of England in the Reigns of George I and George II*, see Eric Newby, *A Book of Traveller's Tales*, Viking, 1986.

George Bernard Shaw, article in the *Star*, 1890. Reprinted by permission of the Society of Authors on behalf of the George Bernard Shaw estate.

Robert E. Sherwood, *The Worlds of Robert E. Sherwood*, New York, 1965.

Andrew Sinclair, *King Ludd*, 1968: *Magog*, 1972. Reprinted by permission of the author.

Iain Sinclair, *Downriver*, Paladin, 1991. Reprinted by permission of HarperCollins Publishers Ltd.

Edith Sitwell, *I Live Under a Black Sun*, Gollancz, 1937. Reprinted by permission of David Higham Associates Ltd.

Osbert Sitwell, *Laughter in the Next Room*, Quartet Ltd, 1949. Reprinted by permission of David Higham Associates Ltd.

John Thomas Smith, *A Book for a Rainy Day*, 1845.

Stevie Smith, *Over the Frontier*, 1938. Reprinted by permission of James MacGibbon.

Tobias Smollett, *Humphry Clinker*, 1771.

C.P. Snow, *Corridors of Power*, Macmillan Ltd, 1964. Reprinted by permission of Curtis Brown Ltd.

Muriel Spark, *The Girls of Slender Means*, Penguin, 1963. Reprinted by permission of David Higham Associates Ltd.

Bernard Spencer, *Poetry London*, 1943.

Stephen Spender, *World Within World*, 1951; 'Epilogue to a Human Drama' in *The Edge of Being*, Faber & Faber Ltd, 1949. Reprinted by permission of the author.

Ernest Stadler, 'Children in Front of a London Soup Kitchen' in *German Poetry 1910–75*, ed. Michael Hamburger, New York, 1976.

Lawrence Stone, *The Family, Sex and Marriage 1500–1800*, George Weidenfeld & Nicolson, 1977.

John Summerson, *The Microcosm of London*, 1943.

Jonathan Swift, 'Description of the Morning' in *Complete Poems*, 1983; *Journal to Stella*, ed. H. Williams, 1948.

Frank Swinnerton, *The Georgian Literary Scene*, 1935.

Alfred Lord Tennyson, 'Ode for the Opening of the International Exhibition', occasional poem, 1862.

William Makepeace Thackeray, *Vanity Fair*, 1847; *The Four Georges*, 1860.

Dunstan Thompson, 'A Visit to Deptford' in *Penguin New Writing*, ed. John Lehmann, 1947.

Edith Thompson, see René Weiss, *Criminal Justice*, Hamish Hamilton, 1988.

Chidiock Tichborne, untitled poem published in *Messages*, ed. Naomi Lewis, 1985.

Thomas Tickell, 'Kensington Gardens', 1772.

Gillian Tindall, *The Born Exile*, New York, 1974.

H.M. Tomlinson, *All Our Yesterdays*, William Heinemann Ltd, 1930. Reprinted by permission of the estate of H.M. Tomlinson.

Philip Toynbee, see Peter Vansittart, *Paths from a White Horse*, Quartet, 1985.

Anthony Trollope, *Phineas Finn*, 1869.

Henri Troyat, *Tolstoy*, Pelican, 1970.

Jules Verne, *Around the World in Eighty Days*, 1873.

Baron Waldstein, *Diary of Baron Waldstein*, 1602.

Horace Walpole, see *Letters of Horace Walpole*, New York, 1937–81.

Jill Paton Walsh, *Fireweed*, Macmillan, 1969.

Ned Ward, *The London Spy*, 1699.

Cornelius Webb, poem published in Anna Maxwell, *Hampstead* (undated).

Stanley Weintraub, *A Stillness Heard Around the World*, Unwin Hyman Ltd, 1986. Reprinted by permission of HarperCollins Publisher Ltd; *Victoria*, Unwin Hyman Ltd, 1987. Reprinted by permission of Peters Fraser & Dunlop Ltd.

H.G. Wells, *Tono Bungay*, Macmillan Ltd, 1909; *The Passionate Friends*, Macmillan Ltd, 1913; *The Work, Wealth and Happiness of Mankind*, Macmillan Ltd, 1932. Reprinted by permission of A.P. Watt Ltd on behalf of the literary executors of the estate of H.G. Wells.

Edith Wharton, *A Backward Glance*, New York, 1934.

Antonia White, *The Lost Traveller*, 1950.

Oscar Wilde, *The Decay of Lying*, 1889; *De Profundis*, 1905; 'The Harlot's House' in *Poems*, 1881.

A.N. Wilson, *Hilaire Belloc*, Hamish Hamilton Ltd, 1984.

Angus Wilson, *The Wrong Set*, Martin Secker & Warburg Ltd, 1949.

Stephen Winsten, *Days with Bernard Shaw*, Hutchinson Ltd, 1957.

Diana Witherby, 'St James's Park' in *Collected Poems*, Derek Verschoyle, 1954.

P.G. Wodehouse, *Mike*, 1903 (reprinted 1953); 'Bingo and the Little Woman' in *The Jeeves Omnibus*, 1967 (see also 'The Clicking of Cuthbert'; *Mulliner Nights*, 1932. Published by Herbert Jenkins Ltd and reprinted by permission of the Random Century Group on behalf of the estate of P.G. Wodehouse.

Humbert Wolfe, poem (untitled) from *Augustan Books of Poetry*, 1926.

Virginia Woolf, *The Years*, 1937; *Flush*, 1933; *Orlando*, 1928; *Mrs Dalloway*, 1925; *The Waves*, 1931; *Jacob's Room*, 1922; *The Death of a Moth*, 1942.

INDEX